KALASHNIKOV CULTURE

KALASHNIKOV CULTURE

Small Arms Proliferation and Irregular Warfare

CHRISTOPHER CARR

PSI Reports

PRAEGER SECURITY INTERNATIONAL
Westport, Connecticut • London

Library of Congress Cataloging-in-Publication Data

Carr, Christopher, 1947–
    Kalashnikov culture : small arms proliferation and irregular warfare / Christopher Carr.
        p.   cm.
    Includes bibliographical references and index.
    ISBN: 978–0–313–34614–9 (alk. paper)
    1. Arms control.   2. AK–47 rifle.   3. Asymmetric warfare.   4. Firearms industry and trade.
5. Illegal arms transfers.   I. Title.
    JZ5645.C37   2008
    355.4′2—dc22   2008010129

British Library Cataloguing in Publication Data is available.

Library of Congress Catalog Card Number: 2008010129
ISBN-13: 978–0–313–34614–9

First published in 2008

Praeger Security International, 88 Post Road West, Westport, CT 06881
An imprint of Greenwood Publishing Group, Inc.
www.praeger.com

Printed in the United States of America

The paper used in this book complies with the
Permanent Paper Standard issued by the National
Information Standards Organization (Z39.48–1984).

10 9 8 7 6 5 4 3 2 1

Contents

Introduction

In the late 1980s officials in Pakistan began to refer to a condition or phenomenon that they called the "Kalashnikov culture." The reference was to an amalgam of problems that together were contributing to chronic insecurity within Pakistan and most particularly to conditions of social and political violence then prevailing in the North West Frontier Province and in the city of Karachi in the south of the country. As articulated by then-Pakistani Prime Minister Benazir Bhutto (and by others), this Kalashnikov culture was an admixture of tribal discontent, urban political factionalism, organized crime, corruption, drugs and, given the descriptor, the proliferation of military-type weapons throughout Pakistan. This corrosive mixture was, when placed in the context of an already weakened society, deemed to pose a threat to the authority of the central government and to the security of the populace of Pakistan as a whole. In short, the Kalashnikov culture was overwhelming the state and substituting dysfunctionalism and chaos for order and governance.

Although the term may have been coined in South Asia in the 1980s, the condition itself had been prevailing elsewhere and in earlier times. Most of the constituents and their effects had been readily discernible during the Lebanese civil war in the 1970s. With the substitution of sectarian clans for tribes, the definition promoted by the Pakistani authorities could have been directly applied to the Lebanese situation. In the latter case, of course, the state was not simply threatened but temporarily made violently moot by the parties to the war. It was precisely this fragmentation that the representatives of the status quo in Pakistan were afraid would result from the pressures of their own Kalashnikov culture. In Karachi and in the tribal provinces armed groups that were representatives of the "culture" were beyond outlawry. They threatened to exploit the existing schisms within the society and to fragment the power of the state along the fault lines that already existed within Pakistan. Some would do so for reasons relating to territory and sovereignty (in the tribal provinces), some over religion and identity (in Karachi), some for aggrandizement and power (in the political parties and security forces), and some simply for profit (the traffickers and criminal syndicates). Although few wished to destroy the state of Pakistan, the desired effect by most of the players was to create an ambience of insecurity and threat that intimidated the state and allowed them to conduct their affairs without let or hindrance from the agents of government. In this they were and remain successful.

Kalashnikov enculturation has proliferated without regard for geography or even for levels of development. Kalashnikov cultures have become fixtures in Europe (the Balkans), in the Americas (Caribbean, Central America, South America), in the Caucasus, in South Asia, in Southeast Asia (Cambodia, Papua New Guinea), and most apparently in Africa (Liberia, Sierra Leone, Central Africa, the Horn of Africa.) They can be rurally based or urban in nature. They can take the form of militia armies or of organized city gangs. Their motivations range from ideological fervor, religious conviction, irredentist passion, or simply from acquisitive consumerism. What they all have in common is strength of purpose in confrontation with a weak state and the arms and will necessary to challenge the state into stalemate or submission.

These are not Eric Hobsbawm's "social bandits," who may have been nonconformist and violent but rarely posed a threat to the state. Neither are Kalashnikov cultures easily dismissable as Kaplanesque anarchies or Conradian horrors. The cultures themselves are often complex, have their own codes of behavior and can be creatively managed by energetic leaders. They have their own economic dynamic, in which commerce, albeit of an aberrant nature, is conducted with sometimes enviable skill. The values of these cultures are often evolved from traditional, pre-nation/state periods with an emphasis upon family and obligation to blood lineage. But Kalashnikov cultures are not benign alternatives to the Westphalian model. Violence, intimidation, and insecurity are the hallmarks of these cultures and their victims are, preternaturally, the most vulnerable in their thrall.

This work attempts to define Kalashnikov cultures through the constituent parts that form their dynamic. The format is one of alternating chapters in which an element of the phenomenon, for example the nexus between gun and drug cultures, is paired with a case study chapter. Most of the cultures contain many or all of the elements that were identified in the context of Pakistan and so the pairings of element and case study are relatively arbitrary. However, an attempt has been made to be as geographically broad as possible when choosing the cases. There is a danger that Kalashnikov cultures might simply be seen as shorthand for the chronic problems that afflict the less developed countries of the southern hemisphere. This is not the intent of this work. The condition is not restricted to the South and while less developed states are the most vulnerable there are plenty of Northern actors who have contributed to this vulnerability and must bear some responsibility for Kalashnikov enculturation and its ramifications.

Small arms proliferation and weaponization is, of course, a key component of Kalashnikov enculturation. Uniquely, for the U.S. audience this creates something of a "cultural" dilemma. For many in the United States an armed society is not necessarily an insecure or unstable society. The Second Amendment to the U.S. constitution implies that an armed populace might act as a guarantee against tyranny. Many in the United States also believe in the principle of self-determination through self-defense and that an armed society fosters order based upon an extrapolation of deterrence theory. But there are major differences between a U.S. "gun culture" and Kalashnikov culture. The weaponization inherent in Kalashnikov cultures is of a type and within a context that is not analogous to that prevailing in the United States. The gun in America may sometimes challenge order but it does not challenge government. The instruments themselves range from handguns to rifle to shotguns but they do not include (except under strict license and control) automatic military weapons, grenades, grenade launchers and other ordnance. What abides in the United States is a unique experiment in the ownership of guns in the context of an orderly society. What exists in Kalashnikov cultures is the proliferation of weapons in the context of weak societies. How much the weapons have contributed to that weakness and how much they may be a response to conditions engendered by that weakness will be discussed in this work.

This author did not invent the appellation "Kalashnikov culture" but it is both the title of this work and it is used extensively throughout. Some responsibility must be borne, therefore, for the perpetuation of the image of the Soviet/Russian rifle that is the identifier of the mostly negative aspects of Kalashnikov cultures. The use of Mihail Kalashnikov's rifle as the poster symbol for these cultures is partly unfair but it is also wholly relevant. It is unfair because weapons from the United States, Western Europe, and China can be found in the cultures, as well as locally produced arms from factories and from primitive workshops. It is relevant because aspects of the weapon itself, together with the numbers and the wide geographical dispersion of the firearm, are tangible contributory factors to the evolution of the cultures that bear its name. The ergonomics, firepower, and durability of the Kalashnikov or AK are not simply casual footnotes to the definition of the culture. As well as being highly symbolic representations of a type of power that poses a challenge to the primacy of the state, they are also very real instruments without which the challengers to the state would be sterile and impotent. The "Kalashnikov" in Kalashnikov culture is not the totality of the firepower inherent in the culture, nor are arms the only element that defines the culture. But the proliferation of light military weapons has ensured that the distinction between professional soldiers and armed but untrained groups has diminished and in certain cases been nullified. The Kalashnikov and its effects are not to be blamed but they should be studied.

Within Kalashnikov cultures the guns are not simply obvious tools of real violence but they are also symbols of respect and primacy. They represent power, wealth and the way to wealth, eligibility for marriage and for group membership, the dividing line between childhood and adulthood, the illusion of security, and the reality of intimidation. It is the arms that encourage the police in Rio de Janeiro into attacking the favelas or slums as if they were storming military objectives. It is the arms that ensure that the young women of the Kerio Valley in Kenya will not countenance marrying a man unless he possesses a Kalashnikov. In Afghanistan the opium grower, when asked what he will do with the money from his crop, states that he will buy a four-wheel drive vehicle and more Kalashnikovs. In North Ossetia pensioners are directed toward the purchase of hand grenades because, at $5–7 each, they are more affordable than Kalashnikovs. In Mozambique the rusting but serviceable AK buried beneath a village hut might be the only consumer durable that the peasant may have owned or may hope to own. In northern Uganda the child soldiers of the Lord's Resistance Army may be underfed and exhausted but the ergonomics and simplicity of the Kalashnikov ensure that these undisciplined and feral "soldiers" are just as intimidating and potentially lethal as any product of West Point or Sandhurst.

The first chapter is concerned with what makes Kalashnikov cultures into distinctive "cultures." Constant and chronic insecurity is a hallmark of this phenomenon, to the degree that it creates its own rules of existence and its own framework of order. These cultures are not simply variations on a theme of degrees of centralized state control; they have evolved in a manner that eschews such control. The reality of authority is invested in the lords of chaos, those who have mastered the climate of insecurity and violence and leveraged it into a peculiar form of opportunity. In this chapter such diverse issues as vigilantism, global popular culture, vendettas, witchcraft, and the impact of drugs and alcohol are used to illustrate how Kalashnikov cultures are a mosaic of traditional, elemental traits and postmodern aspirations. The insecurity milieu is both restrictive—in the way that it imposes limits on movement and access—but it is also, for those who master the environment, a liberating experience that is full of promise.

The next chapter of this work is devoted to the Kalashnikov and other light weapons and their role in changing the balance between armed groups and the agents of the state. The evolution of the assault rifle and the rocket propelled grenade launcher is considered, as is the impact of the change from aimed fire to prophylactic automatic firing. The history of the proliferation of light weapons in the post-World War II period is outlined, with an emphasis on their pedigree as the tools of guerrillas and militias. The relationship between numbers of arms and their relative environments is also considered. Where in Yemen the numbers of arms might be crucial to an understanding of the particular levels and types of violence in that society, in Northern Ireland the dynamic is not so much tied to the size of the inventory under the control of the insurgents but rather the symbolism inherent in their very presence in an advanced industrial society.

Kalashnikov cultures are not simply social phenomena. There are financial and economic aspects attendant on them that are related to the movement of arms and also to the market environment that the climate of insecurity encourages. In two chapters, one on arms trafficking and the other on Kalashnikov economics, the commercial elements of the cultures are examined in some detail. The economic dimension includes the illicit exploitation of natural resources in the Congo, smuggling in the Iguacu Triangle in Latin America and the establishment of an unsanctioned economic free zone in Somalia. Each of these activities relies upon a cofferdam of insecurity and intimidation in order to allow them to exist beyond the control of governments or the international community. Kalashnikov economics may be aberrant or even perverse but it is also robust and, in its own way, successful.

The weapons that help create the ambience of insecurity have their origins and reach their users in many ways. Many are the small change of the Cold War, having been allocated to client liberation armies and insurgent groups by one or other of the protagonists in that conflict. Certainly the majority of arms that are present in Africa, Southeast Asia and in South Asia are the detritus of the 1945–1991 campaign between the superpowers. But arms have also been trafficked into the conflict regions by private entrepreneurs and venal officials. The chapter on trafficking will include an extensive vignette that indicates, through the prism of South Africa's "Wazan affair," how arms are moved through the efforts of brokers, moneymen, document providers, and transport specialists. It will also look at how arms leak from military and police organizations. Perhaps one of the most important elements of this particular chapter is how, through charting the movement of arms, it is possible to discern a contagion effect as a result of the migration of arms between one country to another. Lastly, the question will be posed as to whether arms that are produced in artisan workshops in Pakistan, the Philippines, and other countries are simply curiosities or are major contributions to the levels of violence and insecurity in their communities.

The first case study chapter takes the prototypical Pakistani example and investigates whether the contentions made by indigenous politicians and security force officials in the 1980s were merited. The linkage with the conflicts in Afghanistan is explored, as is the role of Afghani refugee communities in Pakistan in the evolution of Kalashnikov cultures. The role of arms in the maintenance of tribal autonomy is discussed and the linkage between that autonomy and the drug trade is also investigated. The city of Karachi and its devolution into chronic violence and insecurity in the mid-1990s is outlined in terms of the connection between political movements, criminal groups, and the security apparatus. The role that the influx of arms and drugs played as an exacerbating agent in the escalating violence in Karachi is considered in this chapter and indeed this cohabitational relationship is considered throughout the work.

The second and third case studies relate the impact of Kalashnikov enculturation upon the deeply traditional societies of the East African pastoralists and of the West African states of Liberia and Sierra Leone. A true warrior culture, the nomadic pastoralists had existed in an environment of carefully managed violence until the advent of large numbers of modern weapons in the 1980s. Stock raiding was an aspect of the managed violence but what was a finely balanced social dance in earlier times became, after the Kalashnikovs, a massively disruptive and commercially oriented enterprise. Nomadism was interrupted, grazing was inhibited and women and children, who in the past had been at least partially protected by a warrior code, were increasingly placed at risk. Migration to the cities was encouraged by the level of insecurity, with the concomitant destruction of the familial ties that bound the pastoral tribes and an increase in urban dysfunctionalism in such cities as Nairobi. In this chapter this accelerated evolution is catalogued, together with an assessment as to how the arms were proliferated into that conflict.

The fourth case study is that of Yemen. Renowned or notorious as perhaps the most heavily weaponized state, Yemen is the repository of most of the discernible elements of a Kalashnikov culture. Armed clans compete with the government for political power and this conflict creates a vacuum in which law and order are usurped by custom and force of arms. Existing in this vacuum is the trade in the narcotic qat and an energetic kidnapping industry. Camouflaged within this opaque setting are representative elements of regional and global terror groups and observing them (and occasionally doing more so) are forces representing the counterterrorist states. As with the other case studies, Yemen has evolved a complex set of psychological and practical control mechanisms that militate against constant, debilitating violence but these mechanisms often fail and when they do the nature of the failure is often to be found in the form of long-term blood feuds and in armed warfare against the state.

The fifth case study does not focus upon one state but instead concentrates upon three "islands" of Kalashnikov culture : Jamaica, Papua New Guinea (PNG), and the favelas of Rio de Janeiro. All three of these locations are typical of Kalashnikov cultures that are evolving criminal enterprises and that have surpassed the normative understanding of "gang" activities. Each of the elements that make up the criminal core of these cultures poses a distinct threat to the political and social cohesion of the host state and each of them had political roots that ended up undermining the structure that they were supposed to serve. In Jamaica the "garrisons" of the capital Kingston were originally designed to be fortress bases from which party hard men sallied forth to do the bidding of their political masters. Those same hard men then became the "yardie" gangsters who challenged the politicians for the control of the drug trade and who created their own fiefdoms out of the garrison structure. In PNG the "big man" tradition that provided the structural integrity of tribalism evolved into an urban-based patronage system that required enforcers to regulate the lines of authority and to control the distribution of the looted national wealth. But, as in Jamaica, the enforcers, in the form of raskol gangs, grew beyond the control of their patrons and reduced PNG to a virtual civil war state, with the violent young bloods challenging the status quo through an unrelenting campaign of theft and rapine. In Rio the political genesis was less frantic than in PNG and Jamaica but the outcome was the same. The favelas were originally ghettoes of internally displaced rural people who after World War II gravitated to the cities in search of work. During the 1950s and 1960s these slums were the proselytic base for the socialist dogma of such revolutionaries as Carlos Marighella. To these left-wing activists the imprisoned criminal class was fertile ground for the establishment of a counter to the moneyed and security establishment that dominated Brazil during this time. But, as with Jamaica and PNG, what began as an adjunct of the political process soon metamorphosed into a well-structured and well-armed criminal community. The drug economy of the favelas allowed the gangs to arm themselves to a level of successful intimidation not only of the populace of the slums but also over the security forces. The latter, whose legitimacy had been undermined by decades of military dictatorship and pervasive corruption, were relegated to the level of an external enemy by a slum population that was forced to rely upon the omnipresent gangs for their security and economic well-being.

The forces arrayed against the Kalashnikov cultures are not simply those of the military, police, and intelligence communities. They include elements of the United Nations and other intergovernmental organizations and nongovernmental (NGO) bodies ranging from Human Rights Watch and Amnesty International to a group of a few individuals fashioning Kalashnikovs into political art in Mozambique. The concern and interest of the worldwide academic community is also suitably broad. It includes social anthropologists who conduct fieldwork amongst the Kuria cattle raiders along the Tanzania-Kenya border; experts in international security who compile the annual Small Arms Survey at the Graduate Institute of International Studies in Geneva; and researchers from the RAND Corporation who catalog the nexus between drug traders, paramilitary groups, insurgents, and small arms proliferation in Colombia. Journalists, writers, bloggers, and the purveyors of popular culture have also played a role as investigators and commentators upon Kalashnikov enculturation. However, the actor that, for the most part, is missing from this soup of concern is the global community of nation-states.

During the 1990s the campaign against the manufacture and deployment of landmines was, with a certain exception, a triumph of post-Cold war arms control. A grassroots cause celebre became a mass movement that itself begat a binding commitment. The United States, for its own security reasons, may have been partially outside the final agreement but this did not lessen the triumphalist mood in the ban-the-landmines community. Bouyed by their success, many in the anti-landmines movement turned their attention to small arms proliferation. But small arms and light weapons (SALW) proved to be only passingly analogous to landmines. Outside of the U.S. national security community, landmines had no constituency of support. Their profligate and unmanaged use on nonconventional battlefields had created enduring images of maimed innocents from Cambodia to Angola. In contrast, small arms were a far more complex organism. They had an economic, political, and military utility that made many states, from producers to consumers, loath to tamper with the status quo. Rationales for state reluctance ranged from high politics to high-level corruption but what appeared, at the turn of the century, to be a logical transition by the community of nations from the control of landmines to SALW became instead a protracted campaign by non-state actors to raise popular awareness of the issues created by Kalashnikov enculturation.

The chapter on the counterculture details that campaign and catalogs its successes and failures, including attempts by Sierra Leone and Liberia to rid themselves of elements that made them into the quintessential "gangsta" cultures.

Violence, threatened or real, is the hallmark of the Kalashnikov culture. In most orderly societies the threat of violence is usually bounded by a belief that social convention and a functioning legal and judicial system will insulate most citizens from the effects of violence. In Kalashnikov cultures the constancy and pervasiveness of violence dictates most of the actions of most of the populace for much of the time. As abject poverty forces people away from hope and into a subsistence mentality, the violence inherent in a Kalashnikov culture forces people to think in terms of physical security and to foreswear any expectation of peaceful coexistence. Instead of operating from a plateau of security the citizens within Kalashnikov cultures learn how to tolerate and even exploit an environment of insecurity. There are lessons to be learned from the spirit of adaptation that is often found in the Kalashnikov cultures, as well as object lessons in how to prevent their inception.

For those that live outside of the Kalashnikov cultures it might be comforting to believe that this phenomenon can be contained and isolated. But the infective aspect of these cultures has already ensured that they have touched almost every one of the untouchable advanced post-industrial societies. Globalization is a two-way street and the "Rambo"-watching, Tupac t-shirt-wearing militias of West Africa have created eddies that affect the price of a diamond ring in China, the numbers of refugees moving into Europe across the Straits of Gibraltar and the ability of al-Qaeda to mount attacks against the U.S. mainland. Australia has been forced to intervene in PNG in order to protect its own security interests and the chronic insecurity in the Caucasus could yet bring Russia and the United States into confrontation. Drugs, human trafficking, and the counterfeiting of products have all moved out of their safe havens within Kalashnikov cultures and have become global issues. The degradation of living conditions in these places has also led to the encouragement of existing and new strains of epidemic disease. There is no coffer dam of wealth and military power that is high enough to contain these outreach aspects of Kalashnikov cultures. What follows, therefore, is not simply the description of a transient anomaly that is geographically limited and only of prurient interest. It is possible that in the future Kalashnikov cultures and Westphalian states may simply have to coexist with each other in a world where the state no longer has a monopoly over the creative use of violence in pursuit of polity and wealth.

1

Kalashnikov Enculturation

Kalashnikov enculturation does not follow a set formula or a distinct chronology. Certain patterns of behavior, governance, and structure are common to the majority of the Kalashnikov cultures but they are not reliable enough to be able to establish an iron equation. Proliferation of small arms is one of the most reliably identifiable factors but the oft-quoted presence of military weapons in Swiss households indicates that the mere existence of such arms in the body of the population does not equate with Kalashnikov enculturation.[1] A weak central authority or government is also prevalent in most of these cultures but the manifestation of weakness may run the gamut from disorderly democracy (Papua New Guinea) to autocracy (Pakistan, Yemen) to collapsed state (Somalia). Virtually all of the Kalashnikov cultures have a history and pedigree of political and social violence that has inflicted a blunt trauma effect upon their societies and yet Sierra Leone and Cambodia were relatively peaceful states until external factors drove them in extremis. Most of the Kalashnikov cultures have played host to long-term refugee or internally displaced populations but this was not a factor in Jamaica or in Northern Ireland. And even when all of these elements are present the chronology is not fixed and evolutionary. Arms may come and promote political instability that in turn creates insecurity that encourages population displacement. Refugees may, as was the case with the Rwandan *interahamwe* moving into eastern Congo, be the prime movers that bring with them the arms and the pedigree that infects a weakened environment with their catalytic presence. Kalashnikov enculturation does not readily allow itself to be identified as a neat paradigm and yet there are sufficient patterns of cause, effect, and behavior that make the phenomenon portable from Africa to Asia to Latin America. Each of the Kalashnikov cultures might be distinct but they all draw from the same limited set of precursors and one of this set is the presence of large quantities of small arms and light weapons in the hands of the civilian population.

The origins and causes of conflict are complex and varied enough to have spawned a broad body of literature and to have fostered entire subdisciplines of study. Similarly, explanations for the deterioration of conflict into physical violence can be found within the disciplines of anthropology, political science, history, criminology, sociology, and a plethora of other intellectual compartments. Occasionally, violent conflict is considered within the context of multidisciplinary or interdisciplinary evaluation rather than as emanating from more discrete, singular rationales. But for the most part a resort to mass violence is rightly seen as the culmination of many varied and disparate phenomena coming together to form a dynamic of destruction. These phenomena, which include poverty, repression, environmental degradation, and the search for cultural identity, to name but a few, all require study in order to understand how conflict becomes confrontation and it is fitting that such study is undertaken. However, this work focuses upon a narrower aspect of the evolution of conflict. It is concerned with how arms, when they devolve into the hands of the general populace, affect the relationship between individual and state and how a certain level of such devolution creates its own, for the want of a better phrase, culture of violence.

It is arguable that arms are simply a catalyst, an inert instrument denoting a willingness to defend identity or principle or livelihood with deadly force. It is certainly true that in most cases of violent conflict the use of arms is less about cause than it is about effect. But it is also true that a proliferation of arms down to the individual level, in all but the most structurally stable of political entities, can in itself create eddies of insecurity that either exacerbate existing problems or, in extreme cases, actually eclipse the authority of centralized governance. In these latter cases the power of the weapons is greater than the sum of their obvious lethal effects. Some would call the result anarchy, others might talk of it in terms of self-determination and power to the people. But when a society or part of a society becomes "weaponized" that is to say, when military-style arms become freely available to the general public, notions of control, stability, and security must undergo radical redefinition. Just as when an individual enters a public place openly carrying arms, a society where the population is armed to the level of para-infantry is obviously redolent of tensions of a particular nature.

It is a cliché but also a truism to talk of guns in terms of being symbols of power. For centuries the evolution of weaponry was one of the ways in which societies assessed their standings in relation to competitors. The ability to produce enough weapons of a sufficient technological sophistication was an accepted indicator of political and economic strength. Indeed, it has been argued that the Cold War was "fought" on just such a basis and that when the Soviet Union could not maintain relative arms parity it was forced to "surrender." Again, using arms inventories as a shorthand for power is an obvious oversimplification. But the residual of such a mentality is to be found in the rhetoric and actions of groups ranging from Palestinian *intifadists* to Pakistani tribesmen to Sierra Leonean militiamen. Just as states use numbers of aircraft, tanks, and warships to indicate latent power, so do tribes, clans, groups, and individuals use their possession of rifles, machine guns, and grenades to denote independence and to invoke respect.

This latter element, the linkage between guns and respect, is one of the most fundamental and visceral aspects of weaponized societies. Respect in this context is of course closely allied to the invocation of fear but it is also in many cases a code word for modernity. In many places where machinery is largely absent, the possession of a modern weapon indicates mastery of technology as well as a certain degree of wealth. Also in societies where young people, particularly young men, cannot compete through upward economic mobility, the ownership and control of arms is one obvious and open way in which relative status can be assessed. Under such conditions the gun takes on all of the attributes that ownership of a vehicle and a house denotes in an advanced postindustrial society. There is, of course, a major difference between the utilitarian aspects of a vehicle and a personal weapon. The former is for the most part benign. The latter is less so.

Arms are not inherently destabilizing nor does their possession by the general population indicate incipient anarchy or even a predisposition to violent conflict. When the institutions of authority are particularly strong and when the rule of law is applied effectively then it is possible for a gun culture to coexist within a wider society. But such coexistence is unusual and not without its detractors. The United States, the best example of a gun culture, continues to debate whether the right to personal firearms ownership overrides the obligation of the state to maintain law and order for the whole. Most countries simply deny the right of unrestricted ownership of arms on the assumption that such a proliferation of arms is prejudicial to good order. Like the conduct of foreign policy, the state is presumed to maintain the monopoly of military weaponry as a function of its fundamental obligation to the citizenry. This is considered by most to be a burden of responsibility borne by a responsible actor rather than an unjust usurpation of authority and those that are the bearers of the burden, the armed forces and the police, are accorded a distinct status within the society.

It is appropriate here to define the difference between "gun cultures" and weaponized societies or "Kalashnikov cultures." The former is epitomized by a civilian population that believes, for historical or legalistic reasons, that firearms may be maintained and used without undue control from governmental authority.[2] The practical result of this contention is that a significant minority within the society owns and has access to a wide variety of guns, ranging from antique weapons to modern military-type small arms. However, in gun cultures the ownership of arms is still a moderated activity. A skein of laws and conventions ensures that what is often termed a "right" is in fact a regulated privilege and that the security of the "state," including the human security of the general populace, takes precedence over the desires of the gun owners. This control element partly relates to concerns relating to the state's monopoly of directed violence and partly it is predicated upon the belief that the more arms that exist within a society the greater likelihood that they will be used in antisocial ways that pose a threat to overall security. The extent and nature of such limitations on the "free" ownership of firearms is at the core of most national gun control debates and while interesting in its own right is tangential to this work. In Kalashnikov cultures the proliferation of weapons into the hands of the general populace has already reached a stage whereby it seriously threatens the primacy of the state and has passed beyond the nuances of legal controls. It is not a culture that has an affinity with guns; it is an environment in which the ownership and use of guns have a sublime and deep impact upon the social, economic, and political functioning of the society.

There are some emotional and psychological elements that appear to be present within both gun cultures and weaponized societies. The idea of self-protection, whereby the individual uses firearms to protect themselves and their families from those that would harm them, is a constant theme in both cultures. In gun cultures it is in many ways an echoing residual of times past when the law and law enforcement were unreliable and often distant. In Kalashnikov cultures, self-defense is often couched in terms relating to self-respect and honor, as well as in the more expected rationales of dealing with a government's failure to protect its charges. In these circumstances failure by the individual to provide for his defense and that of his kin is an emasculating, demeaning position. The problem with this devolved approach to law and order is that a weapon that might be perceived as an instrument of self-protection by its owner might also be seen as an instrument of threat by his neighbor. To counter that threat the neighbor acquires a weapon, this in turn might be seen as a confrontational and escalatory act by others and street-level arms races are the result.

In the Baluchistan province of Pakistan there is a saying that a rifle is "dearer than a son." In rural areas of Kenya and Uganda young women will not countenance courtship with a man who does not own an automatic rifle. In the slums of Kingston, Jamaica, and Rio de Janeiro criminal leaders adopt the noms de guerre "Uzi" and "Kalash" to denote their association with their weapons of choice. These are but a handful of examples that indicate that under certain conditions arms have assumed a role beyond that of simple accessory. They have become an integral element in the daily lives and in the livelihoods of their owners. In an acquisitive sense pride of ownership is one aspect of this special relationship but there is also an emotional attachment that transcends mere ownership. As one observer has commented, in Pakistan's city of Hyderabad the young men have "found an aesthetic pleasure in the technology of modern weapons."[3] The use of Kalashnikovs in celebratory gunfire during weddings, a tradition that is both widespread and often tragic in its results, is more than simply a substitute for fireworks or other less lethal noisemakers. It is a public display of wealth, power, and independence. It is also, in its negative ramifications, very often the genesis of another aspect of Kalashnikov enculturation, that of prolonged vendettas occasioned by accidental death or injury.

The emotional attachment between arms and men in Kalashnikov cultures can easily devolve into a discussion with Freudian overtones but it should not be neglected when deconstructing the culture. In pastoral East Africa and in traditional West Africa the Kalashnikov has been easily absorbed into the fetishistic spiritual mores that suffuse those societies. Tests of manhood that previously involved close contact with dangerous animals with little but a spear have now been supplanted by simple ownership and use of automatic weapons. In these cases the faith of the community has accommodated and adapted to the presence of the weapon. This adaptation has resulted in the redefinition of bravery, self-worth, and the ability to provide for family, clan, and tribe. In societies where firearms have been integrated for a prolonged period of time, such as in Yemen or the NWFP of Pakistan, the emotional attachment to the weaponry in many ways defies logic. This factor is particularly important when attempts are made to regulate, control, or disarm. Even when a high level of autonomy and security can be guaranteed (by a government or intervening power) the attachment to the gun may override any confidence in a peaceful existence that the owners of the arms might have at that time.

This is an aspect of the Kalashnikov culture that often confuses those that, for good or evil, pursue disarmament as an ultimate goal. When the rifle has entered into the spiritual and traditional aspects of the culture any attempt to remove the device is an affront to the identity of the owner. If disarmament is a desirable objective it must take into account degrees of enculturation. In certain societies, such as Liberia and Sierra Leone, the period of enculturation has been short and specific to a distinct period of violence. Disarming or decommissioning the combatants in those places, while not easy, is not hampered by long-term, profoundly held attitudes toward the ownership of the gun. But in Yemen, Afghanistan, or Somalia the enculturation is more complete and the weapon is not simply considered an aberration on the journey toward state primacy and an orderly society. In pure Kalashnikov cultures the gun represents a basket of attributes with a multiplicity of implications. It is an intrinsic element that cannot be readily sub-divided and extracted from these societies without risking resistance and retaliation.

There is a perversely positive side to those societies that have been forced to accept prolonged periods of civil violence. Most of them have created a set of codes of practice that recognize that while peace may be elusive violence can still be managed. The "new" Kalashnikov states, such as Sierra Leone or Jamaica, have not yet developed this fail-safe mentality and as a result their bloodlettings are unbounded by rules of engagement. In Yemen, where inter- and intra clan violence predates the Kalashnikov culture by several centuries, there are elaborate matrices of compensation and regret that are designed to minimize uncontrolled revenge. This is also the case in Pakistan, the Caucasus, the Balkans, in Papua New Guinea, and East Africa. These laws of retribution include such niceties as distinctions between honorable killing and dishonorable murder, sliding scales of recompense according to the wealth and position of the deceased and of the perpetrator, and who may or may not be killed in the family of the guilty party as a "sacrifice" to appease the aggrieved. In this environment justice is less important than is adherence to a formula of interaction that recognizes that violence is endemic but it does not have to be constant.

Where formal law is absent, honor is often raised to a hyper-elevated role in a society. Behind the palisades of the Kalashnikov cultures honor codes supplement religious stricture as the substitute for constitution and ordinance. Often unwritten and therefore eminently malleable, these codes touch upon matters such as how to treat a hostage, bride pricing, the conduct of trade, and the shaming of women. It is true that codes of honor exist in societies that are not Kalashnikov cultures, but in the latter they are refined and advanced in order to accommodate the climate of insecurity and threat that is the psychological mulch of this phenomenon. In later chapters this topic will be covered in some depth because it begs the question as to whether such substate mechanisms as tribal lore, traditional value systems, and honor codes can, in Kalashnikov cultures, perform the same role that law and enforcement achieve in a modern state. An alternative interpretation of the elevated role played by honor in Kalashnikov cultures is that it simply rationalizes prejudices and behavior along lines that allow its practitioners to absolve themselves of guilt. In the case of the *karo kari* code of Pakistan it certainly appears to have morally sanctioned murder and blackmail in the context of marriage and property.[4]

Faith in the supernatural is, like honor codes, present as a positive and negative force within Kalashnikov cultures. Since the cultures are prime examples of temporal delinquency it is natural that people would seek hope and emotional security in the spiritual. However, the perverse instincts that guide behavior in Kalashnikov cultures also have an impact upon the direction and fervency of religiosity in those places. Religious leaders and communities become politicized because the body politic itself is deemed to be an agnostic burden rather than a responsive facilitator. Religious and denominational rivalries, uncontrolled by secular authority, become the basis of communal violence. Spiritual agents become scapegoats and objects of violent recrimination when they fail to deliver on promises made to their constituents. And dormant practices and cultish movements emerge to take advantage of the devotionally vulnerable.

The history and activities of the Lord's Resistance Movement (LRA) of northern Uganda have been well documented.[5] Originating as a spirit-guided religious community in the 1970s it became a guerrilla army that nearly captured the capital of Kampala before being defeated in the field, forcing its original leader, Alice Lakwena, to flee the country. A supposed relative, Joseph Kony, then turned the movement into a violent and peripatetic militia that maintained its numbers by kidnapping children and its reputation by conducting raids and committing massacres along the Ugandan–Sudanese border region. For two decades the LRA used southern Sudan, itself a conflict zone, as a safe haven while exploiting the instabilities and insecurities of a weakened Uganda. The original spiritual roots had become vestigial as the LRA entered its third decade of activities but part of its mystique and thrall still lay in its origins as a cult directed by a long-dead Italian. Again, this form of apocalyptic spiritualism is not unique to Kalashnikov cultures but what might, in normative societies, be considered the dangerous exploitation of psychically vulnerable people was found to be an acceptable alternative to normalcy in the context of riven and damaged Uganda.

Witchcraft and fetishism are most often concerned with protection and in Kalashnikov cultures protection is highly valued. In the LRA and amongst other African armed groups there is a belief that certain rituals can direct away or absorb bullets. Certainly, during the conflicts in Liberia and Sierra Leone militia warriors bolstered their resolve in battle with activities that included attempts at invisibility and even, in relatively rare cases, engagement in ritual eating of human flesh.[6] Even in those communities where the Christian and Muslim faiths appear to have been adopted Kalashnikov enculturation might include reversion to traditional healing and invocation of protective magic. The feeling of invulnerability that these actions perpetuated served as exacerbants to conflicts and helped to create reputations for ferocity and recklessness that could even have an impact upon a modern, disciplined army that came into confrontation with them. British forces in Sierra Leone learned that enemies that felt a sense of impunity did not need body armor or imposed discipline to make them confident in battle and that to denigrate local custom and belief was to risk dangerous underestimation of the capabilities of a foe.[7]

Kidnapping, extralegal imprisonment, and hostage taking are common to nearly all of the Kalashnikov cultures. Control over human life is a commodity enterprise in the cultures and it is often exploited to its fullest. In Yemen kidnapping has become an elaborate combination of uncomfortable theater and destabilizing national epidemic. The kidnapped are held in a parallel prison system and are released after a complex dance of negotiation and ritual. Few people die as a result of this formalized process but travel, commerce, and movement are drastically curtailed because of the insecurity that results from this "sport." In other Kalashnikov cultures the rules governing kidnap and ransom are not so refined and often the victims are brutalized and murdered during the process. As with many other activities Kalashnikov enculturation often degrades and vulgarizes what might have been a mature if anomalous accommodation to living with the threat of violence. Kidnapping, when bounded by a transparent code of honor and with an emphasis on minimizing insult and injury, can be effectively self-controlled. But when it becomes simply an element of criminal conduct or of uncontrolled revenge then it is an instrument of terror, theft, and retribution.

Kidnapping is just one of the criminal enterprises that are given refuge through Kalashnikov enculturation, although perhaps the use of the word "criminal" is inappropriate in the context of Kalashnikov cultures. Since weak or absent law is intrinsic to the cultures, it follows that crime and criminality are redundant concepts. Later in this work there is a chapter on Kalashnikov economics, which catalogs the type of commercial activity that is encouraged and protected within the cultures and most of these would be considered criminal in law-and-order societies. The cultivation and trafficking in drugs is one of these aberrant commercial activities and with the possible exception of the pastoralist communities of East Africa it is the principal source of income, wealth, and power in Kalashnikov cultures. It is also an activity which, through international trafficking, ensures that Kalashnikov cultures are not just a localized phenomenon but that they have a global and regional impact. Opium, heroin, cocaine, marijuana, and *qat* production are all protected by Kalashnikov enculturation, as are counterfeited pharmaceuticals and recreational drugs such as ecstasy and methamphetamine. As an unintended but foreseeable by-product of the trade in drugs Kalashnikov cultures almost always harbor a significant addict population within their domains, and this in turn further undermines the likelihood that a delicate and nuanced system of honor and tradition will be able to exert an influence over society within the Kalashnikov cultures. The estimated two million addicts that are some of the unintended consequences of Kalashnikov enculturation in Pakistan are part of the self-perpetuating cycle of violence and desperation that has enveloped that country for the past quarter century.

Capitalism, even at its most aggressive, is constrained by rules, laws, and agreements. Kalashnikov cultures act and function beyond and outside of rules. This disparity allows the cultures to achieve an advantage in the global marketplace because there are no labor, environmental, or investment regulations to place constraints on their behavior. The mining of conflict diamonds during the civil war in Sierra Leone is perhaps the best reported manifestation of these extra-capitalist investments, but the uncontrolled exploitation of natural resources in the Kalashnikov culture of Eastern Congo may be the most comprehensive. Using a slave population, the parties to the resource rapine extracted coltan, gold, and other minerals and exchanged them for protection, money, and arms. In this manner they have negated the sovereignty of the Democratic Republic of Congo and have been the architects of environmental degradation that will continue to have a profoundly negative effect for perhaps generations.

The movement of goods and people is an innate aspect of Kalashnikov enculturation. Even if arms are already present in a culture there is a continuing need for ammunition and suppliers must bring the product to the consumers. Supplying arms and ammunition do not provide enough of a guaranteed income on their own and so the same networks and purveyors that provide the munitions are usually engaged in other smuggling activities. An arms network in South Ossetia in the Caucasus morphed into a smuggling operation that underwrote the economy of that semiautonomous entity and undermined the viability of the state of Georgia. Arms suppliers in Albania transitioned from supplying weapons to the Kosovars to human and drug trafficking. The arms supply network that supported IRA and loyalist groups in Northern Ireland existed in parallel and with cohabitational links to smuggling that exploited European Union commercial rules, as well as to an extensive drug smuggling activity that has outlived the political campaign in Ulster. Borders do not, as designed under international law, delineate control and sovereignty to the economic speculators in Kalashnikov cultures but instead act as opportunity multipliers in the quest for extra-capitalist gain.

Change, adaptation, and multidimensionality are an important aspect of Kalashnikov enculturation. Even those cultures that are suffused with religious or ideological motivation are prone to criminalization and vulgarization. What might appear to be an irredentist campaign fought to achieve or maintain ethnic identity, such as in the Balkans or Sri Lanka, can take on the attributes of a criminal enterprise without abandoning its broader, long-term goals. But, as seen in Jamaica and the *favelas* of Rio, a political agenda can also be distorted, suppressed, and cast aside as any reformist ideals are overwhelmed by the profit motive. These shifting sands of motivation create particular problems for those agencies that must confront or mitigate the effects of Kalashnikov cultures. The tools and strategies that are appropriate to the containment or defeat of a political animal are quite different from those necessary to intimidate or control criminal organizations. Incentives that might appeal and appease an ideological urban guerrilla movement, such as compromises designed to achieve an equitable peace, are considered threatening to criminal organizations that rely upon chaos and dysfunctionalism in order to protect their activities. As David Keen and others have recognized, an insecure society can provide a cloak of security for those that can see opportunity in dislocation and lawlessness.[8]

Kalashnikov cultures also adapt concepts of order and accountability to the realities of their constantly insecure environments. As well as honor codes and other resorts to traditional conflict management, most Kalashnikov cultures embrace, to a greater or lesser degree, vigilantism at some time in their development. In the period after the end of apartheid in South Africa the arms and the anger that had been the necessary fuel of the antiapartheid movement became a threat to stability of the new republic. Street violence and especially gang rape moved beyond the townships and the firepower in the hands of the street gangs often intimidated the police force into impotence. Vigilante groups, most notably the organization known as PAGAD, emerged to provide community protection and to, at least nominally, engage in policing where the agents of the state were absent or inefficient.[9] The reaction, particularly by a commercial sector of exposed shopkeepers that felt under siege, was arguably understandable. But even if the initial motive was pure and defensible South Africa's vigilante movement, like most of its kind, soon deteriorated into a mirror image of the violent gangs that it was designed to overcome. Meting out beatings and worse, PAGAD lost its credibility as it metamorphosed into a thinly disguised extortion syndicate and became part of the problem rather than part of an idiosyncratic solution. That problem, of unremitting threat regularly punctuated by real violence, is not susceptible to the subtleties and niceties of normal organizational management. Vigilante groups, because they exist as a substitute for a failed formal enforcement process, must impose discipline on themselves as well as upon their targets and most often they fail in this respect. Vigilantism is about the invocation of fear and such fear is not only useful to intimidate antisocial elements but also to hold hostage a pliant and vulnerable population. Fear and the power that it begets is a corrosive combination that tends to destroy even the most well-intentioned vigilante movement.

Periods of vigilantism are usually short in span, buoyed by anger and outrage and without the necessary organization and discipline to provide a reliable long-term alternative to traditional policing. To fulfill this role an industry has developed that has become an entrenched aspect not only of life in Kalashnikov cultures but also of warfighting by functioning and advanced states. Private security companies have gravitated from the policing of shoplifters in retail malls to the guarantors of life in dangerous places and in doing so they have become a self-perpetuating, self-fulfilling phenomenon.

Outside of Kalashnikov cultures security companies perform an adjunct or supplementary role to police forces and military organizations. At the most humble level they protect property under circumstances where law enforcement cannot monitor the integrity of premises on a twenty-four-hour basis. In the military context they are part of an outsourcing philosophy that stresses the privatization of those activities that are not directly related to armed combat. Whether this is a movement toward the mercenarization of law enforcement and warfare is beyond the purview of this work. But in Kalashnikov cultures security companies are not an adjunct to existing state security organs but are a substitute for those organs. In Somalia, the Balkans, Liberia, and Cambodia the activities of nongovernmental organizations and others who choose to maintain a presence in unpoliced places are protected by sometimes imported but most often locally hired bodyguards and facilitators. Relief activities cannot be undertaken or maintained without such protection and the monies that are dispersed to the security companies form an important part of Kalashnikov commerce.

Most of the above relates to the definition of a society after it becomes a Kalashnikov culture. This begs the question as to what makes certain states or societies more vulnerable than others to Kalashnikov enculturation. Is the weight of accelerated weaponization too great for any country to resist and therefore the factors governing enculturation have little or nothing to do with structure or history of the victimized society? Or are there certain fault lines or weaknesses that encourage, after the onset of weaponization, a metamorphosis into the volatile, shape-shifting form that is a Kalashnikov culture? Is Kalashnikov culture simply a variation on the theme of failed or failing states?

As stated above there is no easy definition of a Kalashnikov culture nor are there distinct evolutionary stages that indicate precursor steps toward encultura-tion. There are susceptibilities that are discernible as weaknesses that place some states, nations, or societies at risk but there are no guarantees that these entities will embrace all of the preceding activities. These susceptibilities include unresolved competition for power between a central authority and subgroup actors; corruption that has undermined a belief in the utility and viability of the existing political process; a lumpen youth mass that is trapped between traditional definitions of adulthood and responsibility and the lure of globalized culture; an opportunistic religious or ideological minority. However, even if all of these elements are present and to a high degree it might still take a tsunami of events to boost them to a level of significance. An uncontrolled revolution, an invasion by an extra-regional power, or even a series of natural disasters might create the required catalytic process to encourage a chain reaction and turn a marginal and dysfunctional entity into one plagued by chronic and endemic violence. Without the catalyst the country or region at risk might simply continue to exist as one with social and economic problems but not one in which violent death through armed attack is constant and omnipresent, as it is in a Kalashnikov culture. It would be the difference between Istanbul and Karachi, between Equador and Somalia, and between southern Italy and the North Caucasus. All share a multitude of problems, violence is a part of their social fabric but in three of the cases a period of major uncontrollable conflict has knitted together these problems and helped form a garment of perpetual insecurity.

Even if arms are present in large numbers fingers are still required to manipulate the triggers on the Kalashnikovs. While the ergonomics of the weapon might allow for armies of geriatrics to provide the necessary manpower behind a Kalashnikov culture, the reality is that such manpower is provided by the mass of the global youth bulge. The age group 15- to 29-year-olds are the foot soldiers of the Kalashnikov cultures and the characteristics of this group have had an important effect upon the vulnerability of societies to the devolution into a Kalashnikov culture as well as to the nature of the culture itself. Liberian militias and street gangs in Jamaica and Papua New Guinea do not harbor many members in their thirties and their aggression is palpably tied to the unfulfilled expectations of restless adolescents. With no investment in the maintenance of the status quo they are open to recruitment by whatever group or force promises them gratification and opportunity. For them a Kalashnikov is an agent of change in a world of unchanging poverty and boredom.

In 2001 the U.S. Central Intelligence Agency (CIA) published a document on long-term demographic trends and how they would affect global security.[10] Defining a youth bulge as a disproportionate concentration in the population in the 15 to 29 age range, the CIA sounded an alarm that historically such bulges were likely to "perpetuate the cycle of political instability, ethnic wars, revolutions, and anti-regime activities" that already affected many places with a burgeoning youth population. The CIA report tied youth bulges to periods of unrest in Algeria, Northern Ireland, Gaza, Iran, Turkey, Egypt, Sri Lanka, and Yemen, with high unemployment and educational "shortfalls" contributing to the disquietude. In sub-Saharan Africa the agency directly tied youth bulges to elements of Kalashnikov enculturation (warfare, crime, terrorism, etc.) and pointed to that continent as the one which, in the future, would be most affected by the phenomenon.

This thinking was fuelled by a number of well-researched commentaries on the role of young people in Kalashnikov cultures, particularly in Africa. These works emphasized the brutality and ruthlessness of youth militias and gangs in Liberia, Sierra Leone, Rwanda, and the Democratic Republic of Congo and how the combatants were unconstrained by sentiment or propriety. In the words of one researcher, "Liberian youth of the civil war appropriated violent measures for themselves. By taking up arms they were transformed from victims of gerontocratic violence to social masters."[11] A subtext in most of the research was an analysis of the underlying violence in ritual and daily life that pervaded many of these places prior to the onset of major civil unrest. Transitions to manhood were accompanied by painful ritual and the heroes of local mythology were often themselves violent. The youth in these places themselves appropriated modern mythmakers, such as the hero in the "Rambo" movies and gangster rap artists, into their updating of traditional storytelling and then carried these cross-fertilizing fantasies into battle with them. Heroes were "good" or "bad" but even the bad were heroic and therefore worthy of emulation.[12]

The blunt trauma of latent, unresolved conflict is one of the most insidious elements in Kalashnikov cultures. Time is almost an irrelevance when considering this factor. There may be, as in Yugoslavia, long periods of forced quietude that thinly covers animosities that have been harbored for centuries. When the inherently weak government of the strong man is concluded then the animosities become *casus belli*. In cases where arms have not proliferated, the factionalism might take the form of a political struggle that is debilitating but not violent. But if the arms have, as a result of chaos or deliberate policy, been scattered beyond the control of the military or security forces, then civil conflict will most often be the result. The blunt trauma might have been relatively recent, such as the period in Colombia in the 1950s known as *La Violencia*, or it may have been prolonged over a period of time, such as the warfare between the Highland tribes of Papua New Guinea or the pastoralist raiding communities of East Africa. The overlaying scar tissue might, to the casual observer, be well formed but when placed in conjunction with change, uncertainty, and the presence of proliferated arms, its appearance can be unmasked as shallow and cosmetic. This does not condemn such societies to endless cycles of cumulative violence but it does make them more susceptible to the blandishments of Kalashnikov enculturation.

The existence of long-term refugee communities also appears to amplify the effects of the radical shifts that create Kalashnikov cultures. Pakistan was the beneficiary of three refugee waves from Afghanistan, beginning in 1979 with the Soviet invasion and continuing through the overthrow of the Taliban regime and its aftermath. The refugees brought with them customs, despair, poverty, and guns and it was inevitable that these two to three million guests would create their own eddies of tension and violence. Kenya has also played host to long-term refugees from both Somalia and southern Sudan and as a result the conflicts in those places have attached themselves to Kenya's own homegrown security issues.[13] Refugees from Liberia have gravitated into the Ivory Coast and, perhaps most notoriously, *interahamwe* refugees from Rwanda have moved through Eastern Congo infecting a large area with their own particular form of violent interaction.[14] The *mohajir* community in southern Pakistan, which fled the partition of the Indian subcontinent in 1947, has only partially integrated into the state of Pakistan and much of the Kalashnikov enculturation of the city of Karachi in the 1990s can be traced to issues relating to their identity as displaced persons.

Displaced populations are particularly vulnerable to the blandishments of Kalashnikov enculturation. With arms they can protect themselves from elements in the host population, they can use arms to create economic opportunity and they can prepare for armed resistance against the regime from which they have fled. Given the restrictions that are necessarily placed upon them by the host government, much of the activity of refugee communities is clandestine and therefore readily adaptable to criminal enterprises such as smuggling or poaching. Aware of their out-group status, refugee communities also tend to stress traditions and religious affiliations that act as a binding agent to help them to maintain their identity and in doing so they are often at odds with the host state. One way to protect themselves from abuse by the hosts is to make themselves too dangerous to be forcibly returned from whence they came and to be armed will facilitate that effect. Refugees are aware that host governments may use them as scapegoats in the event of political or economic unrest and a level of arms in their community might prevent the possibility of an easy pogrom.

Corruption is a symptom of weak government but it can also be a direct facilitator toward Kalashnikov enculturation. Corrupt politicians virtually created the *raskol* and *yardie* gangs in Papua New Guinea and Jamaica and they elevated the lumpenists in Sierra Leone and Liberia to the status of militias.[15] Corrupt and violent security forces in Pakistan aided in the weaponization of that state and indeed in most of the cultures corrupt police and military personnel have sold weapons to the very forces against which they are marshaled. Add to that the crosscurrents of violent competition and frustration that corruption engenders and the psychological mulch that feeds Kalashnikov enculturation is greatly enriched by endemic corruption. Criminal use of arms to gain wealth is legitimized when it takes place in the context of a corrupt society since, in the philosophy of *raskolism*, the "big men" are using their power to steal through corruption. When the police are corrupt they are often seen in the context of an invading army of economic competitors and to outgun them is simply an astute business strategy.

Where there is corruption there is usually the counterweight of ideological resistance or moral condemnation. In Pakistan the resistance and the condemnation emanated from the *madrassas* and from the mosques of activist, reactionary clerics. In Yemen, with its history of secularism and socialism, the religious resistance was more muted but still strong enough to sustain local fundamentalist forces. In Northern Ireland religion and ideology both played a role in sustaining the conflict but they were really convenient forms of shorthand for a basket of issues that included long-term discrimination, abuse of civil rights, and corruption. In Tajikistan and the Ferghana Valley decades of repressive and corrupt communism did help foster an aggressive religious revival in the mid-1990s but in the Caucasus the violent eruptions mostly centered upon irredentist ethnic issues rather than upon any sense of moral outrage. Elsewhere, in the Balkans and in Southeast Asia, corruption greased the skids of Kalashnikov enculturation but it was only one of the elements that raised the toxic levels necessary to push societies over the brink.

When the military and police became corrupted and diverted from their principal tasks this robbed the state of its ability to withstand Kalashnikov enculturation. The politicization of the military in Pakistan, Somalia, Yemen, and Liberia detracted from their primary role as armed guardians of the state and allowed an armed population to challenge the vestiges of that primacy. Militaries that had weakened themselves through corruption and distraction with power were incapable of reversing this trend and their weakness emboldened those who at the same time were enhancing their own power through the acquisition of arms. In Jamaica and Papua New Guinea there was, by design, little military to oppose the emergence of armed gangs and the police, outnumbered and outgunned, had settled into a siege mentality early in the evolution. In the Balkans and the Caucasus vestigial postsocialist militaries floundered at the edges of conflicts as militias constituted themselves as the new armies of the fragmented states. And even in Northern Ireland the British forces, untarnished by corruption but still distracted by their principal role of defending Western Europe from the Warsaw Pact, were unprepared for the finesse required to fight a protracted urban campaign. Politicization, distraction, and fragmentation among the militaries and police forces provided encouragement to those who, for a myriad of reasons, wished to devolve power away from the center and toward themselves. All that was required for this to take place was the catalytic event that would convert the availability of arms into the opportunity to redefine authority. This too came in many forms and nearly all would have taxed even the most disciplined of societies.

The coming of Kalashnikov enculturation occurred in two forms. The first was the result of a cataclysmic occurrence that took the existing elemental constituents and turned them, in the heat of events, into a new level and form of insecurity and violent interaction. The second form was that of a slow-burning movement that was accelerated at various points by the intrusion of a new factor. The first type is exemplified by the enculturation of Pakistan after 1979, by Sierra Leone during the Liberian civil war, and by Cambodia after the ousting of the Khmer Rouge. The second type, of a more methodical digression to enculturation, might include Yemen, Jamaica, Papua New Guinea, and the pastoralist communities of East Africa. For the most part the behavior and ramifications that were redolent of either the accelerated or evolutionary forms of enculturation were very similar but the shock of the former did create a momentum that, when mobilized, was very difficult to halt. The slow-burn model had its own dynamic; the Kalashnikov enculturation insidiously melded into existing customs and activities and by the time that it was recognized as an agent of real change it had embedded itself into the wider culture.

The accelerants that affected the development of both types of Kalashnikov culture could be externally or internally generated. Clearly, in the case of the Afghanistan/Pakistan enculturation the Soviet invasion and U.S. reaction were external factors. But the schisms within the Pakistani body politic, particularly in regard to the relationship between the military and civilian elite, tended to magnify the effects of the successive Afghan wars. Yemen had in many ways been the Fashoda of the Cold War, not coveted for real strategic reasons by either East or West but manipulated by both so that it would not enter the sphere of influence of the other.[16] Tribal and clan politics certainly contrived to weaken any central authority, as did the division of the country that was only overcome by the 1995 civil war. The insecurity of the Kalashnikov enculturation process also allowed other actors, including those that supported international terrorist agendas, to inhabit Yemen and this in turn drew the renewed attention of the United States and others who were the targets of the terrorists. At each juncture a new infusion of arms took place and a new level of insecurity was established.

One accelerant that hastened enculturation was the collapse of dictatorial regimes. Unvented frustration, combined with the dissolution of atrophied remnants of authority, allowed for both the retrieval of arms from the arsenals of the collapsed regime and an opportunity to use them to create a new order or to promote disorder. The economic opportunists were also emboldened by the blatancy of the sudden insecurity. Liberia, Somalia, Albania, and Cambodia all experienced this postdictatorial decompression and all, to a greater or lesser extent, leached arms and insecurity beyond their borders. It is this latter factor—the fluidity of Kalashnikov enculturation—that is perhaps of most concern to the international community. The neighbors of the decompressing states could not rely upon borders and sovereignty to protect them from events, since by its nature Kalashnikov enculturation represents the antistate. The buoyancy of the armed groups that represent Kalashnikov cultures ensures that they float above such niceties as boundary recognition and law of the sea. Their very strength is in not having to hew to the constraints accepted by the legitimacy-seeking proponents of the state system. The states would call these groups anarchic but they tend to see themselves as liberated.

The slow evolutionary road to Kalashnikov enculturation is itself not devoid of seminal events. In Jamaica these events included independence from Britain, key elections, the creation of garrison communities, and the arrival of arms and drugs in those communities. In Papua New Guinea enculturation was encouraged by independence from Australia, urbanization, the emergence of *raskolism*, and the undermining influence of drugs and alcohol. For the East African pastoralists the journey included the collapse of the Amin regime in Uganda, the civil war in Sudan, the rise of cities such as Nairobi, and the commercialization of cattle raiding. No single event or year can be pointed to and referenced as the beginning of these Kalashnikov cultures but a series of interlinked cause-and-effect relationships are compounded to achieve the level of violence, insecurity, and adjustment of power that signifies the process of enculturation.

Is a Kalashnikov culture simply another way of identifying and describing a failed state? In many ways the concept of a failed state is a subjective and culturally weighted idea. It is as though a country has been tried before the bar of Westphalian definition and has been judged unworthy of a passing grade. Is a state that fragments along well-established and historically supportable lines a failed state or is it reverting to its most sustainable identity? Is a state whose very sovereignty was asserted by colonial cartographers failing if tribes or clans challenge borders by freely moving across them without permission? Even in such transparent cases of "failure" as that of Somalia, is the division of Somalia into three tribally dominated areas an indicator of failure or simply that of logical devolution? Failed state has become a useful way of describing dangerous, complex places that challenge the neatness of the extant international system. Despite the negative connotations attached by Pakistani politicians to their baptism of the phenomenon, Kalashnikov culture is not so much about failure as it is about recognition of a set of events, elements, and actors coming together to create their own milieu of admittedly violent but nonetheless real society. In the following chapters this society will be explored through its constituents and in its realities.

Kalashnikov in the Culture: The Role of the Gun

Of course the gun is not all of it and the Kalashnikov is not always the gun. But the gun is a part of all of it and Kalashnikov is one of the most identifiable brand names from the twentieth century. Although the word "iconic" is much overused, in the case of the Avtomat Kalashnikov, or AK, the appellation is quite appropriate. People who have never seen, never mind fired, any firearm can identify the silhouette of the AK. Writers with no knowledge of weaponry can write glibly of the AK with the certain knowledge that their readership will be able to absorb the reference. In the words of one writer it is the "little black dress" of the gun world; ubiquitous and indispensable when trying to convey lethal intent. Deservedly or not it has become both emblematic and symptomatic of a world of chaos and insecurity. It is the representational image of that class of arms that are loosely characterized as "assault weapons" and as such it is used as shorthand for a particularly indiscriminate type of violence. But beyond the casual generalities that are heaped on the device certain anomalies relating to the AK have helped it to earn its reputation. There are reasons why Benazir Bhutto et al did not refer to an "M16 culture" or to a "FAL culture" and such reasons are worth some investigation.[1]

With the possible exception of Antarctica, the Avtomat Kalashnikov can be found on every continent. Although verifiable numbers of production are unavailable the most quoted estimate is that 70 to 100 million AKs of all variant have been manufactured.[2] The production and distribution of these weapons will be covered in detail below but suffice it to say that this figure, the largest production total for any of the assault rifle arms, is itself one of the reasons that the term "Kalashnikov culture" was coined. Tens of millions of these weapons virtually ensure a high degree of recognition and familiarity, especially when production has spanned more than fifty years. These numbers, when magnified through countless pictorial representations in film and photograph, form the quantitative frame around the Kalashnikov culture. But the numbers are only one factor that predicates the definition. The design and functionality of the weapon itself is another crucial element. In many ways it is a device that helped redefine war, moving it from the monopoly of the state to a level of individualized violence. The AK, born as an instrument of the people's war, became successively an instrument of liberation and of perverse individual empowerment. And it was able to fulfill this role because it worked.

Military arms have passed through many stages of requirement and design over the past two hundred years. In the eighteenth century the smoothbore long-arm, single shot and short of range, required massed, disciplined soldiery to achieve effect. Manufacturing was complex enough to require a certain level of industrial development that toward the end of that century had helped spawn a discrete arms industry. This combination of disciplined force and manufacturing base ensured that the mass effect of individual weaponry could only be achieved as an instrument of state power. To be sure, in the hands of the Minutemen or Montenegrin bandits such primacy could be challenged but these tended to be rule-making exceptions. Intimidation and ultimately lethality required the combination of numbers of arms in the hands of individuals who could overcome the deficiencies of the weapons through control and discipline. In many ways the Square performed the same role that the selector switch on the AK would achieve in the twentieth century, with mass of men substituting for a detachable magazine of six ounces of stamped metal.

In the nineteenth century the advent of the rifled barrel, the bolt action, and self-contained ammunition allowed the soldiery to exchange short-range mass effect for long-range aimed fire. The discipline of rank-based, shoulder-to-shoulder orderliness was replaced by the discipline that was necessary to master the basic fundamentals of ballistics. From ranges that could be counted in tens of yards in the previous period a mastery out to 600 meters and beyond was expected of the rifle-armed infantryman at the beginning of the twentieth century (the Mauser 1896 *handgun* had sights calibrated out to 1,000 meters.) Although mass effect could be achieved with these weapons (troops of the British Expeditionary Force in 1914 were reported to be able to exceed more than fifteen aimed shots per minute), the principal utility of these weapons was in there ability to precisely place lethal fire at extraordinary distances.[3] In order to achieve this the weapons needed to be machined to tight specifications, the ammunition needed to be regulated and inspected and the user needed to be inculcated into the science of maintenance and, amongst many other arcane skills, the art of calculating wind drift. Again, non-state actors could master these skills. The Boers in the South African conflict that bears their name were able to combine bush skills with Mauser rifles and smokeless powder ammunition to a particularly lethal effect against the British forces sent against them. But outside of this idiosyncratic skill set only the training environment provided by a state-based military structure could maximize the potential of the manually manipulated bolt-action rifle.

Even before the end of World War I doubts were beginning to be aired over the doctrine of long-range engagement that placed such demands of skill on the average infantry soldier. Engagements beyond 400 meters were exceptional and most casualties had been caused by machine gun and artillery fire. Storming trenches placed a premium on short, light weapons that could place the right amount of firepower rapidly and with the capacity to "sweep" the interior of the trenches once they had been invested. Various devices had been employed to achieve this effect, ranging from the pump-action trench shotgun employed by U.S. forces (and deemed illegally lethal by the Germans) to the submachine gun, invented by the Italians and firing pistol ammunition in fully automatic mode.[4] Both of these weapons were effective but with their highly limited range they could never do anything but supplement the rifle. What was really needed was a rifle that could combine the short-range utility of a shotgun/submachine gun with a capability to engage an enemy at the useful range of 400 meters. Such a weapon would emerge out of the reinforcing experience of German forces in the World War II.

During the interwar period the German army had settled upon the light machine gun as the core infantry weapon. With very high rates of fire (the MG-42 had a rate of fire of 1,500 rounds per minute) and the mobility required of a blitzkrieg-oriented force, the machine gun was protected by bolt-action armed infantry with support from submachine gun armed troops. In a bow to standardization the ammunition of the rifles and the machine guns were interchangeable, as was that of the submachine gun and the fielded pistols. However, experience in combat, particularly on the Eastern front, indicated that placing the monopoly of firepower in the purview of a crew-served weapon did not address the needs of the individual infantryman. Many observers were of the opinion that what was required was an individual weapon that could combine the high rate of fire of the machine gun with simply sufficient lethality at reasonable distances. Originally termed a machine carbine, later given the faux designation of machine pistol (submachine gun) and finally designated Sturmgewehr or assault rifle, it was this concept that was to metamorphose into the Avtomat Kalashnikov of 1947.

In many respects the importance of the concept of the assault rifle was eclipsed by the method of execution of the original idea. Certainly, portable firepower is an intrinsic element in the evolution of the Kalashnikov culture but the movement away from precise, aimed fire also freed the designers and manufacturers from the tyranny of precise, narrow tolerances. Since firepower was more important than accuracy the new weapon could be fabricated from pressed sheet metal rather than machined laboriously from steel billets. The internal mechanism needed to be robust in order to support high rates of fire but it did not need to be elegant or complex. Similarly, the ammunition needed to be lethal to its designated 400 meter range but the recoil of the weapon also needed to be controllable when fired offhand from the shoulder. The result was a weapon that gave the individual the firepower of a seventeenth-century battalion or a nineteenth-century infantry company and that could be manufactured by semiskilled labor on industrial stamping machines.

Germany produced some 426,000 assault rifles during World War II, with the majority being manufactured after D-day.[5] The designers had been forced to create their weapons in a clandestine manner because of resistance from conservative officers who still favored long-distance aimed fire (the designers called their weapon a machine pistol in order to evade detection) and most particularly from Hitler himself, who felt that the infantry was well served by the weapons that were already available. It was not until the conversion of Hitler to the concept in 1944 that the weapon, now named Sturmgewehr (StG) (ostensibly by the Fuhrer himself), was placed into limited production. The rifle itself was just one half of a combination that included the 7.9 Kurz Patrone round. This ammunition was, in comparison to the standard rifle round of the Wehrmacht, drastically reduced in both length and range. However, this reduction allowed thirty rounds of ammunition to be loaded in a detachable curved magazine and to provide control during automatic fire. This controllability was aided by a pistol grip that extended below the receiver. The net result of this configuration is that the Sturmgewehr bears an obvious likeness to the AK series and is clearly in design and function the forerunner of the modern assault rifle.

The StG rifle was heavy (12 pounds) and relatively long (37 inches) but the ergonomics of the weapon overcame these inadequacies.[6] The bolt-action rifle demanded both dexterity and uniform physical characteristics from the shooter in order to maximize its potential. Arms length in relation to the buttstock and forend (called the pull) was particularly important and only the proportions of an adult European/American male conformed to such measurements. Smaller statured people, women, and children were at a distinct disadvantage if required to use such weapons. But the pistol grip, buttstock and forend of the StG (and of the AK) were ergonomically suited to such users. Even if the weapon was too heavy to bring to the shoulder it could be manipulated from the hip and when fired on full automatic it could be an intimidating if not very accurate device. When combined with a sling the architecture of the gun allowed it to be carried with a high degree of readiness and comfort. These facets of design were what would transform the infantry rifle from a device that could only be maximized in the hands of trained soldiery into a utilitarian blunt instrument; less a weapon of the state than of the people.

Mechanically different but conceptually a twin, the AK-47 in its original configuration suffered from the same problems of weight and length that had been an issue with the StG. But more significantly the early versions of the AK did not take advantage of the stamped steel process that had been the true manufacturing breakthrough with the German weapon. It was not until 1959 that the stamped steel AKM was fielded, reducing the weight to seven pounds and similarly reducing cost per unit to a significant degree. When coupled with a steel folding stock and an increase in the durability of the magazine, the AKM became the quintessential assault rifle. Variations were manufactured in China (the Type 56), East Germany, Poland, Bulgaria, Romania, North Korea, Hungary, Yugoslavia, and Finland and in a new caliber, 5.45 millimeter, continued as the standard Russian rifle (AK-74) into the twenty-first century.

An unstated but important facet of the AK series of weapons is to be found in their appearance. The conformation of the pistol grip and the long curved magazine is one of the most widely recognized images of intimidation. When compared to the delicate wood-on-metal lines of the average bolt-action rifle the AK bespeaks raw power potential. The selector switch on the right side of the receiver is a crude but strikingly effective device, with the minor proviso that the audible "clack" when moved from safe to fire has been a signature of the weapon for more than half a century. Internally the AK is simple to maintain and replacing parts in the field from cannibalized weapons can be accomplished with little effort. The sights are equally simple (although graduated to an optimistic 1,000 meters) and the whole gun can be mastered by the mechanically illiterate in a few minutes. It will function without undue lubrication and will remain usefully accurate even with badly degraded barrels. The ammunition is a ballistic match for the venerable thirty-thirty deer rifle, which has taken tens of thousands of deer in North America over the past century. The magazines (always the weak spot in selective fire weapons) have proven durable and forgiving of weak springs and rust. The rate of fire at 600 rounds per minute is optimal for a weapon that will be fired on full automatic from the shoulder. In toto, the AK is not the perfect individual weapon but it is the perfect compromise. To be sure when shaken the internal parts rattle but in many ways this is the secret behind the success of the weapon. With clearances and tolerances that would be considered an example of unacceptable manufacturing practices by most aficionados, the AK can collect dirt and debris within its receiver and continue to function when other weapons would seize and become jammed. It is this inherent mechanical toughness that has proven to be the legacy of the AK and which is why examples that were produced in the 1950s are still as lethal as when they emerged from the factory. In many ways the AK is analogous to the landmine; it never ceases to be active. But unlike the landmine it can be used many times and it is eminently portable.

During the late 1990s Mozambique was attempting, in a modest way, to retrieve some of the estimated 3 million arms that had proliferated in that country during three decades of war. Some of these weapons were collected in warehouse in the capital Maputo prior to destruction. Most of the arms were AKs of various age and manufacture and all the weapons bore the hallmarks of abuse and subjection to Mozambique's tropical climate. In some cases the selector switches were frozen by rust and in others the stocks were cracked and held together with tape. However, a cursory inspection of the internal mechanisms and barrels of these guns indicated that with a liberal application of oil and some work with a hammer nearly all of the rusting firearms could be made to function. Some of the furniture (stocks and forends) on certain of the AKs was manufactured from a light plastic that lent a toylike appearance to them. Some clearly had machined receivers and could be dated to the early 1950 period of production. The collection included Hungarian,

Romanian, Bulgarian, East German, Chinese, and Soviet weapons.[7] This pile of rusting arms represented both the historical origins of the Kalashnikov culture and its current and future legacies. In the case of Mozambique the past included an initial infusion of arms to fuel a war of liberation against the Portugese. The armed and traumatized state that emerged from this conflict then devolved into one of the most intransigent and brutal of Africa's civil wars. An enduring image of the latter conflict was of President Samora Machel dispensing weapons to crowds of rallying supporters with little attempt to monitor to whom they went or how they were employed.[8] For many of the participants in these conflicts the arms that they acquired were the first consumer durable that they had ever possessed. For all of those that had arms there existed some form of empowerment, power potential if not power real. But after the government and rebel RENAMO forces had agreed to peace most of the weapons remained in the hands of the populace. With an economy considered to be one of the most underdeveloped in the world and with a population numbed by the blunt force trauma of thirty years of war, there was a certain inevitability to the nature of postwar society in Mozambique. Intimidation, banditry, and rapine replaced the political conflict without any discernible change in effect or constancy.

Even where serious attempts have been made to collect the detritus weapons in postwar societies, the persistence of the leftover arms has been remarkable. In Cambodia, three years after a major campaign began to disarm the populace one source estimated that there were still 250,000 light weapons in the hands of the general population, roughly equating to one gun per twenty persons.[9] After the end of the war against the Khmer Rouge many people have simply wrapped their AKs in cloth and buried them or sunk them in the mud at the bottom of ponds. Much of this resistance to disarmament was based on the belief that in a highly weaponized society to give up arms was to make victims of yourself and your family. In recognition of this in certain cases the Cambodian police actually gave AKs to vulnerable families, in tacit recognition that they could not provide the level of security that was necessary. Unfortunately such self-defense actions often resulted in an increase in the level of violence. For example, in Banteay Meanchey province of Cambodia, villagers armed with AKs resisted intimidation and robbery by a band of marauding soldiers, only to have the latter return to the village with a tank.[10] But in Kalashnikov cultures sometimes even a tank is vulnerable to the weapons available to the general populace and if the AK rifle is the antipersonnel weapon of choice then the rocket propelled grenade launcher (RPG) is its antimateriel counterpart.

In some areas of warfare the state maintains primacy and dominance, if not exclusivity. The complexity and cost of airpower militate against non-state actors challenging the state in the air, although Biafra during the Nigerian civil war and the LTTE forces in Sri Lanka were able to break the airpower monopoly of their respective foes.[11] Similarly, irregular forces are hindered from deploying heavy artillery by factors that include cost, complexity, size and mobility. In the case of armored warfare, substate actors might fabricate crude fighting vehicles or use captured stock but for the most part their concerns center upon how might light and poorly trained infantry defeat tanks and armored personnel carriers. During World War II this requirement had been met with a variety of devices, the most successful being the American bazooka. In the aftermath of that conflict armies developed recoilless rifles, wire-guided missiles and handheld launchers to attack armored vehicles, with the Soviet Union producing many millions of the latter. The RPG, in its many iterations, could be employed against armor, structures and groups of personnel through the use of a variety of warheads and it could be operated by a single individual. As with the AK, the controls are simple and the sighting arrangement robust and adequate. The launch tube (of the RPG-7 model) weighs less than sixteen pounds and the rockets themselves can be carried in multiples in a backpack. The image of RPGs being launched from the shoulder in conflicts such as Liberia, Bosnia, Lebanon, and Afghanistan is almost as iconic as that of the AK being fired and its power potential is even greater.

In sufficient numbers and against a weak enemy the Kalashnikov rifle can provide an irregular force with enough massed firepower to intimidate and overcome regular forces. Prophylactic firing, rather than aimed fire, can break the will of a force when all of its opponents are armed with automatic weapons. The added dimension of the RPG's explosive warheads can amplify the abilities of an irregular force by injecting destruction of buildings and vehicles into the equation. In many ways the RPG (and the hand grenade and other explosive devices) raises the threat posed by the belligerents within Kalashnikov cultures to the level of an insurgency, even if the owners of these devices have no intention of overthrowing the state. As is evidenced by the problems created for well-disciplined forces in Afghanistan, Iraq, and Somalia, the generation of enough zones of chaos within the battlespace can be an effective strategy to frustrate and even defeat a conventional force. The use of RPGs, mortars, and explosive devices signal to an enemy that an armed community is capable and willing to destroy property as well as to take life.

There is no "M16" culture because the United States sold few of these weapons to their allies and even fewer to non-state actors. When, as with Central America and Afghanistan, the United States did supply arms to insurgent groups, the arms that were most often transferred were Kalashnikovs and other Warsaw Pact weaponry. There were a number of rationales behind this strategy: such arms were "deniable" as being supplied by the United States, the armies of Nicaragua and Afghanistan were armed with Soviet weapons and captured stocks of ammunition could be used by the insurgents, and the weapons themselves were a better technological fit for the insurgents. In respect to the latter point it is significant that the M16 series of rifles has not been adopted and mimicked to the same degree as the AK series. Although M16s have been the subject of cottage industry counterfeiting (most notably in the Philippines) they have not been produced, even under license, by more than half a dozen countries.[12] The tyranny of numbers of AKs has, of course, depressed the market but the M16 itself, and the caliber of the ammunition that it uses, is also partly responsible for this lack of adoption.

The M16 series (and its newer M4 offspring) came into the U.S. small arms inventory almost by accident. In the 1950s U.S. small arms design was controlled from within the military bureaucracy and it was renowned for a conservative approach to the adoption of new weapons. The M1 Garand rifle, which had been the outstanding battle rifle of World War II and the Korean War, had been retained and then modified into a magazine-fed rifle firing the 7.62mm NATO round. Wood stocked, heavy, and largely unmanageable when fired in the fully automatic mode, the M14 represented the U.S. military doctrine that stressed long-distance shooting across European terrain. Aimed fire was still the tenet of infantry warfare and there was no attempt to accommodate the undisciplined or the untrained in the context of rifle design. But outside of the formal design community the America equivalent of Mikhail Kalashnikov, Eugene Stoner, was experimenting with a combination of mechanism and caliber that would become the M16. Using a design in which the gas from a fired cartridge bled directly back into the firing mechanism, thus propelling the bolt rearward in order to load the next cartridge, Stoner was able to put together an elegant weapon that eschewed the forged metal and wood designs of the past and instead could be mass produced from stampings and plastics. But it was the cartridge that broke the mould of U.S. small arms evolution. Unlike the previous battle rifle cartridges, the new .223 (later 5.56mm) round was not designed for long-range fire but rather to fulfill the same function as that of the AK and its 7.62 × 39mm ammunition. The new cartridge (designed around a commercial round used for vermin or varmint hunting) fired a lightweight bullet from a small case and with almost negligible recoil. This in turn allowed for a lightweight rifle that was capable of useful automatic fire and in essence it imposed the American imprimatur upon the Kalashnikov design concept.[13]

The early stage of adoption of the M16 was troubled by failures to feed ammunition and from a misperception that the weapon did not need to be cleaned as assiduously as other weapons (ironically the direct impingement system flooded the firing mechanism with carbon that could, if not cleaned, cause the bolt mechanism to seize.) But after these problems were addressed the weapon went on to become the rifle with the longest history of continuous issue to U.S. forces. For more than forty years, and with very little major change to the design, the M16 has seen service with all branches of the military and in addition tens of thousands of the civilian AR15 model have also been sold. The U.S. armed services still teach aimed fire with the weapon but its ability to be used to provide automatic suppressive fire has also been recognized and utilized. The cartridge that it fires, however, has been a matter of debate since its adoption and although it has increased in bullet weight since the 1960s there is still a belief amongst many that, unlike the robust bullet fired from the AK, the M16 round is not as lethal as it should be.

After the M16 was fielded in Vietnam there began a history of odious comparison between the American weapon and the AK. The weapons acted as Cold War proxies for differences in technology, doctrine, and policy. The Kalashnikov was the weapon for everyman but designed within a conventional state-owned bureau, albeit by a talented individual. The M16 was designed by a talented maverick out side of the system and adopted against the conventional wisdom. The Kalashnikov was a peasant weapon, the M16 was the weapon of professional soldiers. The AK was, in the words of one user "a weapon for men with dignity . . . that can be dropped in the mud, used in the water or clogged with dust and still work. But not the M16. It's for women."[14] In Iraq, where the military and police were traditionally armed with Kalashnikovs, the United States began to arm certain units with the M16. The latter was considered to be superior by many Iraqis and the M16s were certainly newer than most of the AKs in Iraq. But one Iraqi, after trying the M16 responded that he would take the "inferior" AK because "the M16 may be better for the Americans but the AKs are better for Iraqis." [15] Herein may lie a deeper issue: inferior but utilitarian technology (and tactics) can, in context, defeat superior but complex technology (and tactics.) In order to maximize the accuracy of the M16 in the hands of the Iraqi military it was not only necessary to train them on the weapon but also to untrain them in respect to the tactics and attitudes forced upon them by the design of the Kalashnikov. But these tactics and attitudes, while negative in respect to achieving the best from a conventional military, are just those that make insurgent forces so difficult to defeat. The short range of the AK, its hose-like effect on automatic fire and its relative inaccuracy are moot in warfare that stresses ambushes, executions, and the intimidation of civilians. The M16 represents war American-style while the AK represents war for the rest of the world.

The law of unintended, or unconsidered, consequences helped to create Kalashnikov cultures. As a codicil to the belief that the enemy of my enemy is my friend, the insecurity created by the mass proliferation of a simple and enduring weapon appeared to be an ally in the Soviet Union's strategy of destabilization of pro-western governments. That the arms would endure after the collapse of the Soviet Union would not have occurred to the promoters of this strategy. Similarly, when the United States proliferated major weapons systems into Iran during the regime of the late Shah it would not have occurred to those behind such a strategy that they were arming a future member of the "axis of evil." The terrible beauty of Kalashnikov enculturation is not in the elegant and simple design of the weapon that bears its name but rather in the devolution of power that it fostered beyond the era of ideologies. The symbolism represented by the gun, that of people's power growing from its barrel, lived on long after the ideology that promoted it had been eclipsed.

3

Kalashnikov Traffic: Trading Arms

In October 1994 a commission was appointed in South Africa to look into "the alleged arms transactions between Armscor and one Elie Wazan and other related matters."[1] Under the chairmanship of Acting Justice E. Cameron (by whose name the subsequent report would be known) the commission would spend nearly a year looking into what the body itself called the "Wazan debacle" or the "AK47 debacle." For South Africa this investigation, like those of the Truth and Reconciliation Commission, was at least partly a cathartic exercise to signal the break between the policies and ethics of the apartheid regime (Armscor was the state armorer during this period) and that of the new majority government. But as the investigation unfolded it became more than simply an attempt to give an airing to the transgressions of the past in South Africa. The Wazan affair itself was a microcosm of the global trade in gray (illicit) and black (illegal) market arms that fed the Kalashnikov cultures. As such, it will be used here as a convenient device to uncloak the sometimes opaque and often arcane domain of arms trading.

Within the remit of the commission virtually all of the elements of arms trafficking were present in one form or another. The arms in question had been transferred clandestinely into South Africa in contravention of international sanctions; they were re-transferred in contravention of South African law and the destination of the arms (Lebanon, Yugoslavia, and Yemen) were zones of conflict whose extant levels of weaponization had contributed to their devolution into civil war. The cast of characters in the Wazan affair included corrupt public officials, arms brokers, document providers, arms transport specialists, together with a moneyman of royal pedigree. The story itself, even in its incompleteness, was an illustration of how arms, particularly small arms, have multiple existences as they are moved from one theater to another and from one crisis to the next. The Wazan affair, in the great scheme of arms trading, was not a major event involving major transfers but it was typical of the pattern of behavior that contributed to Kalashnikov enculturation. Individuals, organizations, and states, for a variety of motives, came together to form a chain of responsibility linking Kalashnikov cultures on three continents. This was not simply about commerce but about transferring agents of change into volatile arenas with the possibility of changing events.

The onset of the Wazan affair occurred in September 1994 when a team of South African investigative reporters broke a story that South African weapons had been shipped to the Middle East.[2] The initial story linked the arms to the Palestinian Liberation Organization (PLO), with the implication that the new majority government headed by the African National Congress (ANC) was returning favors to the PLO for past support. When it became clear that multiple shipments and multiple destinations were involved, the government commissioned Justice Cameron to conduct an inquiry. It had already been determined that Armscor had acted as the selling agent on behalf of the South African National Defence Force (SANDF) and that the transfers were a holdover from the previous administration, rather than a token of what lay in store from the new ANC government. Indeed, the arms themselves were part of the detritus of the apartheid regime's aggressive defense policy and in many ways were an embarrassing footnote to Pretoria's adventurist forays into Angola and other frontline states. As is often the case with arms transfers, the embarrassment associated with possession became even more acute when attempts were made to rid South Africa of the weapons. Arms and scandal are logical cohabitants and the Wazan affair had all of the elements to appeal to the prurient observer.

The arms in question were, in 1994, in the surplus stock inventory of the SANDF. After a major reorganization in 1992 Armscor had been stripped of most of its previous broad mandate of supplying all the arms to the besieged South African defense community, with the one remaining function in 1994 being the selling of SANDF surplus material. The arms at the center of the Wazan affair were, like all arms that had been supplied to the white minority regime, obtained clandestinely and entered South Africa illegally. South Africa had been under an arms embargo since 1963 and under mandatory prohibition on arms sales since 1977 and as a result had developed a two-pronged strategy in which it created an extensive secret buying network around the world (it had more than 130 front companies) and supplemented this effort with a creative research and manufacturing base within South Africa (its G5 and G6 howitzers were purchased by Iraq). The only unusual aspect of the arms at the center of the Cameron investigation was that the suppliers had been the People's Republic of China (PRC) and Eastern European states that, at the time of the transfer, had been among the most vociferous critics of the apartheid government.[3]

The arms from China were 35,000 AK rifles, or more particularly the Chinese variant Type 56 rifle. They had been secretly acquired in the 1980s by a South African front company, Bowett International, whose managing director was the son of then-South African Prime Minister P.W.Botha. The company had been established, with the assistance of South African military intelligence, to act as a buying agent between the PRC and UNITA, the Angolan insurgency movement. The arms had been purchased on the instructions of South Africa's special forces and had been used to arm UNITA in their struggle against the socialist government of Angola. The PRC was fully aware of the destination and indeed Botha fils had lived in Beijing for two years while the arms pipeline was being established. Between 1976 and 1986 AKs had also been acquired in small lots from Eastern Europe, with Romania and Bulgaria being the two principal suppliers. The final group of arms was G3 battle rifles that had been purchased from Portugal to supplement weapons used by the South African military.[4]

Armscor was directed to find buyers for the AKs in 1992 and one prospective purchaser, the Christian militia movement in Lebanon, was identified. The purchasing agent for the Lebanese militias was identified as one Eli(e) Wazan, also know as Abbas Abdel Kader Abbas or General Abbas. This gentleman, hereafter known as Wazan, had been known to the South Africans as head of G2 or the intelligence section of the Christian Phalangist militia and had been in contact with Armscor representatives since 1984, at the height of the Lebanese civil war. Wazan/Abbas was also known for his close association with the Israelis, which, during the South African arms negotiations, proved to be problematic since his customer was a member of the Saudi royal family. Wazan had overseen South African shipments of arms to the militias in 1989 and by July of that year he had been appointed the exclusive agent for Armscor in its dealings with the Christian militias. By the late 1980s Wazan had become an arms broker on a full-time basis, using his connections with the Lebanese militias to sell their arms in the Balkans after the end of the Lebanese civil war and to solidify his relationship with Armscor.[5]

The arms in the Wazan affair had originated with state actors who were not averse to breaking sanctions in order to earn hard currency. Socialist dogma had so eroded by the middle of the 1980s that ideological strings were no longer applied to arms transfers. One of the rationales behind the sale of Chinese weapons out of the SANDF inventory in 1994 was the belief that the Chinese were about to flood the world market with 3 million Type 56 rifles and that this would depress the value of the South African weapons.[6] Certainly Norinco, the Chinese arms trading corporation, was aggressively pursuing markets in the developing world by the 1980s and with enough zeal that it would become the target of sanctions by the U.S. administration in 2003 (Norinco had been caught smuggling 2,000 rifles through the United States in 1996).[7] But another of the sanctions-breaking supplier of arms to the South Africans, Bulgaria, was perhaps the best example of unconstrained supplier during the 1980s and 1990s.

During the Cold War the Warsaw Pact states were delegated distinct niches within the socialist countries arms production strategy. Bulgaria was allocated the mission to produce small arms for use within the Pact and for export. The defense industrial sector within Bulgaria employed more than 100,000 people by the 1980s and it was exporting more than US$1 billion in arms by the end of that decade. In terms of hard currency earnings the Bulgarian defense sector was one of the few internationally viable and competitive industries that the government in Sofia could count on as the socialist system collapsed. For the state arms trading corporation, Kintex, this meant that Bulgarian arms had to be competitive in a market that was being inundated with arms from the former communist countries and from China. Kintex chose to make itself competitive through a completely uncontrolled and nondiscriminatory sales policy and in this way was able to maintain sales of $250 million during the difficult transition year of 1992.[8]

Small arms reach Kalashnikov cultures through a variety of means. We have addressed the trade and movement of arms within the cultures previously but the manner in which the arms are injected into the cultures is itself complex and diverse. In the case of Pakistan the arms arrived as an unintended consequence of Great Power politics and in the case of the pastoralists the arming of their Kalashnikov culture was the result of seepage from regional civil conflicts. But in much of Africa, including West Africa, the arms came from outside of the region and were supplied as an element in the international gray (illicit) and black market (illegal) in arms. The distinction here is one in which the gray market supplier is a witting and collusive government or its agents, while the black market is private individuals trafficking in arms in contravention of the laws of the supplier state. During the 1990s Bulgaria was a reliable gray market supplier and this made it a source of choice for arms traffickers moving arms into Kalashnikov cultures.

Unconstrained or rogue state sellers of arms are an important supplier into Kalashnikov cultures but they are not the only source. One of the most significant ways in which the cultures receive arms and ammunition is through intra-regional suppliers who act as purveyors of secondhand arms to militias, guerrilla groups, and criminal gangs. The sellers of these arms are almost exclusively black market dealers, engaging in illegal trafficking out of an area in which demand is low and into one in which demand (and therefore price) is higher. It is this supply-demand network that carries with it the elements of arms contagion, when the surplus of resolved conflict becomes the fuel of new confrontations. Examples of this lateral movement of arms include migrations from Liberia to Sierra Leone to Ivory Coast and the flow of arms from Cambodia through Thailand and into Bangladesh and India. These regional networks are often part of a broader trade in smuggled goods but the implications behind their movement from country to country carry political as well as economic ramifications. Trafficking in arms, perhaps more than any other illegal movement of goods, threatens to upset the status quo and is therefore inherently political. In Southeast and South Asia, with their plethora of separatist and irredentist groups, arms migration is an agent of regional instability as well as one of human insecurity.

During the 1990s Cambodia was heavily weaponized. After the occupying Vietnamese forces left the country in 1989 the internal political situation was volatile and violent. The Khmer Rouge still existed in parts of the country, banditry was rife, and the national leadership was fractious and uncertain. Political factions, bandit groups, and common people armed themselves in order to protect their property and persons from competitors and predators. They equipped themselves from the estimated quarter of a million AKs that were available to the general public, allowing for one weapon per twenty people.[9] Perhaps inevitably many of these weapons, even before controls were exerted in 1997, began to gravitate from Cambodia, where they sold from between $5 and $50, to other markets in Southeast and South Asia, where they commanded much higher prices. From Thailand west into Bangladesh and north through Vietnam into the PRC the weapons of Cambodia were moved along well-managed smuggling routes and into the hands of their final end users.

Arms trafficking in Southeast Asia could be very profitable if the arms could be moved cheaply from the area of oversupply to that of high demand. In 1995 the cost of a new AK rifle at the Thai–Cambodian border was approximately $80 to $150.[10] Moving the arms across Thailand to the Burmese border area, where Mon and Karen rebels conducted transborder operations into Burma, the price of the rifle had risen to $350. Passing the rifle into Burma and into the hands of Shan rebels the value rose to $600. Along the trail some rifles were sold to Thai fishermen to help protect them against pirates and others were diverted to Sri Lanka and to Bangladesh. Cambodian arms also passed through Vietnam and into China, where they were used by criminal gangs in robberies and to protect drug territories. The smuggling routes themselves were protected by corrupt officials and by armed security personnel who would guarantee delivery for a fixed price. When, in 1993, the Cambodian prime minister related that "if thirty percent of those involved in (selling) war weapons were soldiers, the rest would be police," he was not contradicted.[11]

The customer base for Cambodian weapons was exceptionally diverse. It included *yakuza* gang members in Japan, separatists in the Indonesian province of Aceh and on the Philippine island of Mindanao, gangsters from Macau, political assassins in Thailand, and political parties in Bangladesh.[12] Some of the transactions were in the thousands of units and others were for tens of AKs but the numbers were less relevant than the potential for disruption that each transfer occasioned. Perhaps nowhere was this potential greater than in Bangladesh, whose fragile political and economic infrastructure was particularly vulnerable to armed factionalism. In the 1990s Bangladesh found itself host to a number of groups that were engaged in political feuds with Burma and India, including Shanti Bahini rebels and members of the Rohingya Solidarity Organization (RSO), both of which conducted cross-border raiding and both of which required arms to continue their struggles. But weapons were also being transported into Bangladesh to arm the supporters of the many political parties and subgroups in that country.[13] With some 165,000 political "thugs" (they are variously described as members of organized crime syndicates or as "mastans" or extortionists) identified in the pay of party "godfathers" the potential for civil war or prolonged armed conflict was omnipresent in Bangladesh. What was not present were sufficient weapons to equip these bands of supporters since Bangladesh had never traditionally been an armed society. It was this factor that made the availability of arms from outside of the country, and particularly from Cambodia, so potentially destabilizing.

Geopolitical anomalies lend themselves to political and commercial exploitation. Between 1912 and 1956, Tangier was an international zone and a haven for smugglers who exploited its tax-free trading potential. Pre-World War II Shanghai, with its own international zones, enjoyed the same reputation for unconstrained entrepreneurialism and lax law enforcement. Cox's Bazaar in Bangladesh is not an international zone but it does, in its isolated position at the end of a peninsular territory alongside the Indian and Burmese borders, share many of the characteristics of the aforementioned. It is in many ways an entrepot for smuggled goods emanating from Southeast Asia and entering the regulated markets of South Asia. The arms are smuggled into Cox's Bazaar by trawlers or other small vessels and are then transshipped to Chittagong and Dhaka, the capital of Bangladesh.[14] With prices for submachine guns and AKs up to four times those achievable at the Thai-Burmese border, the return on investment for the traffickers has been worth the slight possibility of seaborne interception. For the most part the trans-national implications of this trade have been restricted to concerns from India and Burma in respect to the arming of insurgent groups operating against their respective governments. However, the emergence of Islamic extremism within Bangladesh, coupled with the increase in political violence after 2000, made the flow of arms through Cox's Bazaar a regional as well as national issue.

The Latin American equivalent of Cox's Bazaar is the Iguacu Triangle or the Tri-Border area. This geopolitical anomaly, with a population of 700,000, is where Paraguay, Argentina, and Brazil form a confluence around the Iguassu Falls in a region that had traditionally been underdeveloped. In order to encourage development the Paraguayan government created a free-trade zone around the city of Ciudad de Este and this in turn spurred growth in the nearby Brazilian town of Foz do Iguacu (Foz) and the Argentinian city of Puerto Iguazu. The free-trade zone attracted shoppers from Brazil in particular and soon smuggling became the major industry in the region. Entrepreneurs, including some 30,000 Arabs and an equal number of Chinese, established commercial organizations in the three cities to exploit the possibilities of the Tri-Border trafficking and inevitably the activity attracted the interest of organized crime.

By 2001 Ciudad de Este was generating $12 to $13 billion in cash transactions. Money laundering was an important facet of these transactions, as was trafficking in pirated and counterfeited goods from China and drug trafficking with the Colombians.[15] Organized crime elements from the PRC, Korea, Taiwan, Lebanon, Russia, and Nigeria operated within the Triangle and by the 1990s reports of al Qaeda and Hezbullah recruiting and fundraising were also being confirmed. Chinese *triads*, Japanese *yakuza*, Chechen mafia, and Colombian cartel members availed themselves of the relaxed law enforcement and political ambience of the Triangle in order to conduct their business with little interference.[16] One of the most entrenched of these businesses was the trade in small arms and the largest customer for Iguacu Triangle guns were the favela gangs of Brazil.

In 2002 an AK could be purchased in Ciudad del Este for $375.[17] Chechen traffickers were active in bartering arms for drugs with members of the Colombian gangs and groups such as the Argentinian "Local Connection" were beginning to dominate the trade into Brazil.[18] However, by the onset of the new century arms trafficking out of the Triangle was already a mature occupation. As the Brazilian gangs moved from the era of the knife-wielding malandro to the gun-carrying bandido, the demand for arms in Rio and the other Brazilian cities increased exponentially. During the transition period in the 1980s and early 1990s the guns that were most in demand were long-arms and handguns from the United States (in 1997 more than 30 percent of all long-arms seized by the Rio police were U.S. made.)[19] The semiautomatic version of the M16, the AR-15, and Ruger Mini-14 carbines were particularly valued and both of these could be legally purchased in the United States by individuals and were available for legal export with the acquiescence of the U.S. State Department. When thousands of these firearms began to be exported to Paraguay in the 1980s, it was obvious that 500 percent profit margin between the price in Miami and that in Rio had proven to be tempting to the arms traffickers.[20]

Foreign nationals may purchase firearms in the United States, with certain rules applying at the state level. Arms can also be purchased through the illegal "straw man" method, in which local people are paid to acquire guns for those that do not or cannot purchase the guns themselves. Some of the arms that found their way to Brazil were illegally purchased but most of the arms that were exported from the United States to Paraguay were done so legally as an item of trade and were then smuggled through Ciudad del Este and thence to the favela gangs. After being made aware of this conduit the United States banned civilian sales of arms to Paraguay in 1996 and the arms trafficking organizations that supplied the gangs needed to find another supplier.[21] They found the source within Brazil itself. In the first ten months of 1996 Brazilian gun manufacturers exported 21,000 firearms to the Paraguayan town of Puerto Caballero, which had a population of 30,000. By the late 1990s it was estimated that 70 percent of the arms being used by the Brazilian gangs had passed through Paraguay and that many of them had originated from Brazilian arms factories.

Cox's Bazaar and the Iguacu Triangle are two of the more blatantly obvious transshipment centers for arms trafficking. Together with Darra/Peshawar and the Yemeni and Somali arms bazaars, they represent the open face of arms trafficking. In these places the distinction between gray and black markets is blurred by corruption and imprecise laws. They exist in degrees of vacuum that encourage risk-takers to engage in activities that would not be worthwhile in more constraining environments. They also encourage cohabitation between political extremists and criminal groups and help to foster communities of interaction that can become global in reach and implications. Chechens and representatives of Colombian guerrilla groups might have met in Iguacu to trade arms for drugs but they might also come into contact with Hizbullah recruiters, Nigerian money launderers, rogue Argentinian military officers, and Chinese *triad* leaders. These contacts, casual though they might be, could be used in the future to create a loose but eminently useful net of acquaintanceship that could facilitate international organized crime, insurgency, terrorism, and war.

Between arms suppliers, whether gray or black, and customers are the brokers. In the case of the Wazan affair there were in fact two brokers. Wazan was one and the other, acting on behalf of the purchaser, was Joseph der Hovsepian. Variously described as Syrian or Lebanese, Hovsepian had been connected to the arms trade for some years by the time he and Wazan negotiated the purchase of the South African rifles. He was a colleague of one of the most enduring of post-World War II arms traders, Gerhard Mertins, and a partner in his company, Merex.[22] Mertins had begun his brokering career in the 1960s, selling surplus equipment for the West German government (he had been involved in a scandal in which West German aircraft had been transshipped through Iran to Pakistan in contravention of an arms embargo) and had then moved on to broader deal-making, including a role in the Iran-Contra affair. Hovsepian had moved to Germay to work with Mertins and after the death of the latter Hovsepian became an entrepreneur and arms broker in his own right. To the Cameron Commission it was clear that "Hovsepian had a sophisticated appreciation of the international arms business." For at least two of the parties in the Wazan affair Hovsepian was also a man who engendered some fear in his associates.[23]

Brokers have been perhaps the most difficult element to regulate in the chain of arms trafficking. Gray market suppliers can be embarrassed or given incentives to conform to international standards (Bulgaria was encouraged to change its ways as a pre-requisite for membership in NATO and the EU) but brokers rarely act in a manner that is illegal and often never come into contact with the arms shipments or even with the final end user. They are the expediters who bring all of the necessary elements together and then take a fee for services rendered. Attempts have been made to regulate the activities of brokers (the United States has a law, an amendment to the Arms Export Control Act that requires brokers to register) but the amorphous nature of their business means that such regulations are often unenforceable. The arms brokering community is relatively small in number and the idiosyncrasies of the trade in arms ensured that it is a specialist activity that requires mastery in order to pay dividends to the broker. As was to transpire in the Wazan affair, part of the mastery involved a penchant for trickery.

Hovsepian and Wazan, the two brokers involved in the South African case, shared a background and a professional relationship. The professional relationship will be outlined below. The background, that of arms trafficking into Lebanon during the fifteen years of that country's civil war, was shared, to a greater or lesser extent, by nearly every arms broker operating in the 1970s/1980s. All combatants, but particularly the Christian militias, needed a constant supply of arms and ammunition to conduct the attritional warfare that characterized the Lebanese conflict. Often using established elements of the Lebanese diaspora (Lebanese merchants conduct business extensively in Africa, Latin America, the Caribbean as well as in the Middle East) the militia purchasing agents tapped into every available supplier of arms during the civil war. Israel provided arms to favored groups but as the conflict progressed more of the arms of all sides came from the Eastern bloc. To pay for the arms the militias engaged in a number of activities, including counterfeiting and kidnapping, which were easy to conduct within their lawless society. The most lucrative of the fundraising activities, however, was drug trafficking and the transnational nature of this trade encouraged the evolution of Lebanese organized crime, one branch of which had taken root in the Iguacu Triangle. There is no evidence that either Wazan or Hovsepian was involved in drug trafficking but their chief sponsor, known to the Cameron Commisssion as Prince Anwar Bin Fawaz Bin Nawaf Al-Shalaan (hereafter Prince Anwar), was accused before the commission of being involved in drug smuggling.[24]

Prince Anwar was (and is) a member of the Saudi royal family domiciled in Jordan. Active in a number of ventures in Jordan, including foreign exchange and financial services, Anwar had, in the early 1990s, been looking for investment opportunities elsewhere. He had looked at a sporting goods company in Austria and was also interested in doing business in Yemen. A self-professed neophyte in the area of arms trading he was reliant upon Hovsepian, a close friend and sometime partner, to act as his "broker" between Wazan and Armscor. Anwar would provide the money to acquire the weapons, which would then be shipped and sold on to the final purchaser. In respect of the deal that Wazan and Hovsepian brokered in 1994 the identity of the final purchaser was always in some doubt but, given the history of Hovsepian and Wazan's relationship with Armscor, this was not unusual. At least three times before, from 1991 to 1993, arms had left South Africa destined for one country and had ended up in another.

In early 1991 Croatia began to arm itself in preparation for the coming confrontation with the Yugoslav army. Arms were purchased wherever they were available, including Lebanon. Hovsepian, through Wazan, purchased weapons from South Africa, including 10 million rounds of ammunition and nine antitank missile launchers, and shipped them to Europe, with a final destination of Croatia.[25] Armscor, however, had been told that the arms were going to Lebanese Christian militias, which at that time were an acceptable client. It was only when part of a shipment supposedly destined for Lebanon was impounded by the Belgian authorities that the real destination (the arms went to the ports of Rijeka and Marina di Carrara) was made evident. Armscor stated that it was unaware that the destination had been changed to Croatia but the Cameron Commission was openly disbelieving. Prince Anwar had not been involved in these shipments but in 1993 he and Hovsepian, using Wazan as their contact with Armscor, bought another consignment of arms from the South Africans. Again, the stated destination was Lebanon and again the arms ended up elsewhere.

These subterfuges were necessary because South Africa had become increasingly sensitive about who acquired its arms. In 1983 the government in Pretoria had begun to categorize countries according to levels of acceptability as recipients of arms transfers. Group 1 countries had no restrictions placed upon them and could receive any arms from South Africa. Group 2 countries could only receive "non-sensitive" equipment and Group 3 states were not eligible to receive any arms.[26] As an example of how policy was adjusted in the final decade of the apartheid regime, in 1987 the Lebanese Christian militias were in Group 1 and by 1994 they were classified as Group 3. In respect of the real destination of the Hovsepian/Wazan arms, Croatia was a Group 3 destination, as was Yemen. Jordan was a Group 2 state. But this grouping system was not the only problem faced by Wazan et al. In May 1994 South Africa, in conformity with nearly every other country, instituted a process of contract verification known as an end-user certificate (EUC). This was a document transmitted to the transferor state by the would-be recipient confirming that the arms were destined for that country and would be used by its national military or police forces. For Wazan, who had been tasked by his group to provide such a document, this was a problem because the arms in 1994 were not really going to Lebanon, which was their ostensible destination, and therefore no genuine Lebanese EUC could be provided.

There is a trade in EUCs as there is a trade in arms. States that are embargoed or under sanctions, including those engaged in an armed conflict, need to acquire false EUCs in order to acquire arms. Some supplier states are stringent in their requirements for a verifiable EUC on a proactive basis, that is, before the arms are shipped. Other states are less punctilious and do not bother to verify the authenticity of the documents. Perhaps more egregiously, officials from certain countries will sell false EUCs to provide paper cover for illicit and illegal arms shipments. Fake EUCs are documents that, in the words of one of the Wazan affair conspirators, would not be "checkable," that is, they were forgeries that would not withstand an inquiry by the arms seller. In the early 1990s false EUCs, signed by a genuine official of a foreign government and therefore "checkable" were selling in the range of $30,000 to $100,000; the EUC used in 1994 to release weapons ostensibly going to Lebanon cost $50,000 and was a fake document that was a crude forgery.[27]

The conflicts of the 1990s created a buoyant market for EUCs. The Yugoslav civil war, the Somalia conflict, and wars in the Caucasus region all inflated the cost of documentation. In 1991 Croatian arms procurers paid $35,000 for an EUC that had been authorized out of the headquarters of the Nigerian army in Lagos and covered such items as 500,000 AK rifles and 10,000 RPG-7s.[28] The following year a British investigative team paid £1,000 for a blank, that is unsigned, EUC bearing the imprimatur of the Royal Omani Police.[29] Sometimes government agencies that issued EUCs were simply, in the words of a US Senate subcommittee commenting on Belgian practices, "so loosely controlled that they are not worth the paper they are printed on."[30] Sometimes the arms sellers, under pressure to create profits, chose not to inquire too closely into the authenticity of the documentation (in 1989 the British Department of Trade and Industry was made aware that British companies were shipping arms technology to Iraq using false Jordanian EUCs but chose not to act on the information). Bulgaria sold arms to a number of traffickers using false EUCs for munitions supposedly destined to the Philippines or Nigeria with little or no checking of the documentation.[31]

The reason that the EUC used in the Wazan affair was so expensive, even though it was a fake, was because of the greed of Wazan himself. Paid by Hovsepian and Prince Anwar to purchase a "checkable" false EUC, Wazan instead put together a crude counterfeit of a Lebanese EUC and then pocketed the $50,000 that he had been paid to purchase the false-flag document. One of the reasons that Wazan believed he could succeed with this maneuver was that he had, over the previous decade, cultivated a senior member of the Armscor hierarchy. Marius Vermaak was manager of the stock sales department in the company and in this position had been able to exceed his sales goals during the early 1990s by 100 to 400 percent. With almost no oversight, the running costs of the stock sales department were funded out of the money received for sales of surplus South African military equipment and this provided a strong incentive for the department to aid buyers in the clearance procedures required by the South African authorities. In all legitimate and gray-market arms purchases there is an official who acts in the dual role of seller and facilitator. This individual sets the prices, signs the contracts, and assists the buyer in moving the goods out of the country. Establishing a long-term relationship with such a person is clearly to the advantage of a broker such as Wazan and such a relationship perhaps inevitably compromises the judgment of the official.

Corruption occurs in many gradations, from pure avarice to acts resulting from mistaken friendship. In the case of the Wazan affair the level of corruption did not appear to be profoundly venal but nevertheless Vermaak did, according to the judgment of the Cameron Commission, become a partner in the venture rather than remaining an objective outsider. When in 1993 a shipment of Armscor weapons, bought by Prince Anwar and overseen by Wazan, failed to end up in Lebanon and instead went to arm Prince Anwar's "men" in Jordan, Vermaak was aware of this diversion but chose to ignore the possibility that the weapons had been used to equip a private army. In fact, it is most likely that this shipment went to Yemen, as was later attested to by Hovsepian. To give Vermaak credit, however, he did demand to meet with Prince Anwar, Hovsepian, and Wazan in order clarify concerns over the 1993 shipment. Meeting in a hotel in Switzerland, Vermaak spoke with Hovsepian and the prince together and then separately with Wazan. It was at his meeting with Vermaak that the prince informed the South African that Wazan was being dropped from further dealings because of "Wazan's intelligence connections with Israel."[32] It was also at this meeting that the prince, believing that Vermaak's concerns were a ploy to extort money from the prince, offered Vermaak a $100,000 "kickback" (in the word of Hovsepian) that the South African refused.[33]

It would be convenient to state that the intrigues surrounding the Wazan affair were an anomaly and that trading in arms, even gray-market trading, is usually more staid and less dramatic. However, the Wazan affair is really only anomalous in that very few such dealings have been the subject of an open government investigation. Fake documentation, inappropriate relationships, attempted or successful bribery, and distrust amongst the principals are often elements in the conduct of arms trafficking. The invocation or reality of involvement by an intelligence agency is also quite common in the world of arms trading; the traders themselves often forge relationships with the intelligence community in order to protect themselves and intelligence agencies value the access to information that arms traffickers accrue during the course of their business. The multinational aspect of the Wazan affair is also not unusual in such dealings. The involvement of Lebanon, Jordan, Saudi Arabia, Israel, Croatia, Yemen, Switzerland, Germany, and South Africa in the transactions is simply indicative of the complex nature of arms trafficking. But the presence of actors from one other country, Denmark, might be considered uncommon, if it were not for the fact that the representation from that country came in the form of transportation, specifically the ships that carried the arms from South Africa.

Transporting munitions by ship is a specialist activity. It is regulated by international rules and national laws and it requires an understanding of the volatility, real and political, of the cargo. Given the controls and restrictions placed upon this type of cargo the transportation of arms is often carried out by small companies who concentrate on this niche market. These companies operate with ships in the 2,000 ton range that are built for operating out of unimproved ports that have minimal off-loading capabilities. The ships themselves, often part of shallow-draught fleets that ply inshore trading routes in the Baltic and the Black Sea, almost always have an onboard crane that allows them egress and ingress into places that are structurally primitive and marginally policed. The ship that transported the AKs out of South Africa in 1994, the *Arktis Pioneer*, was just such a ship and her owners, Elite Shipping of Denmark, had extensive previous experience in moving munitions under clandestine arrangements. In 1985 Elite, using sister ships of the *Arktis Pioneer*, was the carrier that secretly transported munitions from the Israeli port of Eilat to the Iranian port of Bandar Abbas in an arms-for-hostages transaction that became part of the Iran-Contra affair.[34]

Shipping arms often involves transportation brokers and in the case of the Wazan affair this role was filled by Michael Steenberg, whose companies specialized in hazardous shipping. Steenberg, a Danish-American resident in North Carolina, used his skills to help move difficult cargo into difficult places. During the early 1990s he had been involved in shipping goods into Russia at a time when trade with that country was adventurous and indeed the Cameron Commission was to characterize Steenberg as a "modern-day buccaneer and a rogue."[35] He was the charterer on the earlier contracts when the arms ended up in Croatia and Jordan/Yemen and he had proven adept at massaging the necessary paperwork. The operator of vessels (the *Skybird* and the *Anke*) on these earlier trips was another Danish citizen, Jorgen Pouosen, who had been fined in the 1980s for breaching South African sanctions. He was also the operator of the vessel involved in the 1994 shipment, the *Arktis Pioneer*. Steenberg's contacts with the Danish fleet operators was one of the reasons that Wazan needed the charterer but there was another reason involving documentation and clearance that required Steenberg's talents.

During the negotiations in 1993 for the weapons that would eventually end up in Yemen, Prince Anwar had demanded that Wazan include all shipping, insurance, and freight charges in his contract with Armscor. However, Wazan's arrangement with Armscor was a free on board (FOB) contract, in which the burden of arranging shipping was on Wazan. It was therefore up to Wazan to provide documentation as to the final destination of the goods and this was where Steenberg was needed. Using false names and a false destination (Beirut) Steenberg drafted a bill of lading that was accepted as genuine by Armscor. For the shipping company he then drafted a bill of lading that identified the real destination, Yemen, but that was kept secret from Armscor. Wazan also needed Steenberg as a front man in the 1994 dealings because Prince Anwar had stopped his association with the Lebanese by that time. Steenberg therefore became the ostensible agent for Anwar on the 1994 shipment and he again took care of the bills of lading. The owner of the *Arktis Pioneer* would not accept Steenberg's destination as simply a Red Sea port and demanded that Yemen be on the bill of lading that they had in their possession (this bill was not released to the South Africans until after the ship had left their shores). Steenberg then made false bills of lading for Armscor, as he had done for the previous shipments and the *Arktis Pioneer* sailed for Yemen with 24,000 rifles and 14 million rounds of ammunition on board.[36]

The transportation saga of the South African arms centered on maritime arrangements but by the mid-1990s Kalashnikov cultures were being supplied by an informal air bridge of companies that, often using Russian and Eastern European personnel and aircraft, provided a more responsive and far-reaching service than that offered by their maritime competitors. Much has been written of the most notorious of these aerial traffickers, Victor Bout, but in reality he was just one of many entrepreneurs who were willing to exploit the demand for transport companies who would fly arms into conflict zones or to support embargoed customers.[37]

The United Nations had itself cause to investigate airborne arms traffickers throughout Africa on a number of occasions and as a result it was able to establish their modus operandi. Under the heading of deceptive practices, the UN cataloged the manner in which these air carriers avoided or evaded oversight by monitoring authorities. Subterfuges included the use of false flight plans, fraudulent use of call signs and flight numbers, constant changes of company name and registration, forged registration and airworthiness certificates, false declarations on cargo manifests, refusal of pilots to contact control towers in the countries that they overflew, and the use of complex company structures that defied identification of the rightful owner of the aircraft. After inspecting the documentation of twenty-four aircraft at Bukavu and Goma airports in the Democratic Republic of Congo (DRC), UN investigators found that there were problems with either certificates of registration, airworthiness certificates, or insurance coverage on nearly all the aircraft. UN teams found documents that were out of date, invalid for operating in a war zone or had simply been fabricated.[38]

It would seem possible to control the activities of aircraft that must use prepared fields to land and that need fuel and some form of support in order to deliver their cargo. But in an environment like the DRC, with its 350 to 400 airfields and with almost no radar coverage, even a United Nations monitoring force could not oversee the activities of the aerial arms traffickers. In a country where roads were used as airstrips, where new runways were carved out of the jungle by militias, and where arms were dropped by parachute, the interception of arms trafficking flights was likely to occur more by accident than design. In an analysis of arms flow into Eastern DRC, a British All Parliamentary group determined that some legitimate airlines had even been forced to transport arms by local militias under threat of violence and destruction of property.[39] On other occasions aircraft were found masquerading as UN relief planes. Aircraft flying into Angola were found to be using airfields after officials had left for the day and where radar facilities had been closed.

Shallow-draught ships and errant air carriers take advantage of the dislocation and disorderliness that is inherent in Kalashnikov cultures. Some of the cultures themselves facilitate the suppliers by engaging in document or accreditation schemes that provide the necessary fig leaf to allow transportation companies to flout international regulations. Liberia flagged both ships and aircraft throughout its civil war and this facilitated arms traffickers as well as providing money for the national exchequer. Other countries establish free zones that allow airlines of dubious pedigree and deceptive practices to operate from a politically protected environment. The aforementioned Victor Bout was identified in six UN investigations as trafficking arms into areas under embargo but, operating from his base in a Gulf state, he managed to avoid arrest or personal sanction as he continued to ply his trade with the largest private fleet of Antonov aircraft in the world.[40]

The *Arktis Pioneer* sailed for Yemen on August 25, 1994, and three weeks later a news report appeared in South Africa outlining what became known as the Wazan affair. On September 22, Armscor was informed that the shipment had not gone to Beirut but instead the *Arktis Warrior* had docked in Hodeida, Yemen, where the consignee had inspected and rejected the cargo. Between the arrival of the first of the shipments to Yemen and that of the last shipment the country had been through a short but deadly civil war that had ended in July 1994 and it is plausible that these events had some effect upon the acceptability of the weapons (the consignment was also made up mostly of AKs that were of the full-stock configuration and it was known that the folding-stock version had been requested.) The arms were returned to South Africa, where they were subject to litigation.[41]

There were few ramifications from the Cameron Commission report. Most of the principals to the Wazan affair had been questioned but no individual was charged or suffered legal penalty from the events. Vermaak, the Armscor official, was proven to have accepted money on behalf of his daughter's school and there were charges that he had accepted use of a time-share in Cyprus by the conspirators.

Steenberg continued to operate his charter companies and although Hovsepian was under investigation by the German police for illegal activities he was not brought to trial. Prince Anwar also continued with his business ventures in Jordan and did not appear to have suffered from the publicity surrounding the Wazan affair. The Lebanese broker himself was wanted by the authorities in his home country and had not been available to the Cameron Commission, which estimated that he had made perhaps $200,000 for the deals. Prince Anwar, Hovsepian, and Steenberg had also profited from their mutual involvement in the sale of the South African arms but it was not known by how much.[42]

The arms from the Wazan affair ended up in two Kalashnikov cultures; the Balkans at the onset of its civil conflict and Yemen on the eve of its own civil war. They left the inventory of a pariah state at the end of its own internal strife and their transition was expedited by a man who learned his trade during the Lebanese civil war. This is not an untypical pattern in the supply of arms to the cultures. The arms go from where they are no longer valued or needed to places where continuing or incipient conflict creates demand. The traffickers use knowledge gained in conflicts in which they are involved, often in the procurement or intelligence sectors (Wazan was in both), and they parlay this knowledge into the profession of arms trading. The transportation of arms attracts brokers and shippers who understand the idiosyncratic nature of the business and who believe that they are discreet and small enough to avoid attention. All parties are attracted by the premiums attached to arms sales that are the result of the trade's risks and cyclical nature. Some may be attracted to the Byzantine nature of the trade, which in many ways is more dramatic than the way that it is portrayed in fiction. Certainly few arms traffickers appear to be stricken by conscience in respect of the likely outcome of their actions. As the Cameron Commission noted in the afterword to its report: "Throughout the proceedings we were struck by the detached way in which the witnesses described their business of selling weapons. We wondered whether any of them had ever given thought to who used their weapons, against whom, for what reason, and with what consequences. Finally, we put this question to Vermaak. He told us frankly that he never thought about such issues. He was a salesman after all, not a politician."[43]

Kalashnikov Commerce:
The AK as Economic Instrument

In his work on the economic functions of civil wars David Keen observes that "at the top and at the bottom of society, violence can be an opportunity rather than a problem."[1] Similarly, Paul Collier, while working at the World Bank, concluded that "rebellion is large-scale predation of productive economic activities."[2] This view of conflict can be taken to extremes (it tends to overlook the confused mixed motivations behind many wars and insurgencies) but in Kalashnikov cultures the gun is certainly both itself an item of commercial opportunity and a facilitator of predation. The gun and its ammunition are an item of barter, an instrument of intimidation, a tool of aggression, and a promise of security. In each of these guises it can be used to acquire wealth or to sustain life, even as it destroys the prospects of long-term development and takes the lives of the innocent. Kalashnikov enculturation provides a bubble of insecurity and threat under which those who can exploit this volatile milieu can become, in the words of a former British prime minister, "the unacceptable face of capitalism."[3] But even this descriptor does not adequately cover the commerce that evolved in Mogadishu, Peshawar, the favelas of Rio, or on the streets of Port Moresby. In such places the economics could best be described as postcapitalistic, freed as it is from the rules and regulations that constrain the flow of capital in disciplined markets.

Kalashnikov commerce is found in two forms. One is the trade of the gun, that is the buying and selling of small arms and ammunition within the Kalashnikov culture. The other is a broader category of trading that is parasitic upon the conditions prevailing in anxious, unstable, and ungoverned societies. The trade in guns within the cultures, of course, is part of the chain of challenge that weakens central authority and creates the conditions that allow for the other aspect of Kalashnikov commerce to thrive. A buoyant and open market in small arms is an indicator that the threat of violence is high enough to encourage purchasing weapons and that whatever authority may exist is too weak to stop the trading. That indicator of weakness is also an encouragement to engage in what some have called a "war economy" but which is in effect a naked economy, denuded of everything except the pursuit of profitability. That is not to say that there are not rules within this naked economy but rather that such rules that exist assume that the threat of violence substitutes for the threat of state sanction. Given the role of violence in the conduct of business it is tempting to compare Kalashnikov commerce with that of the organized crime but the Sicilian mafia or the N'drangheta or the yakuza have always had to operate clandestinely, in fear of higher authority. The stallholders and shopkeepers in the market of Bakaaraha in Mogadishu might still have to look over their shoulders but it is their customer base that creates anxiety rather than the agents of government.

Bakaaraha, even more than the Iguacu Triangle in South America or Peshawar in Pakistan, was the archetypal bazaar of the Kalashnikov culture. Established in 1972 as an alternative to existing overcrowded markets, from its inception it had a reputation as a place where law enforcement was loath to intrude. The rules governing the activities of the more than 10,000 people who work in the market were predicated not upon the laws of the land, which became moot after the beginning of hostilities throughout Somalia in 1991, but upon the protection, physical and regulatory, provided by traditional clan-based organization and order. Constantly evolving, Bakaaraha went through periods of a genuine war economy and then, after 1995, settled into a hybrid of globalized trading center, dominated by cartels, and the small stallholders who fed into a network of street-sellers, many of them women.[4] Within Bakaaraha were many submarkets, most of which would be found in any market or bazaar throughout the developing world. The pricing of goods and the ready and open availability of counterfeit products, including pharmaceuticals, reflected the idiosyncratic nature of trade in the market but it was the section of the market named Cir-toogte that set Bakaaraha apart from others of its ilk.

Cir-toogte (literally shoot in the sky; buyers test their weapons by firing in the air) formed the arms trading section of Bakaaraha. Together with the Argentina arms market in the north of the city, Cir-toogte, with its fifty stores and booths, provided a barometer of security and insecurity within Mogadishu and Somalia. The availability and prices of arms, many of them Kalashnikovs, indicated whether the clans were preparing for armed confrontation (in early 2005 prices rose by 85 percent as the clans prepared to confront forces of the Transitional Federal Government), whether the flow of arms from Yemen had been interrupted (a maritime force patrols the Somali coast enforcing a United Nations embargo), or whether the market was glutted as militia members sell their weapons because of relative peacefulness and they need the money for purchases of qat or other commodities.[5] As the factional fighting ebbed and flowed in different parts of southern Somalia so the arms traders propositioned the warring factions with the contents of their inventories. In this way arms circulated as a form of currency, substituting for cash in a society where cash itself was suspect (counterfeiting was rife and the national currency almost nonexistent.) As the arms wore out they were cannibalized, with many weapons being the sum total of three or four previous incarnations, and existing stocks of weapons were supplemented by new arrivals, many of which pass through Yemen on their way to Mogadishu. Stockpiling of weapons by the Cir-toogte traders ensured that even when attempts were made to stop the flow of new weapons coming in to Somalia the impact was lessened.

Some of the arms that were sold in Bakaaraha were provided to Somali warlords by Ethiopia and Eritrea in an outreach example of the rivalry between those two states. The United Nations team that monitored arms trafficking into Somalia traced arms in the market to shipments of small arms made by Ethiopia to favored militia leaders, who then traded them for larger weapons. But most of the new weapons were acquired from Yemen, in a clear example of how one Kalashnikov culture interconnects with another on matters of arms and commerce. Some of the Yemeni arms might have come from Yemeni government stocks but most were acquired from the souks such as that at Al-Talh and shipped in dhows across the Gulf of Aden to Puntland, the de facto state that lies to the north of Somalia.[6] Adapting to the possibility of interception by foreign naval task forces operating in the Gulf of Aden, the trafficking syndicates split their cargoes into smaller consignments, joining them back together after they reached Puntland, and then shipping them in truck convoys down to Mogadishu. Similarly, Djibouti allowed itself to be used as a transshipment point for arms destined for Somalia, with significant numbers of Bulgarian arms being passed through Djibouti on a false end-user certificate.[7]

Not all arms in the Horn of Africa passed through vendors in large markets. There was a lower level of arms trading that was not as dramatic in its impact as Bakaaraha but which in many ways illustrated how deeply weapons have become part of economic life in Kalashnikov cultures. Somaliland, to the north of Puntland and one of the three para-states that emerged after 1991, was not the place of violence and militia thrall that typifies Mogadishu and southern Somalia. Militia-led conflict did occur in Somaliland during 1991–1996 but in relative terms peace was maintained after this period. Nevertheless, the society had been weaponized during this time, with arms being deposited within the body of the population from militias, government forces, and arms markets supplied from outside of Somaliland. Most families acquired multiple weapons during this period of insecurity and they kept the guns as a hedge against future violence. The guns were also a hedge against the uncertainties of what, even in Somaliland, was an uncertain economy. Ownership of multiple weapons allowed a surplus item to be sold (or bartered) should it be necessary and this trafficking fueled networks that often fed into the markets in Mogadishu.[8]

While trading in one or two rifles might not appear to be at the heart of Kalashnikov enculturation, the rationales and actions that accompany the acts of sale and transportation are quite fundamental to an understanding of the phenomenon. The fungibility of arms makes them a viable investment in places where the arms have helped to create political instability and economic uncertainty. The duality of the Kalashnikov, as guarantor of physical security and as transportable wealth, is highly valued and in societies with few consumer durables the gun's intrinsic qualities are important. One observer of arms ownership in Somaliland has identified this form of ownership as "passive," in that arms "constitute a reserve," both against future physical threat and economic hardship.

In Somaliland the transfer of arms was conducted in an illicit context, with none of the openness found in Mogadishu. Women were often involved in the trade, with the assumption that they are less likely to be suspected and far less likely to be searched at roadblocks. Traveling on buses or on trucks (often sharing the space with cargoes of qat) the gunrunners (the term is appropriate here) moved small amounts of ammunition or one or two rifles from one town to another, taking advantage of price differentials (in the late 1990s an AK sold for between $100 and $300 in Somaliland) within their area of trade.[9] In certain parts of the country camels and donkeys were used extensively to transport weapons, while in other places qat planes moved arms in a mixed cargo. The arms themselves were considered a commodity and although they required a certain amount of special treatment they had been fully integrated into the economy of Somaliland. Nevertheless, the level of insecurity and violence in both Puntland and Somaliland, where arms were available to those that want them, was deemed to be significantly less than in the Somalia/Mogadishu. Access to arms, even in the Horn of Africa, did not readily translate into full Kalashnikov enculturation. However, in the rump of Somalia a full representation of the phenomenon had matured during the 1990s and after the turn of the century the economic activity beyond the simple trade in arms was discernibly aberrant.

One aspect of Kalashnikov commerce that was absent in Somalia was the manufacturing of local weapons. In Bakaaraha there were former soldiers who fixed unserviceable weapons and cannibalization of guns was quite common but there was no indication that a cottage industry of gun making existed. But in many weaponized societies the supply of factory arms was not as guaranteed as it was in Somalia and demand for weapons created, as in Darra, a manufacturing sector. For the most part this activity was limited to supplementing expensive factory arms that might have been available on a limited basis but which were often beyond the purchasing power of the local population. However, the very evidence of these attempts at furnishing weapons without an external supplier does raise the issue as to whether Kalashnikov culture is a misnomer. If enough military-type weapons of sufficient quality can be manufactured in the environs of a conflict then it is possible that the movement of arms into the area is not necessary in order to create a pseudo-Kalashnikov culture.

The city of Danao on the Philippines island of Cebu is the center of *paltik* or homemade gun making in the archipelago. Since the beginning of the twentieth century family based groups of artisans have produced substantial quantities (it was estimated that 6,000 guns a year were manufactured locally by the beginning of the twenty-first century) of both copied and original firearms designs.[10] The metal for the arms comes from the ship-breaking yards in Cebu City and the guns themselves range in price from $375 for a submachine gun to $15 for a crude revolver. The products of the Danao workshops (which are illicit but uncontrolled) feed into a weapons culture in the Philippines that consists of some 900,000 registered firearms owners and an estimated 600,000 unlicensed owners. The customers range from local police forces to the militias of political strongmen to *yakuza* gangs from Japan. The arms from Cebu also crossed over to Mindanao island, where insurgents used the arms to continue their actions against the Philippine armed forces.[11]

It is estimated that the paltik trade supports 20 percent of the population of Danao and this made any attempt by the national government to permanently close the workshops politically problematic.[12] Hoping to control without alienating the population, the approach from the government in Manila followed closely that of Islamabad's attempts to control the gun makers of Darra; they co-opted the paltik by establishing a legal entity that would manufacture and sell the guns under a license from the government.[13] As with the Pakistani situation, undercapitalization and a poor sales strategy (the workforce could not support large orders for arms because their workshops were not equipped to make quantities of weapons) undermined this attempt and many of the paltik makers reverted to supplying the illegal market. Much of that market centered on providing armed support for local political leaders and many of those that carried the arms were young lumpenists recruited to provide protection for their clan or kinship associates. Periods prior to elections see an increase in the number of paltiks sold and the number of incidents in which the guns are used.

In India the local equivalent of the paltik weapon is the *katta* or country-made gun. Unlike Pakistan, India has maintained strict gun control laws since partition (for example, no handgun over .32 caliber may be privately owned) and as a result there has evolved a trade in illegal weapons, many of which are kattas.[14] These weapons, crude when compared to the guns of Darra or Danao, sell for $10 to $20 and they are most often used for criminal purposes (less than 1 percent of the weapons used in crimes in the city of New Delhi are licensed.) The trade is particularly active in the state of Uttar Pradesh, where the small town of Bamgaur in the east of the state has a reputation for gun making that mirrors that of Danao.[15] The manufacturing process, in which artisans fashion the different parts of the guns in separate locations in order to confuse the police, is ponderous but still allows for the production of 150 kattas for criminal groups per month. The gun makers are proud enough of their work that they stamp the name of their town on the weapons and "Bamaur" weapons have become valued for their craftsmanship, even though many are made from such materials as bicycle frames. There are also some 9,000 katta-makers in the state of Bihar, many of which cater to the demands of political leaders and their factions.[16]

In Africa the availability of factory-built arms has tended to suppress the development of locally-built firearms but where prices are high cottage industries have evolved. In South Africa the *kraal* shotgun is made in bush factories that produce five or six guns a week. Using hacksaws and metal from ploughs and piping (which has no rifling and therefore leaves no ballistic evidence), the gun makers forge receivers over charcoal fires in one-room shacks. The end result is a weapon whose crudity makes it almost as dangerous to the user as it is to the target but the intimidation factor remains and at short ranges it is still lethal.[17] The limitations of these weapons predicate their manner of usage and for the most part they are carried more than used and used only in circumstances in which the victim is unarmed and vulnerable. Unlike the Kalashnikov, the paltik, katta, and kraal do not imbue the owner with the capacity to confront armed militias, police, or military at the same level of firepower (although many paltiks are equivalent to the AK in their firepower, if not their durability). These are the weapons of the poor and the predatory and their style of usage reflects their limitations.

In Burundi the locally manufactured firearm is the *mugobore* or artisan rifle. These devices were first fabricated during the civil war that began in 1994 and they were used to supplement machetes, which were cheap and universally available. As with kraal guns the mugobore were manufactured in rural villages, mostly by farmers attempting to supplement their incomes. Made from pieces of wood and pipe and fired by a spring striker mechanism, the gun sold for $10 and was the preferred weapon of the bandit community that added to Burundi's insecurity during the ten years of civil conflict in that country.[18] But it was its use as a weapon by the ethnic militias in Burundi (similar weapons were also used in Rwanda during the genocide) that again raises the issue of whether these types of guns are more than simply an interesting but fundamentally irrelevant footnote to understanding Kalashnikov enculturation. While it is true that in both Rwanda and Burundi it was troops armed with imported small arms that stood behind the militias and allowed them to conduct the mass killings, under certain conditions the crudity of the weapons matters less than the fact that those employing them are willing to take life. In Burundi this form of aggressive resolve has become ritualized to the point that when a woman is approached by a man brandishing a mugobore, she acquiesces to rape based upon the assumption that death is the alternative.[19] In both Burundi and the Philippines young men rush into marketplaces, firing their locally made arms in the air. After the population is stampeded out of the area, the gangs in both countries steal product and money from the stalls. Again, the efficiency of the arms and the proficiency of their users are less important than the effect of the assault upon the victims. In many ways this is a crude variation upon the very result that the German military was trying to achieve with the Sturmgewehr; the shock of attack was as important as the infliction of casualties.

Industrialized nations often have skill levels and raw materials that can provide weapons to insurgent groups or militia armies that allow them to confront conventional militaries. In the Caucasus the conflicts in Nagorno-Karabakh, and Chechnya saw much use of sophisticated light weapons that were manufactured by engineers and metal workers who had no background in gun making but whose creativity made up for their lack of specialist knowledge.[20] Making mortars from the drive shafts of trucks and submachine guns out of the ubiquitous domestic piping, Chechen rebels and Armenian militias were able to confront and hold conventionally armed opponents at low cost and with tactical effect.[21] Similarly, in the 1990s Irish authorities found small factories in their country that were manufacturing mortars and handheld rockets for the Provisional Irish Republican army (PIRA).[22] In England machinists servicing the criminal world re-activated weapons that had been legally deactivated and in some cases converted toys into viable weapons.[23] In the United States, where selective-fire military weapons are tightly controlled, machinists and rogue gunsmiths have used spare-parts kits and illegally manufactured receivers to create arms for a relatively small (legal arms are so available in the United States that procuring illegally manufactured weapons makes little sense) collector and criminal market.

On a local basis the cottage industry of gun making may create income and employ artisans but the overall impact on national economies is small. Even in the United States the commercial manufacturing of firearms employs only some 17,000 workers (in contrast, there are 61,000 floral designers in the United States).[24] But the numbers employed and wealth created is only one aspect that inhibits governments from controlling or curtailing this activity. Kattas and paltiks are symbols of empowerment for the poor and unprotected within their societies and to stop their manufacture might be seen to discriminate against those who cannot afford to purchase factory-made arms. In a real way the arms made in shacks and sheds represent the divide between those that are protected by the weapons in the hands of the authorities and those that must defend themselves. It is ironic, therefore, that the homemade weapons are also those most likely to be used by bandits, dacoits, and others who might prey upon the poor. The kattas, paltik, kraal, and mugobore guns may lack the prestige and recognition factor of the Kalashnikov, but they share the ambiguous traits with which the latter is burdened. The homemade weapons are not sold with a limiting device that restricts them to hunting and self-defense and therefore they are as susceptible to unconstrained and aggressive use as is any factory-made weapon.

In 2003 the UN panel of experts tasked with the reviewing affairs within Somalia were moved to characterize the nature of the "war" economy of that country: "On the margins of the international community, the Somali people have been left at the mercy of 'governments' who pay their bills in counterfeit currency; faction leaders who demand tribute for the use of public assets like ports, airports and even sections of road: commanders who reward their troops with ammunition or *khat* (sic); people traffickers who smuggle economic migrants on rickety boats to Yemen or on aircraft to Europe; and foreign interests that bestow arms, cash or political legitimacy upon their proxies of the moment."[25] Within this terse analysis is the embodiment of Kalashnikov commerce. Where national governments provide services as an obligation of representation, in Kalashnikov cultures such services are provided by those that control territory through force of arms. Formal taxation is supplanted by informal extortion and threat of retaliation substitutes for legal recourse on issues of breach of contract. That which is illegal in orderly societies, such as trafficking in people, is an element of the service sector in those places where economic and physical insecurity drives people to illicit emigration. Drugs, arms, and ammunition become acceptable tender in a society where any relief from threat, whether through the consumption of mood-altering drugs or the ownership of weaponry, is valued.

The naked economics of Kalashnikov commerce are, by definition, lacking in subtlety but they refer to the same set of needs that are to be found in any trading community. What is supplied (and how it reaches the marketplace) and what is demanded may sometimes be unusual but the fundamentals of supply and demand are still what drives the internal economies of such places as Somalia. But there is another aspect of these places that the United Nations and other bodies have found even less acceptable than the Darwinian nature of their domestic economies. The trade in stripped natural resources, such as logs and minerals, not only degrades the environment within the Kalashnikov cultures but the manner in which the products enter the marketplace creates issues that have global ramifications. Perhaps even more importantly, the uncontrolled exploitation of these resources has encouraged conflicts to cascade into areas not originally fought over but whose promise of loot motivates the belligerents to expand their areas of operation. The expansion of the Liberian conflict into Sierra Leone is one such example of this cascading effect but perhaps a more blatant example occurred in Africa's Great Lakes wars, when the eastern provinces of the Democratic Republic of Congo (DRC) were subjected to economic rapine by militias and militaries from throughout the region.

Trees form part of the naked economy of Somalia but it is not logs but charcoal that is the most valuable export commodity of the entity. The charcoal that is exported from Somalia to Saudi Arabia and the Gulf states is prepared from acacia trees harvested within Somalia. During the first four months of 2005 some 40,000 metric tons of charcoal (culled from approximately a quarter of a million trees) was shipped from Somalia's seaports and the $8 million of revenue from these shipments was spread among the thousands of producers, collectors, and traders who maintain the unregulated trade.[26] A 25-kilogram bag of charcoal sold for $5 at the Somali port of exit and for between $15 and $20 at the point of consumption in the Gulf States or Saudi Arabia. The United Nations group monitoring the trade traced most of the activities, from production to wholesaling, to various militias in Somalia and estimated that the profits were "used to buy arms and reinforce the security apparatus of the militias."[27] The consequence of uncontrolled cutting for charcoal production was an elimination of some species of acacia, with the effect of creeping desertification and loss of grazing for the pastoralist community. As a result the export of animal stock, which was once the largest earner of revenue for Somalia, was surpassed by that of charcoal, which then placed pressure on rural people to destroy more areas of scrub and woodland.

The exploitation of agricultural resources in a Kalashnikov culture is fraught with difficulties. As previously noted, the freedom that is required to graze and manage herds in semiarid locations is severely restricted by the insecurity inherent in the cultures. But even where traditional farming is an economic mainstay there are still opportunities for armed parasitic groups to extract wealth from behind the walls of insecurity. In Abkhazia in the Caucasus, for example, the hazelnut and mandarin orange farmers were subject to the predations of armed militias and "mafias" who, taking advantage of the complex security situation in the region, gained control of much of the harvests through intimidation and hijacking.[28] Harvesting the sea can also be problematic within the environs of Kalashnikov cultures: the United Nations characterized Somalia's fishing industry as having "deteriorated into a 'free for all' among the world's fishing fleets."[29] Even along the relatively peaceful coast of Puntland fishing boats were armed with heavy antiaircraft cannon as they plied the dual occupation of fishing and arms smuggling.

Plundering natural resources behind the walls of Kalashnikov insecurity was taken to extremes in eastern Democratic Republic of Congo (DRC). It was here that armies from seven African states fought a war over the control of the resources of the DRC and used their respective armies to engage in hyper-pillage. Ugandan and Rwandan soldiers encouraged unrest among the tribes of the area and then used the resultant conflict as the raison d'etre for a maintained presence, which in turn allowed them to control trade and extract resources. Zimbabwean forces, aligned with the DRC government in Kinshasa, signed lucrative commercial contracts in return for their support and established an elite network of Zimbabwean, Congolese, and foreign businessmen to asset-strip the region. The foreign partners included Ukrainian organized crime figures, Belgian arms manufacturers, a Zimbabwean arms dealer/sports promoter, and Lebanese criminal "clans" of diamond smugglers and counterfeiters. The Zimbabwean-Congolese connection was primarily interested in diamonds, cobalt, and copper and operated sophisticated and violent theft rings that looted private and state-owned mines throughout eastern DRC. Revenue from mining in the areas controlled by the armed force of the DRC was used to acquire arms, as were monies collected within the Ugandan and Rwandan controlled areas.[30]

Perhaps the most transparent example of DRC's klepto-economy was the illicit mining of coltan. This ore, from which the mineral tantalite is obtained, came into prominence in the 1990s as demand accelerated because of its use in the manufacture of cell phones and other electronic devices. The DRC held the world's largest deposits of the mineral and as the price rose to $345 per pound the armies and militias within eastern DRC began to export the ore by aircraft out of bush airstrips. Investigators estimated that between November 1998 and April 1999 Rwandans removed 1,500 tons of coltan from DRC, using their own military and the militias that they supported.[31] The air bridge that was required to move the ore from DRC to Rwanda was conducted by airlines whose shareholders included major Rwandan political figures and whose operators included Russian and Ukrainian personnel. Even the tempo of the conflict in the area was dictated by coltan mining; Rwandan forces would fight their way into an area with coltan deposits, using intelligence on when the ore was ready for shipment, and then withdraw with the spoils. Ethnic and political rationales that had existed as casus belli disappeared as the looting of resources became the principal reason for continuing the hostilities.[32]

The conditions that existed in DRC and Somalia are locust events. Every resource and human activity is open to predatory practices. What occurs is not so much illegal as beyond law (the United Nations found itself having to attempt to define "illegal" in its report on "illegal" exploitation of DRC resources) and the arms that are an element of the commercial interplay in these places are the instrument of enforcement in this lawless environment. Without the arms and ammunition the armies and militias could not "enforce the lawlessness" necessary to conduct their strategy of loot and resource extraction. The aircraft that took coltan, diamonds, and gold out of DRC returned with arms, which were then dispensed to militias who continued their warfare that in turn perpetuated the instability that allowed for continued "illegal" resource theft. This symmetry of perpetual upheaval was in many ways the perfect storm of Kalashnikov commerce. The arms were both a currency in the conflict and a creator of wealth opportunity.

The warlord economics of Somalia and the Congo are definable examples of the informalization of war. It is, of course, arguable that the conditions were as much about the formalization or regularization of criminal behavior as they were about redefining war. Semantics aside, civil conflicts, in Africa and elsewhere, are fought for a variety of mixed motives, many of which undergo transformation during a period of open warfare. These transformative movements often involve existing elements that may be dormant within the society and that are given new life from the soup of instability and insecurity inherent to Kalashnikov cultures. The reemergence of witch-hunting in both East and West Africa is one such man-ifestation, as was the strange metamorphosis of student fraternities in Nigeria.[33] In the latter case, a movement that began as an exercise in identity development during the colonial period mutated into university-based urban gangs with po-litical attachments and economic motivations. These fraternities, dubbed "cults" by the Nigerian media, had been established in the 1950s by the Nobel Laureate Wole Soyinka with the intent of helping to form a Nigerian national identity as a prelude to independence from Britain. In the postindependence period the fra-ternity movement spread across university campuses in Nigeria and by the 1990s most campuses hosted thirty or forty of these secretive organizations. The original benign intent behind the fraternities had changed over the previous forty years and the newer versions were more gang-like than intellectual debate societies. Initiations often involved rape and robbery and the faculty and administrators of the universities were subjected to bribery, blackmail, injury, or even death if they challenged the cults.

The metamorphosis of the Nigerian "cults" is an essay in how social muta-tions form within the boundaries of deeply insecure societies. After independence Nigeria suffered through a debilitating civil war over the oil-rich state of Biafra and then the oil itself helped to create the quintessential kleptocracy. By the 1990s Nigeria had become renowned for its globally oriented confidence tricksters, its "pen robber" bureaucrats and increasingly for its diverse forms of civil violence. In the north of the country religious conflicts took the lives off thousands and in the south tribal clashes over access to power and the oil wealth became increasingly common. Political strongmen searched for supportive constituencies and during the 1980s they turned their attention to the university secret societies. Increasingly the societies or cults became tools of politicians and university administrators in their confrontations with reform-minded students and it was at this time that "the guns came into the picture."[34] Like most of the former British colonies Nigeria had not been a gun culture before independence but the Biafran conflict had helped to spread a knowledge of guns and to proliferate a certain number of weapons within the country. But, as with Jamaica and other Kalashnikov cultures, the arms that created the chronic instability in the south of Nigeria were dispensed as political largesse by the lords of insecurity within the country's body politic. Inevitably, once the cults were armed and protected by their sponsors they became unmanageable and a threat to the wider community. By the beginning of the twenty-first century these cults had become part of what Human Rights Watch termed the "prevailing culture of immunity" in Nigeria.[35]

The economic impact of the tribal, religious, and political violence within Nigeria was profound and widespread. Extortion took place at every level of government and the roads of Nigeria were intersected with the checkpoints of illegal "tax" gatherers. When security forces were deployed to chronically violent areas the police and soldiers demanded money from the twice-victimized population in order to perform their duties. But the dislocation and violence did, of course, provide opportunities of a nontraditional nature. Arms, including AKs, were smuggled into the country from the battlefields of West Africa and security forces sold their weapons to the cults and other gangs. Blacksmiths worked on locally manufactured arms and political parties continued to supply their supporters with guns in return for practicing intimidation against rivals. Nigeria's pattern of intimidation, extortion, smuggling, and paid thuggery were quite traditional elements of Kalashnikov commerce but there was another activity, that of bunkering, which was particular to that country.

Bunkering is the theft of oil (including crude) and petroleum products from pipelines or installations.[36] Oil had been discovered in Nigeria in the 1950s but it was not until the 1970s that the country had become a major exporter. With a production capacity of 2 million barrels a day, Nigeria relied upon oil revenue for 90 percent of its foreign earnings and 80 percent of its budget. However, little of the oil wealth reached the people and the combination of gross corruption by oil officials and environmental damage became a political cause celebre in Nigeria. When the chief critic of corruption, Ken Sar-Wiwa was executed in 1995 the tribes occupying the oil-producing Rivers State began a low-level insurgency against the oil companies and their installations. Again, what may have begun as a protest movement quickly became an arena of economic exploitation as attacking pipelines gave way to tapping into the lines and selling the crude to a network of middlemen. By 2002 between 60 and 150,000 barrels a day were being stolen or "bunkered" from the oil lines in the Niger Delta, with the whole enterprise being guarded and fought over by tribal militias, cultists, and vigilante groups.[37] For some of these groups, most notably those of the local Ijaw tribe, bunkering was a way of funding their struggle against the federal government and for others it was simply about gaining access to an illegal trade that in 2005 was worth some $1 billion.

Stealing oil from pipelines, some of which were buried, required a particular level of corruption and instability. Unlike eastern DRC or Somalia the state had not collapsed in Nigeria and the federal government still had the power to commit the Nigerian army into the hinterland. But the combination of cultist violence, tribal disaffection, political warlordism, and aggressive criminality was enough to "create a state of anarchy" in the Niger Delta region. Oil workers were ambushed and kidnapped, installations were vandalized and the Nigerian military and security forces responded with increasingly harsh measures. Attempts were made to broker a peace with the major tribal groups but the theft of oil had become an economic rather than a political activity. By 2004 the situation had become precarious enough that a threat by one of the Ijaw groups to launch an "all-out war" in the oil region was enough to raise the global price of oil above the $50 per barrel price for the first time.[38]

Kalashnikov commerce is centered upon a construct that obeys the laws of supply and demand but which eschews the laws of imposed economic discipline. Within Kalashnikov cultures taxation by the centralized authority is often unenforced and what taxation does occur is simply part of the predatory enterprises of gangs and militias. Counterfeit products are openly marketed because there are no authorities to enforce regulations. The physical and economic untenability of life in places such as Somalia encourages human trafficking, with resultant depopulation and incidents of forced labor.[39] Insecurity interrupts planting and harvesting cycles and drives people to rely upon food sources such as bush meat from wild animals, with a concomitant increase in zoonotic diseases.[40] Work conditions in the logging and mining camps under the control of militias in the Congo have lowered the resistance of the workers and made them likely to be exposed to the conditions that encourage outbreaks of ebola and other hemorrhagic diseases.[41] The breaking of taboos against mass killing of women and children during cattle raids in East Africa force women to seek the safety of urban areas, where they may engage in prostitution to support themselves and their families and thus expose themselves to HIV and other sexually transmitted diseases. All of these are ramifications of Kalashnikov commerce and, together with the trading in drugs in uncontrolled areas and the ebb and flow of the weapons themselves, constitute elements of an economic process that is beyond capitalism.

Pakistan: The Prototypical Kalashnikov Culture

The inception of the prototypical Kalashnikov culture did not spring fully formed from Afghanistan in 1979 or even from the dislocative violence of South Asian partition in 1947. The growth culture had matured across centuries, perhaps millennia, so that when the admixtures of the twentieth century were added they found a well-established, fertile environment from which to develop their own variation on a theme. It was an environment that had forced both the British and Russian empires to recognize limits to their acquisitive agendas and it was one of the rare corners where the concept of the modern state foundered on the rocks of tribe, clan, and family affiliation. Power was always very personal in the lands of the Pathan (Pashtun) and the Baluch and any attempt to create institutions beyond that ring of personal association was considered by the locals to be a zero-sum equation that had to be resisted. Indeed, resistance became a tradition and an avenue of opportunity for the nations, tribes, and clans of Afghanistan and northern Pakistan. The Great Game was as much about the manipulation of Russia and Britain by the locals as it was about competitive espionage between the great powers themselves. And whenever the tribes were depicted as participants in this drama they were never without their rifles and their knives.

The British lost 16,000 men during the retreat from Kabul in 1842. If this disaster had not been the subject of nineteenth-century spin (the British public was very sympathetic to the portrayal of disaster as heroic, poetic tragedy), it could have severely undermined the program of expansion that impelled British imperial ambition. The fact that it came at the hands of non-Christian, unmodernized and state-rejectionist forces only served to worsen the impact and to force the British, after successive campaigns in Afghanistan, into a tacit recognition of the limits of their imperial power. What was tacit became concrete in November 1893 when British official H.M. Durand and Amir Abdur Rachman Khan signed what became known as the Durand Line agreement. This agreement, the Hadrian's Wall of its time, recognized that it was better to buy off and leave to their own devices those fractious elements that would not recognize the beneficence of colonial authority. Unfortunately, as with many attempts to solve complex matters through the tyranny of cartography, the Durand Line created as many problems as it solved, most notably through an arbitrary division of Pashtun tribes between those who were citizens of the Raj and those who were Afghanis. But the overall significance of the Durand agreement was not lost in the details; if a group can make itself dangerous enough then it can use its penchant for violence to wrest money, influence and recognition from a nominally greater power. The Pashtun and other tribes who lay beyond the Durand Line were simply too willing to resort to the aggressive defense of their marginal lands for it to be worth conquering and policing them by an overstretched colonial power.

In many ways the modern state of Pakistan drew its own Durand Line when confronted with the issue of tribal areas at the time of the construction of the Pakistani constitution. The Federally Administered Tribal Areas (FATA), including those around the North West Frontier Province (NWFP) and Baluchistan, were placed in an administrative limbo in which they lay within the sovereignty of Pakistan but outside of its direct control. This was a legacy of the approach that gave birth to the Durand Line and it was itself, at a time when the very existence of Pakistan was threatened, a pragmatic response to the need to maintain internal cohesion. For Mohammed Ali Jinnah and the other architects of modern Pakistani identity the compromise on the tribal areas was a necessarily deferred problem that could be addressed when the immediate problems of partition had been resolved. Unfortunately, those problems had not been resolved more than fifty years later and the ambiguity surrounding the tribal areas had itself become part of the identity issue. If this had been the only identity-related problem confronting Pakistan, it might alone have been sufficient to have encouraged Kalashnikov enculturation. But in the south, in the province of Sindh and particularly in the cities of Hyderabad and Karachi, partition had created a long-term displacement dilemma that in the 1990s was to become violently schismatic.

The partition of the Indian subcontinent was acute in its creation of refugees. By conservative accounts some 15 million people were encouraged by events to gravitate to the Indian or Pakistani side by dint of their religious or ethnic identity. Those that came to Pakistan and who were overwhelmingly Muslim (but mostly secular in political viewpoint) were identified by the term *mohajir* and for the most part they settled in the provinces of Punjab and Sindh. These transplants shared a language, Urdu, and a cultural background that separated many of them from those already living within the borders of the new Pakistan. Across the decades of postindependence they also shared an identity and homogeneity that was fed by anger, the anomie shared by displaced persons and a feeling that they were neglected and underappreciated by the power elite of Pakistan. In their concentrations in Hyderabad and Karachi they helped establish centers of commerce and economic power but they always felt vulnerable to the threat of Sindhi (the original inhabitants of the province) backlash and, after the military coup of 1958, to the organs of the security state. By the 1980s this disquietude had begun to crystallize into a political agenda that emphasized defense of community and resistance to a threatening alliance of their enemies that they felt was dedicated to undermining mohajir cohesion.

It was at this time in 1984 that the aggressive Mohajir Quami Movement (MQM) sprung, seemingly fully formed, out of the universities and youth associations of Hyderabad and latterly Karachi. In an analogy with the rise of the Taliban, this instant radicalization of mohajir politics gave rise to speculation that, in tortuously conspiratorial ways, the Pakistani army and intelligence community had underwritten and later armed the MQM in order to use them to further fragment an already fragmented civilian polity and to rationalize military intervention in the political process. Whatever might have been the truth, by 1988 the MQM was galvanizing the lower and middle classes amongst the mohajir into political assertiveness. A transient alliance with the Pakistan People's Party (PPP) served to cement the legitimacy of the MQM and by the early 1990s the military, either because of Frankensteinian regret or out of concern that the MQM might succeed in dominating Pakistani politics, began a campaign to discredit and control the MQM. The movement split into two parts, MQM (A) and MQM (H) and the (A) faction renamed itself the Muttahida Quami Movement in 1997. Infighting within the MQM was added to the sectarian fighting that had already broken out in Hyderabad and Karachi in the late 1980s and the whole was exacerbated by competition between the PPP and MQM. In a divide-and-conquer strategy the Pakistani security establishment first encouraged this melee but later came to realize that the flames that they were fanning might spread beyond their control. However, by 1992, when the army tried to exert control over Karachi, they found that Kalashnikov enculturation had become the dominant pathology in that city.

The guns of the mountain people had found their way into the cities during the war against the Soviets in Afghanistan. They had been released from their traditional environs by a backwash from the refugee enclaves around Peshawar and other northern cities but they had also come to Karachi as the result of a late-twentieth-century variant of the cargo cult. As part of their support for the anti-Soviet mujahedeen the United States engaged in what had been a Moscow strategy throughout most of the Cold War, that is, the supplying of light weapons to guerillas. Washington transferred, and encouraged others to transfer, large quantities of small arms and light weapons to Afghani insurgents on the understandable if somewhat facile basis of the enemy-of-my-enemy. As an encouragement to an understandably nervous Pakistan, the United States helped to support the Afghans who had fled to refugee camps in Pakistan and parenthetically allowed many Pakistanis to grow wealthy from the crumbs that fell from the feast of American support. Many of these crumbs were in the form of arms and ammunition and many of the beneficiaries were members of the Pakistani military, police, and intelligence services.

Given the clandestine nature of U.S. support for anti-Soviet forces in Afghanistan it is not possible to state with any certainty how many weapons were channeled through Pakistan and into Afghanistan during the 1980s. One source postulates that more than 400,000 Kalashnikov variants were delivered into Pakistan during that decade, with other sources quoting a figure ten times higher.[1] What was more important than how many arms were actually delivered to the mujahedeen was the number of arms and the amount of ammunition that were shipped but never reached their intended users. Various sources estimate what became known as the "leakage" at between 20 and 50 percent of the total tonnage of munitions destined for the Afghani insurgents.[2] Given that almost all of the weapons were small arms and light crew-served systems (such as mortars and heavy machine guns), the numbers of arms that remained within Pakistan could be in the millions of weapons and billions of rounds of ammunition. These numbers alone, outside of the volatility of the domestic political milieu in which they were placed, had the capability to create their own insecurity dynamic. When combined with the established weapons culture of the tribal territories and the multidimensional conflict environment in the south of the country, the result was the prototypical "Kalashnikov culture."

By the end of 1980 there were one and a quarter million Afghan refugees in Pakistan.[3] That figure would rise to 3 million by the end of the decade. Most of the refugee camps were in NWFP, with many of the remainder in Baluchistan. Even though nearly all the refugees were Pashtun and most of NWFP was itself Pashtun, the strain upon the Pakistani infrastructure and upon an economy that was always marginal at best was acute. The search for a sustainable stream of income by the refugees was oppressive and perhaps inevitably the partial solution was to be found through the exploitation of two traditional commercial activities. The first, the trade in arms, was an outgrowth of Pashtun warrior culture. The second, the trade in drugs, had a pedigree that was linked to the narrow options available to the agrarian Pashtun. For the most part the growing and cultivation of opium poppies in Afghanistan had been directed toward a small group of domestic users and to a substantial number of addicts in Iran. With the latter market made more unstable after the fall of the Shah, it was perhaps inevitable that the Pashtun population in Pakistan should look to exploit a market that lay closer to their own physical presence. The fact that the addict population in Pakistan went from negligible in 1980 to 5 million in 2005 is testament to their success in finding that market.[4]

Benazir Bhutto, who as PPP leader became prime minister of Pakistan in December 1988, may have had a vested interest in emphasizing the Kalashnikov culture as part of her campaign against the MQM, but by the time she took power most of its elements were well established within Pakistan. The refugee camps of the Afghani Pashtuns were about to start their second decade of existence, opium and heroin from what had become known as the "Golden Crescent" had entered the world market and the incidence of political and sectarian violence (*jang*) was rising. The cities of Peshawar in the north and Karachi in the south became the twin exemplars of the forces that were creating new levels and types of violence within Pakistan, and within their collective persona lay the defining components of the Kalashnikov culture. Clashes of identity, ideology, faith, and criminal competition would, over the following few years, create a nexus of insecurity that would itself challenge the viability of the Pakistani state.

Peshawar, the capital of the NWFP, is as much influenced by Afghanistan, two hours away by road, as it is by Pakistan. Language and custom is that of the Pathan tribes, the "free tribes," which bestride the border between the two countries and whose priorities are less related to the nation-state, as exemplified by Islamabad, than to their own tribe and clan. In terms of religion, most Pathans/Pashtun are members of the Hanafi branch of Sunnism, with an emphasis upon a conservative and basic interpretation of the Koran. It is difficult to assess whether Pashtun religion reinforces cultural values or vice versa, since the vaunted Pathan code of behavior is probably as important to the tribes as is their religious faith. The spiritual guidance of the one reinforces the temporal discipline of the other. The code itself stresses, in the words of one observer, "rigorous standards of bravery and risk-taking, defence of honour, responsibility and aggressiveness."[5] As with other aggressive, tribally based societies the code also has complex rituals and requirements in respect of hospitality and protection of guests. But it is the aggressiveness that has historically marked the Pathan personality and that has led them to be termed a martial race by both the British and the Pakistanis.

Twenty-five miles from Peshawar is a village that has come to symbolize, almost to the point of cliché, both the independence and the assertiveness of the Pashtun. Darra Adamkhel is in the tribal areas, under the most indirect control of the Pakistani authorities and it is the center of a cottage industry that concentrates on the manufacturing and trade in light weapons. Nonfactory arms production is covered elsewhere in this work but Darra represents more than simply an example of artisan accomplishment. In many ways this village, with its shifting population in the range of 10,000 to 20,000, epitomizes the majority of the seminal aspects of Kalashnikov enculturation. For the past one hundred and fifty years Darra has benefited from political ambiguity, physical proximity, and almost mythical reputation. The village is in the domain of one of the so-called assimilated clans of the Afridi tribe, generally known for their aggression and for their nomadic lifestyle. Ironically, the settled Afridis in Darra in many ways represent one of the few examples of successful industrialization in an area not renowned for manufacturing. Using foot-treddled presses and boring machines, the Darra gun makers have been creating and copying firearms for the Pashtun and other customers since the time of the Raj and by doing so they have helped perpetuate the belief that arms can guarantee independence and vice versa.

For the Pashtun and other mountain tribes acquiring arms was always difficult. They had little to trade for modern weapons and thus were reduced to innovative means to arm themselves. During the time of black-powder weapons artisans were able to repair and even construct single-shot rifles (*jezail*) whose ornateness, if not their reliability, was valued as a wall hanging from Lahore to London. But supplying arms for a clan or tribe required reliable sources and, with the onset of the cartridge period, access to ammunition. After the beginning of the twentieth century, captured and purloined Lee-Metford and Lee-Enfield bolt-action rifles were repaired, modified, and finally copied in the workshops of Darra and other villages. Ammunition, either stolen or remanufactured, was provided along with the weapons. Steel from railroad tracks was used for the barrels and actions of the guns and each weapon was individually crafted and fitted.[6] Always considered inferior to the original, nevertheless, Darra guns were important because they represented an uncontrolled source for arms within the tribal areas. To this end by the 1980s the workshops of Darra were producing some 20,000 weapons per year, including creditable facsimiles of the AK rifle.

When the United States and its supporters began providing arms to the anti-Soviet forces in Afghanistan the gun makers of Darra faced a dilemma. Millions of manufactured arms were transiting their way through the tribal areas on their way to Afghanistan and naturally this depressed the prices of the Darra guns. But the Afridis had not only specialized in manufacturing arms, they had also become experts in smuggling arms and other merchandise into Afghanistan and into the nontribal areas of Pakistan. The Pashtun were a dominant force in the trucking and transportation sector in Pakistan and were well-placed to expedite the movement of arms and supplies into Afghanistan for the Americans and Pakistani security elements. They were also well-placed to move people and products out of Afghan-Pakistani border areas and down into southern Pakistan. The people were primarily Afghani refugees on their way south to Karachi and Hyderabad. The products were arms, ammunition, and opium. Some of the arms were Darra guns destined for the criminal markets in Pakistani cities and villages. Others of the arms were "leaked" U.S.-supplied weapons that found their way into the arsenals of the MQM and its political rivals. The drugs, like the Darra arms, were homegrown beyond the edges of state control in Afghanistan and the tribal areas of Pakistan and as with the U.S.-supplied arms they leaked at every transit point on their way to their European (it was estimated in 1997 that this area supplied 80 percent of the heroin for the UK market) and U.S. destinations.[7]

The violence and dislocation that are redolent of Kalashnikov cultures are distinctive not simply in the frequency of incidents but in the scope and nature of the incidents. In December 1999 two women, identified as beggars, entered the home of a friend in the Pishtakhara area of Peshawar and were blown up by a landmine that had been planted as part of a long-running feud. One Pakistani commentator opined that "due to the kalashnikov culture (sic) the use of landmines was increased (sic) in the country because mines were cheaper than ammunition."[8] In 2003 a landmine or grenade sold for $6 in NWFP. On another day in Peshawar and in the same month three persons, including a woman, were beheaded by assassins, and in a further case assailants opened fire on a crowd and killed a man and a young girl. In all cases the reason for the killings was given as an "old enmity."[9] In January 2000 in the Hangu district of NWFP four people, including two children, were killed when men with whom the occupants were feuding attacked and demolished a house with hand grenades. In the refugee camps around

Peshawar, such as that at Jalaozai, gun battles in which Kalashnikovs, grenades, and machine guns were used were frequent during the 1980s and 1990s, with the firing often being termed "indiscriminate."[10] In virtually all cases where members of the local police or paramilitary forces were able to intercept the perpetrators a gunfight ensued, with fatalities on both sides. In rural areas of NWFP, police posts were frequently attacked by groups using automatic weapons and rocket-propelled grenade launchers. Disputes over land and water quickly gravitated into violence, often ending in multiple fatalities and no arrests by the authorities.

This record of quick and easy resort to aggression is a symptom of Kalashnikov enculturation. The ready availability of weapons helps to create an ambience in which old feuds and seemingly trivial slights are magnified through the prism of general insecurity. Weapons such as the AK are placed in fully automatic mode and the resultant spray of uncontrolled gunfire takes the lives of innocents and this in turn becomes the basis for more feuding. Hand grenades, mines, and explosives are used to settle disputes with inevitable collateral damage and heightening of tension. Police and security forces adopt a war footing and come to treat the population that they are supposed to serve as a belligerent enemy. The "enemy" reacts by attacking the police and security forces and the result is often an outbreak of extralegal killing that mirrors the intertribal feud mentality. When this spiral of aggression reaches the level of a parainsurgency, as it did in Karachi in the 1990s, then intervention by a military force, with all the implications that such a drastic measure implies, is almost inevitable.

Kalashnikov enculturation, as achieved by the mid-1980s in Peshawar and by the early 1990s in Karachi, pushes behavior into the realm of hypersensitivity in regard to perceived threat and at the same time dulls sensitivity, through repetitive acts of violence, to the implications of such acts. It is here that deterrence theory, as applied to a Kalashnikov culture, fails. In a Kalashnikov culture proliferated arms are not agents of moderation that force discipline and control upon the owners through fear of catastrophic violence and insecurity. Instead they are instruments that must be used on a regular basis in order to establish intent. To own the weapon is not enough; the actual use of the arm is what denotes power. But the use of the weapon, particularly one firing at the rate of 600 rounds per minute, is itself an undisciplined act prone to second-order consequences. Many of the hundreds of Peshawar citizens who were killed in 1989 died as the result of demonstrative fire with automatic weapons between rival groups or because of celebratory fire at weddings. As one local observer noted, " . . . before the rapid-fire guns, we were fine. This (level of killing) only came after the Kalashnikov. It's part of the Kalashnikov culture."[11] For the inhabitants of Peshawar this was the equivalent of the change between the agrarian and the industrial age but in their case it was not the machine that caused dislocation but rather the machine gun, or more precisely the assault rifle, the rocket-propelled grenade launcher, and the hand grenade. Vulgar firepower had pushed through the delicate membrane of honor code and warrior ethic and had created its own modern, less manageable subculture.

In Pakistan the word "mafia" had begun to be used in the 1980s to describe the loose criminal network that spliced Pashtun commercial entrepreneurialism into the trade in arms and the traffic in drugs. As exemplified by sometime-parliamentary deputy Haji Ayub Afridi, this network drew together the disparate elements of the Kalashnikov culture and turned them into a subeconomy. Operating from his fortified home in the tribal areas close by Peshawar, Ayub Afridi organized the transportation of opium from within Afghanistan, processed it in laboratories guarded by members of his clan, shipped it in trucks owned by himself or fellow Pashtun, and arranged for distribution in North America and Europe. The whole operation was protected by an arrangement of Afghan warlords, refugee gangs, corrupt law enforcement and customs officials, flexible Pakistani and foreign intelligence officials, and venal politicians. Only when Ayub Afridi became too wealthy and too dangerous (in 1993 it was rumored that the drug "mafia" had acquired "Stinger" manportable air defense missiles) as a trafficker did the Pakistani and U.S. governments decide to make an example of him with arrest and imprisonment in both the United States and Pakistan. The "mafia" or organized crime network of which he was a part continued after his eclipse and its existence helped to blur the distinctions between violence that was political in nature and that which was designed to facilitate criminal activities.[12]

The so-called mafia syndicates were the result of tribal cohesion and traditional smuggling activities coming together with the internationalization of Afghan opium harvesting, with all elements protected by the insecurity perimeter created by Kalashnikov enculturation. All of the parts had existed before the 1980s but the acceleration and intensification of their development had resulted in a mutated form of outlawry that Benazir Bhutto and others always included in their denunciation of the Kalashnikov culture. There was also another traditional form of lawlessness that benefited from the ambience of insecurity and instability. Dacoits or bandits had been a staple of reality and folklore in South Asia since before the coming of the Europeans. Defying caste and social order, dacoits were shunned as outcast criminals and at the same time romanticized as rebels fighting against an oppressive status quo. In reality, dacoits robbed from the poor as much as from the wealthy and in Pakistan their specialty was a form of collective extortion known as the *ghunda* tax. This "tax" was in fact nothing more than receiving money and goods by menacing the population of a village with threats of death and destruction. In one representative case in the Upper Dir district of NWFP an army of some 200 dacoits invaded two villages, robbed the villagers and burned more than thirty structures, including a school. The dacoits then decamped, taking hostages with them. The villagers complained that this army, commanded by one Haji Muhammed (a proclaimed offender or wanted man), had so intimidated the police (and allegedly bribed some) that they never intervened when contacted by the villagers. Perhaps one of the most interesting aspects of Haji Muhammed's "tax" gathering enterprise was that he had reportedly sent his son to Saudi Arabia to collect taxes from villagers who were working in that country. This dacoitism was far removed from the traditional image of knife-wielding desperadoes falling upon travelers in the night (although that form of banditry still took place). Dacoits with grenades and automatic weapons who traveled internationally to engage in extortion were competitors with the state for power and presence.[13]

Apart from targeting the heads of criminal syndicates and dacoit gangs, the government in Islamabad made attempts to control the Kalashnikov culture in the northwest by controlling the arms that originated from the region. Darra had always been an irksome symbol of contrarianism to the Pakistani state and as the arms from the tribal areas began to underwrite the insecurity in Karachi successive Pakistani administrations decided that there should be limits to the independence of the Darra arms sellers. In the 1990s this approach included proposals to co-opt the arms makers of Darra by absorbing them into the government-owned Pakistan Ordnance Factories (POF) and having them make arms for the Pakistani military and for export. A program of "de-weaponization" was also proposed, in which heavier weapons such as grenade launchers, mortars, rocket launchers, and light artillery would be banned but individuals would be allowed to possess rifles and handguns. There was also to be a ban on the public display of guns. In return for these concessions the inhabitants of the tribal areas were promised security guarantees, job prospects, social services, and investment in infrastructure.[14]

The initial response from the Afridi gun makers of Darra was predictable and it lay at the heart of the dilemma faced by all state actors when they feel compelled to confront Kalashnikov enculturation. As one Darra resident succinctly stated: "There are a hundred thousand guns in this town and five million tribesmen in the hills around us. Everyone has carried a weapon since he was a child, every one is a warrior and every one is a Pathan before he is a Pakistani. If the Pakistani army want to come, let them. It will not be a very pleasant sight."[15] Even allowing for a healthy dose of bravado, this statement echoed a reality that prevailed in Kalashnikov cultures from Yemen to Somalia to Abkhazia. An armed population is an army-in-waiting and attempts to disarm it is tantamount to declaring a war on its identity and independence. Inputs of money and assistance would certainly have been welcomed in the congenitally poor tribal areas but to trade independence for promises required a level of trust that had never been present in Darra . To quote another gun dealer from Darra, "The whole point is that we look after ourselves and don't answer to some fat bureaucrat or policeman. If the government takes over then a few big people far away will make a lot of money and the rest of us will be left with nothing."[16]

The issue of de-weaponization and the banning of openly carried arms were also problematic. The omnipresent threats from intertribal feuding, armed street crime, dacoitism and "mafia" clan activities did not inspire enough confidence to encourage voluntary disarmament. The real or perceived corruption of the police force and the reality of their inefficiency mitigated against deferring protection to that body and any way in FATA they had little or no presence or legitimacy. For arms control or disarmament to be attractive to the tribes they had to be offered both sufficient incentive and credible penalties if they failed to comply. In 1995 the death penalty had been extended to cover arms trading but, of course, this only applied outside of the tribal areas. In 2000 a ban on the issuing of arms licenses was instituted within Pakistan, as was a nationwide prohibition on the public display of arms. The latter had been attempted before but a ban on licenses to own arms was new. As a follow-on to the licensing restriction it was further decided that arms of certain calibers, most notably those that conformed to the description of military weapons, would be made illegal throughout the country and that these illegal arms should be surrendered to the authorities. This surrender of arms would take the form of a "buy-back" scheme. In addition, the government in Islamabad announced in 2001 that they would "de-weaponise" the Afghan refugee camps in the country.[17]

There had been many such attempts to control arms in the past. In 1991 the government had instituted mandatory life imprisonment for the ownership of illegal, military-type weapons and demanded that such weapons be turned in to the authorities. In Karachi, with a population of 5 million and with an estimated 40,000 AKs in private hands, just twenty firearms were handed in to the police, partly because the PPP saw the measure as being directed at its supporters.[18] But the bans instituted in 2000 did have at least a surface effect upon the northern areas. Public displays of weaponry tended to be restricted to private security personnel (in 2003 there were thirty-five security companies registered in Peshawar alone) and to bodyguards, of which there were many. Even in the FATA the ban was at least partially observed (previously one observer had stated that such a ban would not succeed in the tribal areas because "guns are like our jewelry").[19] However, prohibited arms were not surrendered by the tribes and the buyback program stalled with some 210,000 weapons surrendered. In 2005, a Peshawar-based nongovernmental organization announced that by their estimate there were 10 million illegal arms remaining in Pakistan, of which 4 to 7 million were held within the tribal areas and the northern provinces. These totals were more than the combined arms held by the Pakistani military and police forces. The guns may not have appeared in public as much after the 2000 campaign but they still remained available for use.[20]

Darra was also affected by the attempts to exert control over the availability of arms. The decision to try to absorb the Darra gunsmiths into the Pakistani Ordinance Factories had only had limited success because of the low salaries offered to the Darra artisans. By 2005 most of the workers had returned to Darra but the trade in locally manufactured guns was depressed and likely to remain so for the foreseeable future. The problem with arms dealing in the tribal areas was that it was prone to cycles of demand that stretched the resources of the Darra dealers during the low-demand periods. Although they themselves traded in factory weapons, the glut of arms that occurred during the 1980s and then again after the fall of the Taliban regime in 2002 had undermined the local industry to the point of insolvency. The current generation was discouraging their offspring from learning the art of gunsmithing and in many ways Darra and some 300 work-shops that made the "Khyber Pass Specials" had become a victim of a saturated market.[21]

In December 1999 the police in Peshawar raided the premises of the Shalimar Arms Factory on the Kohat Road in that city. They confiscated 110 pistols, 180 rifles and nearly 20,000 rounds of ammunition, all of which the police believed had come from Darra. In the Machiavellian world of arms trafficking out of the tribal areas, the arms had been smuggled out of Darra and then stamped with Shalimar factory code and serial numbers in order to legitimize the guns as legal Peshawar arms rather than illicit Darra guns. Given the millions of arms extant in the region this was not a major haul. But the destination of the arms was more important than the number of weapons; the guns were to be sold in Punjab and Sindh provinces in the south of Pakistan.[22] As such, this small consignment was a useful example of the infective and fluid nature of the Kalashnikov culture. In the north of the country the AK and its ilk were used in inter- and intratribal disputes, in feuds over "old enmities," within the refugee camps by competing groups, by "mafia" organizations to protect their trafficking business, and by dacoits to intimidate their victims and the police. In the south of the country all of these conflicts prevailed and there were two important additional casus belli. Sectarian and ethnopolitical warfare, beginning in the late 1980s, had taken the lives of thousands of victims in the cities and countryside of Sindh and Punjab provinces and it was into this environment that the consignment of arms from Darra, via the Shalimar Arms Factory, was to be directed.

Sectarian conflict did exist in the northern provinces and in the FATA, but it was generally commingled with intertribal and interclan competition. The puritanical streak within the tribes in the north was well served by the Deobandist dogma that had attracted the Taliban but pragmatic entrepreneurialism had still allowed pornographic movie theaters, seating up to 1,000 patrons each, to flourish in Peshawar during the 1990s. Sharia courts certainly existed in the north but so did a certain lusty independence. Nevertheless, as an explosion at a mosque in Quetta in 2003 that killed forty-seven people illustrated, religious extremism, in both the Sunni and Shia communities of the northwest, can be counted as yet another exacerbant to violence in the north.[23] But in Sindh province, and particularly in Karachi, sectarianism became one of the twin pillars, along with ethnically based political extremism, of Kalashnikov enculturation. Attendant upon these "big two" were all of the ills that existed in the remainder of the country: dacoitism, urban gangs, corrupt and violent police, honor killings, drug trafficking, and a politicized military. Add to this the crime and street violence that occurs in any city of more than 12 million, then there is a certain inevitability to the devolution of Karachi into the archetypal Kalashnikov culture.

Karachi is a seaport, commercial center, and a place of some energy. Since partition it has proved to be a magnet for all of the ethnic groups and tribes of Pakistan and as a result has become a reflection of all of the tensions and competitions within the wider society. From the northwest the Pashtun, with their knowledge of transportation, came and became the dominant force in the taxi and trucking sectors of Karachi. This brought them into conflict with both the Sindhi population and with the mohajirs and this competition was one of the first irritants that resulted in communal violence in the 1980s. The fact that the Pashtun were also deemed responsible for bringing drugs and guns into the city (there were rumors that the drug "mafia" encouraged the violence to mask their activities) made them easy scapegoats and targets but by the late 1980s this type of ethnic tension would be absorbed into the war between the MQM and its political rivals. Shortly after the formation of the MQM, in August 1986, political rallies were turning into riots, with violence against property and persons in both Hyderabad and Karachi. Pashtun, Sindhis and mohajirs died in these early clashes and by 1990 the PPP and MQM were engaged in an insurgency in which kidnapping and assassination were commonplace. To add to the level of insecurity, in late 1990 police opened fire on an MQM rally and more than 100 demonstrators were killed.

Rumor and innuendo has played an important part in the evolution of violence in Karachi. From the persistent belief by some that the MQM was a thing of Inter-Service Intelligence (ISI), the highly political internal and external Pakistani security service, to the equally fervently held belief that India was fomenting the troubles, there has been a tendency to give credence to any conspiracy theory. The "hidden hand" of the ISI, the Pakistani military, drug "mafias" and foreign agitators was readily discerned by those affected by the disorder and dislocation in Karachi. The fact that it took the MQM less than three years to dominate the political landscape of Karachi helped to fuel the sense that the Pakistani military had groomed and fostered the mohajirs as a malleable alternative to the distrusted PPP. This particular interpretation of the rise of the MQM was, however, severely tested when, in August 1992, the Pakistani army "invaded" Karachi and broke up the MQM (A), sending its leader into exile in London.

For nearly two years the Pakistani army occupied Karachi but, instead of the army imposing its will on Karachi, the city placed its imprimatur on the military. The military became caught between the PPP and the MQM, between the two MQM factions, between Sunni and Shia sectarian groups and between "mafia" gangs engaged in turf wars. As conventional interventionist forces found in like circumstances the Pakistani military found itself caught on the horns of an operational dilemma. Too heavy to do ordinary policing and too doctrinally rigid for the delicate and complex regimen of counter-insurgency, the Pakistan army could suppress open warfare by its presence but it could not provide solutions to depress the violence. When the army withdrew from the streets in 1994 the police in Karachi, together with the paramilitary ranger force, were overwhelmed by the now-heavily armed groups whose different agendas and internecine struggles did not preclude concerted attacks upon the representatives of local law enforcement.

If the tribal areas and provinces of the northwest provided the traditional backdrop to Kalashnikov enculturation, then Karachi in 1994–1995 was its modern face. The mores and codes of the rural tribes might have failed to accommodate the effects that Kalashnikov proliferation had achieved but the societies of the north were still more prepared for the Kalashnikov culture than were the cities to the south. In Karachi, as in Beirut in the 1970s, frustrated youth coagulated with criminal opportunists and committed ideologues to form a complex of militias whose strategy was to control the presence of law enforcement in order to allow them the freedom to fight each other. After the military withdrew in 1994 the campaign to intimidate the police and government paramilitaries became one in which terror was the principal ingredient. Not only were the police attacked as they patrolled, they were targeted for assassination, kidnapping, and torture in an unremitting process that forced them to relinquish the streets to the insurgents. Complicating the position of the police was the fact that many of them (and other civil servants) held their jobs because of a quota system that was used to protect Sindhis from pressures from the mohajirs and other latecomers who made up the majority population in Karachi. To target the police, therefore, was to target the representatives of an unfair and discriminatory system.

Prior to the bloodletting of the mid-1990s Karachi and Hyderabad had been moving slowly in the direction of Kalashnikov enculturation. In 1991 some 460 murders had been cataloged, together with 140 kidnappings (the average ransom was US$100,000) and 420 assorted shooting incidents.[24] Most of the ills of the city could be traced to generic problems that could as easily be applied to Rio de Janeiro, Port Moresby, or Nairobi as to Karachi. The physical infrastructure of the city had been overwhelmed by successive waves of urban immigration, squatter camps (more than a third of the city lived in such camps by 1990) had become unserviced and permanent, corruption amongst city officials was endemic, and education and social service support was itself corrupted and inefficient. With virtually no garbage collection and with the streets clogged with an uncontrolled mass of buses and minibuses (most owned by Pashtuns), the physical environment contributed to tensions that were often relieved through domestic abuse and drug taking. The rich and middle class withdrew to suburban gated communities protected by the ubiquitous private security guards, while the day-laborer class, comprised mostly of unattached males, was housed in decrepit and dangerous high-rise slum buildings. A general sense of insecurity had, by 1993, begun to affect the movement of people outside of their communities and the release valve provided by entertainment (Karachi had a famed nightlife in the 1980s) was often supplanted by drug-use and petty crime.[25] But Islamabad could not afford to completely neglect Karachi, because even during the worst of the troubles the city was still providing between 60 and 70 percent of the national tax revenue.

Education can provide the antidote to despair but in Karachi that avenue of escape had also suffered from policies of ethnic discrimination (university admission quotas favored Sindhis) as well as from the onset of Kalashnikov enculturation. By 1990 students were bringing AKs to class in order to intimidate both teachers and other students and exam proctors were threatened with weapons if they tried to stop cheating during examinations. School buses were often attacked by gunmen and Karachi University became a military enclave after assaults by armed gangs. Schools were closed for weeks and in the western and northern parts of the city gangs of armed children as young as ten occupied their time with intimidation and extortion. Even the elite prep schools in the city suffered from gang warfare, with paramilitary Rangers having to be deployed within the school grounds. In addition to the omnipresence of insecurity the education system itself was rampant with corruption. A government survey estimated that in 1998 in Punjab province alone there were more than 4,000 "ghost schools," where there were no students and the teachers never taught and often the money for the school buildings had been purloined by local officials.[26] Given these impediments to learning, the official literacy rate of 45 percent was deemed to be inflated by a third. It is also against this background that the number of madrasas in Karachi expanded from twenty in 1971 to 979 in 2005.

The young people of Karachi adapted to Kalashnikov enculturation in a variety of ways. The sons and daughters of the wealthy adopted a form of "militia chic," in which they mimicked the struggles of the MQM and the sectarian groups but within their own sphere. This type of behavior, which emphasized style (U.S. gangsta rap was particularly popular) as an element of the conduct of violence, was reminiscent of that which certain Falangist militias had adopted in the early days of the Lebanese civil war.[27] For those that were young and poor style was less of an issue. By the end of the century there were 80,000 heroin-addicted children in Karachi, all of them trying to earn the $4 a day that were required for them to buy their "medicine." Other young people gravitated toward those armed groups that would allow them to become camp followers, carrying their "machines" (Kalashnikovs) and remaining on watch for the police or rival armed groups. As one social worker remarked about these children: "They are the product of Kalashnikov culture and an intolerant society. Today they are lookouts, tomorrow they might be terrorists."[28] In Hyderabad many of the youth belonging to MQM factions embraced the description of "terrorist" as one of distinction and coolness.

After the withdrawal of the army in 1994 all of the actors in Karachi's tableau of violence fell upon each other and upon the police. More than 150 police officers (out of a total force of 3,000 officers) were killed during 1995 and overall the violence of that year claimed more than 2,000 lives. The weapons used had come from a variety of sources. Political leaders had handed out weapons, or licenses for weapons, to their supporters (Benazir Bhutto accused the provincial government of Sindh of handing out 1,600 arms licenses to its supporters in 1991) and items from police and military inventories were available. But the Kalashnikov culture of Karachi was also inventive in the manner that it armed its citizenry. The AK, grenade launchers, handguns, and grenades could be rented from such places as the Afghan refugee camp at Gadap, near Karachi, with a fee for a Kalashnikov being $90 and a deposit of $455 (contract killers could also be hired for a fee.)[29] After the withdrawal of Soviet forces from Afghanistan, and before the onset of the civil war in that country, the price of a Kalashnikov in Karachi had been as low as $680 but this price was still far too high for the average Karachi citizen to find affordable. In Hyderabad, Kalashnikovs could be purchased on the installment plan, with a third of the price demanded at purchase and the rest paid over a period of time. The problem with both this approach and the rental plan was that it encouraged the purchasers to "take the Kalashnikov, go rob somebody at gunpoint and use the loot to pay off the rest of the purchase."[30] One of the preferred methods of raising the money was through armed carjackings, of which there were nearly 8,000 in 1999.[31]

As the death toll among the police began to rise, it encouraged a responsive countermeasure from the force. This took the form of "encounter killings," in which the police shot suspects as they attempted to flee or killed them while they were in police custody. This form of extrajudicial execution is an indicator of siege mentality taking the place of normative law enforcement and it can be found in other urban environments such as Rio de Janeiro and Port Moresby. Some of the killings were directly related to attacks made on the police but others were part of a counterterror strategy designed to intimidate the gangs and factions. Encounter killings were not restricted to Karachi (there were fifty-six such killings in the city of Lahore in 1999) but after the insurgency in 1995 they occurred with regularity in that city.[32] The police, even with support from the paramilitary Rangers, were aware of their vulnerability in a city where they were outgunned and outnumbered and permanently under pressure from those that perceived of them as examples of Sindhi discrimination against the mohajir. Encounter killings was one of the ways that they could attempt to fight back, albeit extralegally and often against the innocent.

In the decade after 1995 the MQM continued to fight but mostly in an internecine fashion. Members of the two factions engaged in turf wars that were often about spoils rather than about ideology. But even though the political warfare might have waned sectarian conflict continued to worsen during the same decade. The 25 percent of Karachi's population that is Shiite believes, much as the mohajirs believe about the Sindhi, that they have suffered permanent discrimination at the hands of the 70 percent majority Sunni population. As *jihadists* began to return to Karachi from Afghanistan in the late 1990s they brought their extremist dogma, their proficiency in arms, and the weapons themselves with them. These Sunni extremists either infiltrated existing religious parties, such as the Jamiat-e-Ulema-e-Islam (JUI), or established new organizations such as the Herkatul Mujahideen. Shiite groups, including the aggressive Sipah-e-Mohammedi Pakistan (SMP), emerged in the 1990s to protect the Shia community and to promote their own theological position. The sectarian conflict also had tribal undertones, external exacerbants (al-Qaeda had been present in Karachi since the 1990s) and linkages to criminal activities that were used to fund the sectarian agenda.[33]

The landscape of Pakistani sectarianism is too complex to address here but it has led to certain distinct behaviors linked to Kalashnikov enculturation. The first, the use of explosives for mass effect, is an indicator that war mentality, rather than simply desultory violence, had taken hold within the community. The second behavior, that of assassination of representatives of the religious and secular professional class, is a form of what in Karachi is termed "target killing." Both of these aspects of sectarian violence began to appear with regularity in the 1990s but they accelerated considerably after the year 2000. The bombing of religious institutions, including Christian churches as well as mosques and *imambargahs*, became commonplace and formed a large part of the more than 1,100 bombings that took place in Karachi during the period 1990–2003. The mosque bombings were most often timed to detonate during prayers, with the result that the number of dead and injured were often in double figures (a bomb detonated at Imambargah Ali Raza in Karachi in May 2004 took the lives of twenty-four worshippers.)[34] Initially many of these blasts were the result of hand grenades being tossed into buildings but after 2000 explosives were being used, sometimes attached to the bodies of suicide bombers. (The first suicide bombing took place in Karachi in November 2000.)[35]

Bombing campaigns conform to two types of strategy. The first, exemplified by the Irish Republican Army (IRA) campaign in Northern Ireland, is designed to destabilize and to act as an amplifier of demands. Casualties occur during these campaigns but the desired effect is one of noisy statement rather than the deliberate death and destruction. The second type of campaign, as exemplified by the bombings in Karachi and elsewhere in Pakistan, is designed to destroy the fabric of the targeted community. Killing people and destroying meaningful buildings is the operational means to achieve the end of eradicating the enemy. In the first campaign the bombers must be aware of backlashes that might erode sympathy for their cause and as a result they often communicate that a bomb has been placed before it detonates so as to avoid the complication of casualties. But in the second campaign terror is not theater but rather the simple side effect of destruction. The bombing campaigns in Karachi included hospitals, bazaars, post offices, buses, restaurants (including Western fast-food outlets) and shops, as well as religious buildings. Rocket-propelled grenades were also used in attacks on buildings but the preferred method was a hand-delivered explosive device. The overall effect of the Karachi bombings was to further restrict the communal activities and personal interplay that are a necessary part of the functioning of a healthy society. The emotional impact of terror may be transient but residual elements of fearfulness and unease are permanent and corrosive.

Target killing is assassination by another name. As the bombings were designed to kill and intimidate the mass of the population, target killings are a strategy of leadership decapitation. The leadership in question may be political, or in the case of Karachi clerical, or it may simply be symbolic of the power and prestige of the targeted group. In the ten years prior to 2002 more than seventy doctors, mostly Shia, were victims of target killing in Karachi. It is estimated that there are 7,000 doctors in Karachi, averaging one per 2,000 people. Apart from those that have been killed many doctors have simply left the city or drastically curtailed their professional activities.[36] Most of the killings have occurred as the doctors moved between their homes and surgeries, with the preferred method being assassination by gunfire from gunmen riding pillion on motorcycles (pillion riding was banned for a time in Karachi). Similarly, religious ulema or teachers were a preferred target amongst the clerical class, with students often being collateral damage.

After visiting Peshawar in 1989 one reporter attempted to define "Kalashnikov culture." It was, he observed, "a patchwork of skullduggery stitched together with the universal weapon of late twentieth-century wars, the AK-47 automatic rifle."[37]

Thirteen years later a former Pakistani general ventured that during the 1990s "Pakistan developed a sort of Kalashnikov culture. Weapons became a power symbol for politicians and others."[38] An Afghan psychologist characterized Kalashnikov culture as a situation in which two decades of violence had so degraded morality and ethics that "impulses to bully, fight and kill go unchecked . . . The Kalashnikov means more than anything else. If there is no security, there is no social contract between the people."[39] All three of these comments have in common the perception that the gun itself contained the seeds of a new and different form of violence. The weapon was not simply a manifestation of an existing phenomenon but the Kalashnikov carried within it a form of contagion that infected Pakistan. Clearly, this inert combination of wood and metal could not be blamed for what happened during the past quarter century but the implication of these observations is important. Pakistan might have been a fractious, violent, divided gun culture before the coming of the Kalashnikovs, but when the latter came they created a different and unmanageable dynamic that demanded a new definition that was satisfied by the title "Kalashnikov culture."

The soil into which the Kalashnikovs fell after 1979 was culturally fertile. Nearly every element of schism and division was present in Pakistan, running the gamut from ideological through tribal to religious and class. Successive military and civilian governments had been unable to provide for the needs of the abject poor and both rural and urban communities wrestled with assaults on traditional values by modernizing and globalist trends. Competition with India, including lost wars and territory, undermined the national treasury and blunted national honor. Insecurity and uncertainty prevailed at every level from the political elite through chronically feuding tribes down to the day laborers on the streets of Karachi. When the Kalashnikovs were added to this stew of discontent they acted as a catalyst around which gathered the crowds of the disaffected. Thus, when supplied with the guns the crowds became the militias and armies of the "Kalashnikov culture."

Pastoral Warriors: Cattle Raiders of East Africa

The weaponization of the NWFP were logical, albeit extreme in nature, evolutionary trends in the development of warrior societies. In contrast, the "gangsta warriors" of West Africa were a perverse and aberrant corruption of traditional warrior values. And somewhere in between are cultures whose traditional warrior roots, when exposed to modern weaponry, result in a form of contaminated but recognizable outgrowth of that which went before. The impact of such weapons on the Zulu of South Africa and upon the hill tribes of Papua New Guinea has been profound. In both areas centuries-old patterns of stylized and controlled approaches to conflict have often been supplanted by profligate acts of gun violence. But even though the Kalashnikov may have taken the place of the thrusting spear, there still exists the vestigial elements of the cohesion and discipline that made both these groups into archetypes of traditional warrior societies. Such has not always been the outcome when guns have been introduced into like environments; in northern Uganda and Kenya firearms have served to destroy one of the most finely balanced of all conflict arenas and to help create one of the most enduringly unstable interstate areas in the world.

Karamoja in northern "upcountry" Uganda occupies a triangular territory abutting the Sudanese border to the north and Kenya to the east. The land is semi-arid, with rolling hills and some deep ravines. Few roads cross the district and the only towns are Kitgum and Moroto. Economic development is almost nonexistent and the mandate of the central government in Kampala is only desultorily enforced. By most definitions Karamoja would constitute, in Western parlance, a nation without the status of a state. And like many such entities the "nation" of Karamoja is not wedded to such concepts as respect for state borders or for written trade regulations. In essence, the people of Karamoja are, in a world dominated by both state-centrism and postindustrial globalism, both a throwback to an old world and the potential harbingers of a new one. However, the people of Karamoja may not provide the best example for the prospects of evolving traditionalism.

The two districts that constitute Karamoja, together with much of the area in Kenya that borders Uganda, Sudan, and Ethiopia, are pastoral societies. Wealth, power, and lifestyle are dictated by the quantity and quality of herds of animals controlled by tribes, clans, and individuals. Goats and camels constitute a percentage of this wealth but it is cattle that provide the base currency of life. Cattle are bartered in trade and the bridewealth or bride-price (paid by young men to the families of their prospective brides) is usually between twenty to forty head of cattle. But more than a substitute for money, cattle are a source of spiritual as well as physical sustenance, with the blood and viscera being used in many religious rituals.[1] As a result, when cattle raids occur, as they have increasingly over the past decades, the effect is traumatic upon those tribes and subgroups who lose their animals. They must respond either by retrieving their cattle from the raiders or by becoming raiders themselves. In this way a ritual of almost continuous raiding has become a facet of life in the region. But what had been in the past a "dance" of raid and response has, in the past twenty years, metamorphosed into unabated vendetta, with loss of life counted annually in the thousands.

The tribes and subgroups of the Karamoja have raided and stolen cattle in a casual manner for generations.[2] Most young men could not afford the bride-price and stealing cattle was a way to both obtain the necessary "dowry" and to demonstrate courage and fortitude. Before the 1980s such raiding was constant but its scope and nature were in harmony with the political and cultural environment. The raids were framed in ritual and the violence was, in context, minimized. For example, in the first seven months of 1958 the Karimojong raided neighboring tribes more than 200 times, seizing more than 12,000 head of cattle. Approximately fifty people were killed on all sides in these raids. Mortality figures for raids in the years 1954–1957 indicate that on average one person died for every three raids conducted. Very rarely was a female a victim of such raids (Karimojong raiders killed two women in the 1958 raids) and even rarer was a child harmed, even though the cattle herds were often tended by boys.[3] In contrast, by 1997 more than seventy people were being killed during a single raid, of whom fifty were children and thirty-six were female.[4] In the first seven months of 1997 more than 500 Karimojong were killed in raids, a tenfold increase over the same period forty years previously.[5]

Several factors contributed to the quantum leap in mortality figures. Uganda itself had gravitated from colonialism through despotism and civil war into a postcolonial generation riven with concerns over the impact of AIDS and involved in regional conflicts that had diverted security interests toward Rwanda and the Democratic Republic of Congo (DRC). The central government in Kampala had over twenty years gradually abrogated its control over the Karimojong, concentrating instead upon the guerrilla movements such as the Lord's Resistance Army (LRA) which, using southern Sudan as a safe haven, made forays into Karamoja.

Also during this time the tribes and subgroups of the Karimojong suffered through a number of famines, including one such in 1980 in which an estimated 20 percent of the population of Karamoja died. Their cattle herds had also been decimated during the famines and as a result they had little to trade for grain and other necessary foodstuffs. By the early 1990s the ratio of cattle per person had dropped from 6 in 1920 to less than 2.[6]

It was during these times, between the late 1970s and the early 1990s, that raiding itself went through a distinct change of dynamic. The traditional form of raiding, sometimes called "redistributive raiding," was considered by many observers to be at the core of the stability to be found within many pastoral communities. To quote a study conducted in the late 1990s, the authors stated their belief that ". . . in the absence of any over-arching authority in pastoral society, (redistributive) raiding and other forms of warfare serve to maintain separate identities and rule-governed relations between different groups as well as acting as a balance." But the same authors also recognized a form of raiding, dubbed "predatory," that was far less benign. Specifically referring to raiding in northern Kenya, in lands adjacent to Karamoja, such activities and their high death tolls were linked to a criminalization of rustling and to the involvement of political figures and entrepreneurs in the disposal of stolen cattle in Kenya. The high mortality rate amongst raided tribes and clans was ascribed to the willingness of the sponsors of such raids to make part payment to the raiders in military weapons, many of which emanated from war-ridden Ethiopia and Somalia. The rise in "predatory raiding" and the eclipse of "redistributive raiding" was yet another element of change that served to increase the vulnerability of the Karimojong.[7]

This period of despair in Karamoja coincided with certain key political changes both within Uganda and on its borders. Sudan, which had been engaged in internal warfare almost constantly since its independence in 1956, had since 1983 been fighting what amounted to a civil war against the Sudan People's Liberation Army (SPLA) in the south of the country in an area that abutted the Ugandan border. The SPLA had in turn split and factionalized over the years, with the internecine warfare spilling over into neighboring countries. But it was the changes inside Uganda that exacerbated the problems of the Karimojong and that had provided them with the tools and the opportunity to evolve into a cattle raiding society rather than a cattle raising society.

Uganda had achieved independence from Britain in October 1962. Between that time and the 1971 coup that brought Idi Amin to power the government of Milton Obote attempted to forge a national identity within the state, using his own blend of socialism and nationalism to appeal to the tribal groups who were the real power within Uganda. But his style and intransigence had served to alienate many within the ruling elite, which included the Ugandan military, and on January 15, 1971, Milton Obote was ousted by the Ugandan armed forces. For the next eight years Uganda would be ruled by the quixotically dangerous Idi Amin, who was to use applied violence as an instrument of internal state policy. Although directed mostly toward the tribes and elites in the south of the country, Amin's policies of subjugation and control also affected the Karimojong. The Ugandan military used draconian tactics to stop the cattle raiders and, much as Mussolini had been able to temporarily suppress the Sicilian mafia in the 1930s, was able to inhibit the raiders by outterrorizing them. But Amin's forces did not undertake such activities for altruistic reasons. As part of the campaign they confiscated many herds of cattle and then sold them and divided the spoils amongst themselves.[8]

By 1979, when a Tanzanian army overthrew Idi Amin, the Karimojong were desperate and disenchanted. The promise of nationhood and of benefits from state- enforced stability had been unfulfilled and, now near destitution, they were more than ever being driven toward an autonomy whose economic sustainability was based, as it had been in the past, upon the ownership of livestock. Perhaps ironically, it was a residual of the Amin regime that gave them the opportunity to resurrect their standing among the pastoral tribes of Uganda and Kenya. When the Tanzanian army invaded Uganda the latter's armed forces collapsed and the soldiers fled. Garrisons were abandoned and armories lay open to whoever claimed them. The barracks at Moroto in Karamoja contained such an armory and, loading the guns and ammunition on donkeys, the Karimojong looted every weapon from the base. This single act, more than any other, changed the nature of cattle raiding in the region.[9]

It is uncertain when and under what circumstances firearms first appeared among the pastoralists of Uganda, Kenya, Sudan, and Ethiopia. Europeans certainly owned guns when they arrived in the late nineteenth century and there is evidence that arms also filtered down into Kenya and Sudan from Ethiopia in the last quarter of that century. What is certain is that in 1900, in an agreement signed between the then kingdom of Buganda and the British, the colonists included a provision that acted as both a control on the number of firearms available to the population as well as placing a tax or license fee on each firearm owned, up to the maximum of five such weapons. In essence, the British taxed guns away from the ordinary people and made them the exclusive tools of the wealthy and in doing so made arms into a symbol of power and political potency. The Karimojong, who were considered by the British to be beyond civilizing (Karamoja was declared a "closed district" by them and all people entering required a special permit), were forbidden firearms and therefore were restricted to carrying the traditional weapons of their tribe, the long spear and bows and arrows.[10]

The limitations of these traditional weapons acted as agents of discipline and ritual upon the conduct of cattle raiding. The closeness of combat allowed for a certain code of chivalry to evolve, so that when overwhelmed in a raid the defeated group could lay down their spears and surrender with dignity. These weapons also required physical prowess to master their use and this was recognized in the ritual of body scarring that took place after each raid was successfully accomplished. The British too recognized the proficiency with which the Karimojong used their weapons, particularly the long spear. No Karimojong warrior was allowed to carry more than one spear at a time, since it was believed that a warrior with two spears was inevitably engaged in cattle raiding.[11]

By the late 1960s firearms began to be used in increasing numbers during the raids. Initially they were sparse enough so that they were incorporated as adjuncts to the larger numbers of traditional weapons. But an influx of bolt-action rifles into the hands of the Turkana in Kenya and the Toposa in Sudan allowed for all members of raiding parties from those tribes to be armed and this drastically changed the balance of power amongst the pastoralists. The Karimojong particularly felt disadvantaged, since they were still, even after independence, banned from legitimate firearms ownership, even if funds had been available for the purchase of guns. Initially the Karimojong tribes attempted a local variant upon the Darra approach to weaponization. They stole metal furniture from government buildings and made the chair legs into crude shotguns.[12] They also vandalized boreholes, using the metal and rubber to create single-shot homemade weapons called amatida.[13] But such devices were only useful in ambushes and to further the acquisition of weapons from rivals or from the police. Therefore, the guns from the Moroto barracks not only enabled the Karimojong to provide for their own defense and to mount their own successful cattle raids but, given the military nature of the arms, allowed them to technologically leapfrog such groups as the Turkana. With machine guns, grenades, mortars, and particularly the assault rifles, the Karimojong had, within a very short period of time, transformed themselves from victims into a reasonable facsimile of a modern army. This fact was not lost on those tribes and subgroups upon whom the Karimojong now preyed and they too went in search of modern weapons.

The pastoralists of Uganda and Kenya were, by the 1980s, virtually surrounded by conflicts. To the south, the embattled regime of Milton Obote fell to an army coup in 1985 and the coup plotters themselves were defeated in battle by the National Resistance Army (NRA) of Yoweri Museveni. To the north, the SPLA continued its fight against the government in Khartoum, with various factions fighting amongst themselves over power within the SPLA. In addition, the LRA, first under the leadership of Alice Lakwena and then under Joseph Kony, used Sudanese safe havens from which to raid into northern Uganda and kidnap recruits for their child army. To the northeast, the regime of Mengistu Haile Mariam collapsed in 1981 and destitute soldiers sold their arms at the border crossings between Kenya and Ethiopia. And along the Kenyan border with Somalia old smuggling routes were increasingly being used to facilitate the traffic in arms. In this way, by the 1990s all of the pastoralists had access to modern military weapons and it was this arms race that had been the principal contributing factor to the quantum increase in death rates during the cattle raids.

The militarization of cattle raiding had ramifications within the pastoralists' own territories and beyond. In Karamoja the subtle elements of leadership that had existed in the past had been replaced by a formula in which firepower, and the cattle that were acquired with it, defined status. The concept of individual employment supplanted the established community-oriented work ethic, with raid "warlords" recruiting armies of youth from the clans and subgroups that had been unable to adapt to the changes. Karimojong women turned to prostitution and men to scavenging in garbage dumps as the fabric of support dissipated and social cohesion waned.

The weapons from Moroto had also changed the Karimojongs relationship with the Ugandan government. After Idi Amin fled, Milton Obote again took power in Kampala. He was from the north of the country but not a Karimojong and when complaints from tribes that were being raided by the Karimojong began to increase he made the pacification of Karamoja a priority. The preferred approach of the Obote regime was in the tradition of Kampala's historical response to problems in Karamoja. Announcements were made ordering the tribes to surrender their arms and when the desired response was not forthcoming the Ugandan authorities sent security forces into the district. But unlike on other occasions, the Karimojong engaged the police and military in skirmishes that often resulted in the routing of the government troops. As a result of the failure of this new strategy, when the Museveni government came into power in January 1986, the Karimojong had a level of armaments and a history of successful engagements that made them both a threat and a formidable opponent.

The Museveni government had a choice of strategies in relation to Karamoja. It could abdicate power over and responsibility for the district and place a cordon sanitaire around the area. But Museveni was not willing to adopt that course for two reasons. First, he was unwilling as a matter of national honor to allow for de facto Karimojong secession. And on a practical basis, an autonomous Karamoja would allow Ugandan anti-government guerrillas operating from Sudan to move in an unconstrained manner and to come very close to southern Uganda and the capital.

The second available strategy was the use of brute force and suppression. Idi Amin had successfully applied such a strategy ten years previously but that was before the Karimojong had access to modern weaponry. Milton Obote's attempts to intimidate and disarm the Karimojong had been signally unsuccessful and by 1986 the number of arms in the hands of the northern tribes had increased. Nevertheless, Museveni's National Resistance Army (NRA) did attempt to pacify Karamoja through force in the first three years of the regime, with varying degrees of success. Herds of cattle were confiscated and the NRA, now metamorphosed into the Ugandan armed forces, made desultory attacks upon the tribes. But Museveni was not only fighting the Karimojong during this period. As well as the LRA, Kampala was fighting the Western Nile Bank Front in the north and the Allied Democratic Forces in the west of the country, together with smaller groups such as National Army for Liberation of Uganda and the Ugandan Salvation Front. It was obvious, therefore, that the concentration of forces necessary to defeat the Karimojong was not available to the Ugandan government.

As is evident from the NWFP and Yemeni cases, when Kalashnikov cultures reach a certain stage of development they pose a significant management dilemma for centralized authorities. Curtailing the activities of armed and fractious peoples even, as in the case of Northern Ireland, when there is a dependable professional military available, is a long-term strategy requiring political continuity, patience, and popular support. If the threat posed to the body of the population is widespread and demonstrable then support of the people may be present for a period of time but it will diminish as the people learn to live with the psychological discomfort. Patience and political continuity are themselves strained by the often glacial movement of an incremental strategy. Therefore, even if a "winning" strategic approach may be recognized it cannot always be implemented. It is this reality that often forces centralized authorities into what appear, out of context, to be dangerous and desperate approaches to the problem of weaponized societies. One such approach, tried in Uganda during the 1990s, is to legitimize the enemy through co-option.

An old aphorism states that if you cannot beat the enemy then joining them should be an option. Somewhat short of such a drastic step is the tactic of imbuing the enemy with the right to maintain their own security. In reality, they already have that capability but this allows all sides to retain some dignity from the circumstances. As an element of this approach, it is usual for the forces of government to establish or recognize a "militia," formed from the forces of the recent antagonist. What took place in Uganda was a variation upon this theme, with the added dimension of a manifestation that has occurred within Kalashnikov cultures on all continents: vigilantism.

A fundamental element of the social contract between a government and an individual relates to security. In exchange for restrictions on the right of self-defense, an individual expects the organs of government to provide for his or her physical security. This security includes the obligation of the state to protect its territory and, through the institution of laws and enforcement machinery, to provide for the safety of its citizenry within the borders of the state. The individual then abrogates the right to provide for their own security to the state, often including the right to use deadly force in the protection of the community. In most cases, this contract is an accepted and supported element of a progressive society. However, when the government fails in its obligation to provide for the security of its citizenry then the abrogated right of self-protection may be reinstated by individuals and groups. This is the core rationale behind the emergence of vigilantism in a society.

It has been said that vigilantism is the law of the lawless. That it emerges from a primal instinct of self-defense and that the group manifestation of vigilantism provides for strength of purpose in the face of accusations that vigilantes are themselves outside of the law. If the community is sufficiently represented within the body of the vigilantist group, then such catholicism imbues the activities of the vigilantes with pseudo-legalistic and moral legitimacy. This sense of shared purpose, coupled with the instinct of self-preservation, allows vigilantes to proselytize the belief that they are manifestations of incipient order, rather than being the harbingers of anarchy themselves. Unfortunately, the presence of vigilante groups within Kalashnikov societies usually denotes slippage into chaos rather than a positive movement toward stability and security.

There is enough of a negative connotation toward vigilantism in advanced industrial societies for such activities to be masked by euphemism. Descriptions like "protective association" and "community response" enable such societies to avoid the possibility that the threat to public safety may be beyond the control of governmental authorities. But movements in other communities are not as concerned about such niceties. Indeed, they may need a heightened sense of incipient anarchy in order to achieve popular support and to help with fund-raising and recruitment. Perhaps some of the best examples of such "open" vigilante organizations are also to be found in Africa, albeit in South Africa.

Groups such as Pagad and Mapogo a Matamaga in that country have, in attracting tens of thousands of members, led to a national sense that crime is beyond the control of the authorities and that only "kangaroo courts" and "people's justice" can ensure personal security. In a country where private security guards outnumber police in a ratio of seven to one, the privatization of justice and punishment might seem a logical evolutionary trend. But far from ameliorating the conditions within South Africa, Pagad and Mapogo have simply added another dimension to the threat environment within the country. As with many like organizations in Latin America and elsewhere, the vigilante groups of South Africa became vehicles for the agendas of their founders and their acolytes and the organs of the state became even more stretched and tested.

Pagad (People Against Gangsterism and Drugs) was founded in 1996 in Cape Town, South Africa. Primarily a response to violent crime emanating from the Cape Flats township (where in 1996 it was estimated that 35,000 to 80,000 inhabitants belonged to 137 separate gangs), the organization was closely identified with the Muslim community in the Cape region and by 1997 claimed a membership of over 100,000, with the majority being from the 2 percent of the South African population that is identified as Sunni Muslims. As a group the Muslims, predominantly descended from immigrants that had left India for South Africa in the nineteenth century, lay claim to being an integral part of the antiapartheid movement. This pedigree of resistance allowed many in Pagad to exhort that their sacrifices allowed them to be especially concerned about the lawlessnes that had been a hallmark of the first two years of Nelson Mandela's administration. But disappointment in the new government was not the only residual of the antiapartheid struggle that helped to fuel the founding of Pagad. Direct action, in the form of covert and overt opposition to the white government in Pretoria, had become an acceptable and heroic form of expression during the period of the "Struggle." Reflecting an attitude that also helped with recruitment into township gangs, Pagad disseminated the propaganda that its activities were in the tradition of those that had turned their back on the repressive white government and had either fought the authorities or established communities that eschewed government-supplied security and assistance. However, this invocation of their status as "urban warriors" and of plucky self-sufficiency was somewhat offset by a belief among the general population of South Africa that Pagad was an exclusionary organization linked somehow to the Islamic extremist politics.[14]

True vigilante movements, as opposed to extralegal death squads acting as agents of a government, rely upon mass membership to protect themselves from a government and the legal authority that they are attempting to supplant. To paraphrase Stalin, when an individual or small group takes the law into its own hands then that is an act of illegality. When 80,000 do the same thing, then that is an act of community self-help. Pagad and Mopogo a Matamaga, its counterpart in the north of South Africa, had by 1998 both become mass movements and could therefore indulge some of their membership who believed in using violence to address the problems of lawlessness within their communities. But Pagad, with its invocation of Quranic law as the spiritual basis for its actions, appeared to be exclusionary in its membership and this, in a society that had just emerged from a period of hyper-exclusionariness, would always limit the appeal and support for the movement.

Pagad concentrated upon drug dealers as their primary target. But the drug dealers of Cape Flats were at the heart of a parallel economy that had developed during the apartheid years, when unemployment and the restrictive Group Areas Act had forced hundreds of thousands of young men to find nontraditional ways of earning a living. The Cape Flats drug entrepreneurs had by 1998 become so formidable that they felt comfortable in assaulting police stations, engaging in major armed skirmishes with each other, and at the same time establishing themselves as a political force. Rashied Staggie, leader of the 10,000-strong "Hard Living" gang in Cape Flats, even went so far as to compare himself with Nelson Mandela, whom he characterized as "a gangster who used force against the white government."[15] To enhance this image of gangster-as-benefactor, Staggie paid the rents of many people in the township and helped to fund the United Democratic Alliance political party. When Pagad targeted drug dealers for vigilante action they threatened not only street-corner sellers but a narco-economy that was as well entrenched as anything to be found in Latin America or Southeast Asia. They also faced, in the criminals of the townships, an enemy that was more adept than themselves in using the twin tools of publicity and propaganda.

Initially, Pagad used marches, mass meetings, and demonstrations to help expand its membership. Demands were made upon the government to use draconian measures, including the death penalty, against drug dealers, to which the gangs responded that these were exactly the type of repressive actions that had been used by the apartheid regime. Frustrated by its inability to pressure the government, Pagad then began a campaign of violent assaults on the drug gangs. In 1996 Rashied Staggie's brother was killed during a Pagad demonstration and this ushered in a period in which the gangs and Pagad engaged in an escalating series of murders and bombings. During this period Pagad killers made weekly incursions into the townships to assassinate gang members and Asian-owned businesses were themselves targeted in a bombing campaign that by 1998 numbered sixty-seven unsolved incidents.[16] Pagad was also accused of extortion tactics against businessmen in an effort to replenish its war chest. The overwhelmed authorities freely admitted that they were no longer in control of the situation and laid much of the blame for what they termed the "anarchy" on the Pagad organization. It was clear by the end of the decade, after the deaths of more than 800 people in the

Pagad–gangster war, that what had begun as a popular response to gang violence had itself deteriorated into a vendetta between two violently intransigent armies.

In the north of South Africa Mapogo a Matamaga performed the same role as Pagad in the south but without the undertones of religious and ethnic identification. Also established in 1996, Mapogo had a claimed membership of 50,000 by early 2000. The membership included white farmers, Asian businessmen, and poor inhabitants of black townships, all of whom paid an annual subscription fee ranging from a few dollars to $2,000. In return for this investment, members received the protective services of the organization and helped to underwrite Mapogo's vigilante activities. The latter included whipping suspected criminals with the notorious sjambok, a device that resulted in more than twenty deaths during its administration by Mapogo between 1996 and the year 2000.[17]

The attitude of Mapogo's leader, Monhle Magolego, typifies the rationalization that underlies the philosophy of most vigilante organizations. When confronted with evidence that sometimes those who are flogged are innocent or that some die under punishment, he opined that while such occurrences were unfortunate ". . . a doctor does not take the patient to the operating theatre to be killed, but to remove the ills from him . . . If we approach a criminal he tells the truth. You don't have to go to school to learn how to catch a criminal."[18] When members of his own organization demurred over the increase in violent acts committed by Mapogo, Magolego's response was neo-McCarthyite: ". . . these [critics] must start their own organization. They are criminals. That is why they are against my organization. They also know that we know how to deal with criminals." Such an attitude is indicative of one of the inherent dangers of vigilantism. The infectious nature of using violence for the resolution of social problems can cause such practices to become an accepted and general response to all those that are perceived as being threatening nonconformists within the society.

The South African experience with vigilante movements is by no means unique. Groups such as Pagad and Mapogo have been cataloged in societies as disparate as India, Mexico, and Russia. Even if their intentions are honorable, the methods that they are forced to adopt almost invariably add to the climate of violence rather than detract from it. The antigangsterism of Pagad very quickly devolved into killings that were indistinguishable from those being perpetrated by their enemy. The threateningly fascist position of Mapogo may have deterred some criminals but it also helped resurrect some of the very fears that had been engendered by the apartheid regime. Vigilantism is most often the last refuge of desperate people and impotent authorities and so it was in Karamoja in the 1990s.

The armed forces of Uganda had suffered between 300 and 600 casualties in their confrontations with Karimojong cattle raiders in the late 1980s. Such loss of life made the Ugandan military unwilling to prosecute the campaign and this forced President Museveni to find an alternative way of controlling Karamoja. But before the Ugandan authorities could formulate a strategy, events within Karamoja itself appeared to offer a solution to their dilemma.

By 1992 many of the inhabitants of Karamoja had reached the same level of fear and frustration that their counterparts in South Africa would assume some four years later. "Predatory" raiding had now become rampant through the region and whole villages had been displaced into refugee camps around the larger towns. Travel along roads and tracks had been almost halted, further restricting any economic interaction within Karamoja. And livestock diseases had reached epidemic proportions, due in no small part to the transfer of the cattle from one raiding group to another.[19] Together, these factors, exacerbated by the almost total lack of law enforcement within Karamoja, had created a crisis of order that the citizens of Moroto decided to address. The chosen vehicle of their response to the near-anarchic conditions was vigilantism.

Initially, the vigilante movement in Karamoja was very much a reflection of traditional pastoralist virtues. Only weapon-owning men of distinction, with cattle herds of their own and the respect of their communities, could participate. Each of the ninety parishes of Moroto District was required to recruit ten such men and the first task assigned to the militia was to secure the roads. Having accomplished this with a degree of success, by 1994 the vigilantes had attracted the attention of the Museveni government. Realizing that a self-policed Karamoja was preferable to an anarchic one, the government of Uganda decided to underwrite the vigilantes with a $10 a month individual stipend and a uniform each. In return, the vigilantes came under the control of the Ugandan army and were encouraged to expand into an 8,000-man force. This organization, renamed the Anti-Stock Theft Unit, was later placed under the authority of the Ugandan police in 1997.[20]

As part of the arrangement between Museveni and the Karimojong the latter were allowed to retain their arms while they remained within Karamoja itself. Although termed a concession, this was a tacit recognition by Kampala that it was unwilling and unable to disarm the Karimojong. Since it was estimated that by 1996 the tribes and subgroups of the region possessed between 150,000 and 200,000 weapons, this was perhaps a prudent strategy.[21] But this combination of laissez faire management, the number of weapons available to the tribes and the change in authority over the vigilantes was to prove the unmaking of the arrangement between the Ugandan government and the Karimojong.

Confiscation of cattle as a punishment for crimes was widespread in both Uganda and Kenya. An entire village, or wananchi, would have its livestock taken away by the authorities until the suspected culprits were given up to the state authorities. But often corrupt officials and vigilante leaders would conspire to sell the animals even after the criminals had been surrendered and such a loss would serve to cripple the economies of smaller wananchi. After the police took over from the Ugandan army as Kampala's partners in the security arrangement, such corruption and malfeasance increased and disenchanted by this development, most of the tribal elders withdrew their support for the Ant-Stock Theft Unit and many of the remaining vigilante commanders took the opportunity to convert their gangs into tribally based cattle raiding groups.

The Karimojong subtribes had always fought each other as much as they had attacked the Turkana or the Acholi or the Toposa. Most of their "redistributive raiding" had been within Karamoja and the kinship element had been one of the reasons that the raiders had developed low mortality tactics in order to reduce long-term enmity. But since 1979, when the Matheniko subtribe had been the principal beneficiary of the Moroto arsenal raid, there had been an escalating tension between them and their traditional rivals, the Bokora. The Ugandan military had encouraged this divisiveness, believing that if the Karimojong tribes fought each other then this would be to the advantage of the Museveni administration and of the Ugandan military, who after the collapse of the Anti-Stock Theft Unit were finding themselves under increasing attack from the vigilante groups.[22]

Within Karamoja itself the vigilante groups were engaging in what local authorities termed "mob justice."[23] Suspected thieves and murderers were stoned, axed, lynched, and shot without any form of trial or procedure. Interclan and tribal vendettas were pursued under the guise of cleansing Karamoja of criminals and this served to further increase tensions between such groups as the Bokora and the Matheniko. Police presence in Karamoja was minimal and their involvement in law enforcement activities was desultory. The Ugandan army made pro forma incursions into the region, killing in a seemingly arbitrary manner and confiscating cattle at will. Overall, by the end of 1998 insecurity was chronic in Karamoja and many of the subtribes, bereft of their cattle and of the protection of any authority, had lapsed into dependency on food aid from non-governmental organizations. The well-armed tribes, most notably the Bokora, Matheniko, and the Jie, preyed upon the smaller groups and then attacked each other whenever they felt that the opportunity was ripe.

By mid-1999 the level of tension in Karamoja was high enough that the Ugandan government, for the third time in fifteen years, enacted a law to outlaw ownership of firearms within the district. Both Idi Amin and Milton Obote had tried to implement such laws but without success and this third attempt was met with cynicism within Uganda as a whole (many thought that it was a political ploy related to an upcoming referendum on multipartyism) and with scepticism by the Karimajong.[24] As if to test the government, in July and September 1999 two raids took place in which there were a total of 500 casualties among the raiding tribes who took part. In the first raid, members of the Matheniko tribe raided a Bokora village, killing 140, of whom seventy were children who were tossed alive into burning huts. The children had gathered to be fed by an aid organization. In retaliation, two months later the Bokora attacked a Matheniko village. During this attack a Ugandan military helicopter, converted into a gunship, made repeated assaults on the Bokora raiders, killing several hundred.[25] Although all who participated appeared shocked by the death toll (one Matheniko warrior was quoted as saying that his eyes were "blurred with the blood of people I killed"), within a month of the September encounter most of the tribes of the Karamoja were rearming and preparing to raid once more.[26]

It might be possible to dismiss the warring tribes of Karamoja as a quaintly idiosyncratic manifestation of atavistic behavior. The image of mud-daubed warriors, clad only in their short native skirt and rubber-tire sandals, marauding across a barren landscape appears to fulfill many of the preconceptions that casual observers maintain about Africa. But Karamoja society was, and to a certain extent remains, a highly complex and environmentally adapted organization. To term the Karimojong as "primitive" and to dismiss their actions between 1979 and 2000 as predictably Malthusian is to make an assumption that, once the modern weapons and the mass killings began in earnest, there was a viable alternative to what became known as "predatory" raiding.

As far as being aberrational, Karamoja is not the only pastoralist area of East Africa that has metamorphosed into its own "Kalashnikov culture." In Sudan, Ethiopia, and most particularly Kenya, there are cattle raiding cultures that mirror Karamoja in the intensity of their warfare and the lethality of their firepower. In many ways, one such rivalry, between the Turkana and Pokot of Kenya, involves ramifications that have a greater bearing upon the future of the "host" nation-state than the Karimojong wars have upon Uganda. In the latter case the Ugandan government has been able to physically and politically contain the impact of the cattle raids in Karamoja. But in Kenya the war between the Turkana and the Pokot has threatened to destabilize the fragile set of alliances and associations that form the backbone of Kenyan national polity.

Kenya's population of 28 million is comprised of more than forty ethnic groups. Within each ethnic group are numerous subtribes and clans. The Kalenjin, for example, who account for 12 percent of the overall population, is subdivided into eleven separate subtribes, including the Pokot and the Marakwet. For the most part the Kalenjin are pastoralists and although they often share language and customs it is this shared economic activity that is the prime indicator of their homogeny. In contrast, the Turkana, who inhabit land in northern Kenya that is directly adjacent to Karamoja, are an identifiably separate tribe of nomadic pastoralists who have as much in common with their Ugandan neighbors as they do with the Kalenjin or the Kikuyu or any other Kenyan tribe. Perhaps the most evident of the affinities between the Karimojong and the Turkana is that both groups have a prolonged history of cattle raiding, where for the Pokot and other Kalenjin such activities are a relatively recent, learned experience.

The Turkana played an important role in the history of the arms race amongst pastoralist tribes.[27] An early adopter of firearms, for more than fifty years they used their weapons technology to become the dominant raiding tribe in a belt of territory running from Uganda, through southern Sudan, across northern Kenya and into southern Ethiopia. The firearms were mostly bolt-action rifles that leeched from Sudan and Ethiopia but at a time when the Karimojong were using spears and bows this gave the Turkana a significant advantage. After the raid on the Moroto barracks in 1979 however, the Karimojong, using the automatic weapons that the raid had provided them, began a series of raids against the Turkana that demonstrated that power had shifted. In response to this change, the Turkana began cattle raiding against tribes within Kenya that had not yet acquired firearms. One of these tribes was the Pokot.

The Pokot were traditional enemies of the Turkana and had been used by the British in their attempt to pacify the latter.[28] But, as in Karamoja, the raiding between the two tribes had been of a disciplined and stylized nature until the 1990s. Then the Turkana, newly rearmed from their sources in Sudan, began to engage in "predatory raiding" against the Pokot, Samburu, and Marakwet tribes.[29] The Pokot then began to arm themselves, allegedly sponsored by "entrepreneurs" who encouraged cattle raiding as an economic enterprise.[30] The Pokot and Turkana continued to raid each other but the Pokot also began themselves to raid the Samburu and Marakwet tribes, both of which were poorly armed. In this way the insecurity created by constant raiding began to move south and east across Kenya, causing the central government to resort to the same draconian measures that had failed in Uganda.[31] Vigilantism and mob violence also began to occur in Kenya, with indications that it was at least as widespread as in Uganda.[32]

This cascading effect, in which tribes and clans exploit weakness in order to acquire livestock, contributed to constant and chronic instability in areas that hitherto had been immune to such insecurity. And major urban areas away from the raiding zones were not immune to the effects of the weaponization of the tribes. In Nairobi, assault rifles and handguns could be rented by criminals in 1996 for $150 a day and by the end of the decade the price had been reduced and the availability broadened.[33] Inevitably, violent crime in the capital city increased, tourism was affected and an air of crisis began to permeate the country.

Traditional cattle raiding of the "redistributive" type had not been free of violence. One group of experts cautions that it would "be wrong to romanticise redistributive forms of raiding." But the same group also identified "predatory raiding" as a major factor in the spiral of massacre, vendetta, famine, starvation, and overall decline of the pastoralist communities. The insecurity that sprang from the raiding was, in itself, a corrosive element. Seminomadic tribes such as the Karamajong and the Turkana needed to move their flocks 10–15 times a year in order to find sufficient grazing. With such freedom curtailed by the constant threat of raiding, herds dwindled and starved, were sold for a pittance and clans and subtribes were reduced to living in refugee camps or hiring themselves as mercenaries to the larger raiding tribes.[34]

Several factors were identifiable as encouraging the move from traditional, contained raiding to the depredations of "predatory raiding." Changes in climate, the so-called Sahelization of the semiarid lands, made the grazing of large herds problematic. The wars in Uganda, Sudan, Ethiopia, and Somalia also, through their example of applied violence at the state level, helped set a tone of disorderliness and chaos. However, the radical change in the nature of warfare among the pastoralists can also be directly traced to the influx of modern weapons into the arena. Authorities ranging from local law enforcement, the military, nongovernmental organizations, academics, religious leaders and heads of state identified the increase in numbers and lethality of weaponry as being the single factor that has changed a sophisticated form of social and economic interaction into a series of large-scale massacres. Indeed, the guns themselves have now begun to figure in a countertrade that provides tribes such as the Jie and the Tepeth in Uganda with much of their wealth.

The raid on the Moroto barracks in 1979 provided the impetus behind the weaponization of Karamoja and Turkana. The type and number of weapons (approximately 5,000 assault and battle rifles, machine guns, submachine guns, and grenades) created a demand amongst the tribes of Karamoja and across the border for analogous armaments. By the mid-1980s the most prolific source for modern military-type weapons was Sudan and most specifically the SPLA. The guerrillas received their arms from a variety of sources, including at various times the governments of Ethiopia, Eritrea, and Uganda, and also from the United States.[35] Some local commanders of the SPLA and many individual deserters then sold weapons and ammunition to Jie tribesmen in Karamoja, who transported them to Moroto district, close to the Kenyan border. The weapons were then bartered for cattle with Kenyan Pokot tribesmen, who in turn sold them to the Kalenjin in the interior of Kenya.[36] The Jie sold the bartered cattle to Kenyan dealers, exchanged their Kenyan currency for Ugandan money and then traveled north to Sudan to continue the process. In 1999 the average price of an AK-type rifle at the Sudanese border was US$20, with the price rising to US$135 by the time it reached its destination inside Kenya. In 1997 the barter price paid by the Pokot for each gun was ten head of cattle. In the late 1970s the barter price had been sixty head of cattle per weapon, indicating that the flow of weapons was reliable enough to drive down the price of the guns.[37] Goats and other animals are traded for ammunition. Arms also flow directly into Kenya from Sudan (the price of an assault rifle at the Sudanese-Kenyan border was an inflated US$80 in 1999) and from Somalia.[38]

This illicit supply network was augmented by a Kenyan government policy of supplying Pokot tribesmen with arms in order to protect themselves from the Turkana and the Karimojong. In an action that mirrored the Ugandan government's treatment of the vigilantes in Karamoja, the Kenyan authorities "organized" Pokot tribesmen into home guard units, armed them and encouraged them to police their tribal area. Unfortunately, the Pokot then used their weapons to intimidate other tribes, steal their cattle and sell them to entrepreneurs in the interior of Kenya.[39] The Kenyan authorities' attempts to track down and impound illegal weapons were also less than auspicious. In a major operation in 1998 fewer than 300 firearms were recovered nationwide.[40]

The history of the weaponization of the pastoralists provides a microcosm of an arms race. The seepage of a few bolt-action rifles into Kenya from Ethiopia and Sudan gave the Turkana a technological edge over the Karimojong. The latter used the confusion of the collapse of Idi Amin's government to increase the level of armaments with semiautomatic battle rifles and selective-fire assault rifles. This then created a demand amongst the Turkana for such weapons, which was then satisfied by arms leeching from the conflict in southern Sudan and brokered by the arms-rich Karimojong. The Turkana then turned those weapons on the Pokot, who themselves acquired arms from the Karimojong and then turned those arms on the Marakwet and other tribes, as well as upon the Turkana. Such a spiral of victimology might be amusing if it were not for the fact that the end result has been thousands of deaths and the virtual destruction of a lifestyle.

Several lessons can be learned from the East African experience. Even small numbers of weapons can, under certain conditions, create a technological imbalance that can in turn undermine a subtly balanced but conflict-prone society. Mechanisms of constraint that may have evolved over centuries, even millenia, can be destroyed by weaponry that emphasize the virtue of lethality over a code of warrior behavior. This decline can be exacerbated by arms made available as a result of political chaos. The guns of Moroto may have been a windfall for the Karimojong but they proved to be a Pandora's box for the region. If weapons can be controlled or even destroyed in future such situations, then communities might save themselves from the experience of the pastoralists of Uganda and Kenya. Similarly, when arms are constantly injected into war zones such as southern Sudan it must be recognized that the seepage will contribute to general insecurity in neighboring areas.

Once societies reach the level of weaponization such has occurred in northern Uganda and Kenya the options for amelioration of the situation are few. Any disarmament program by state authorities will require a level of intimidation and use of force that would be distasteful and possibly counterproductive. Even if a group such as the Karimojong were to be successfully disarmed this would simply make them easy victims of the Turkana and other armed tribes. A coordinated approach involving the forces of multiple states would be difficult, costly, and might create a regional crisis. Even if all groups were to be disarmed weapons would still flow in from the surrounding war zones, to be bartered for cattle. Attempts to control the movement of cattle have led to corruption, conflict, and a negative impact on the fundamental structure of nomadic life. The concept of self-policing amongst the tribes through the encouragement of vigilantism has also failed, leading as it did in Uganda and Kenya to revenge killing and mob violence.

The weaponization of the East African pastoralists is a cautionary tale. In a period of barely twenty years a carefully balanced traditional society was structurally altered by the infusion of modern weapons. Once such a saturation level has been reached it is extremely difficult, if not impossible, to reverse the damage that has taken place. Warning signs and precursors do exist but they require prescience and action to forestall the shunt effect of a regional arms race. When state authorities such as the police and the army find themselves outgunned by an armed populace it is probably too late to think in terms of a return to the status quo ante and more appropriate to think in terms of de facto secession and even civil war. And even when such civil wars have abated, the weapons remain like landmines within the communities that formerly embraced them.

Gangsta Warriors

Unlike the North West Frontier Province and Yemen, Liberia and Sierra Leone are not traditional weaponized states. Except for the crude arms possessed by a few hunting tribes, guns have, until the last decade of the twentieth century, been monopolized by state institutions in those countries. Sierra Leone, a former British colony, reflected the restrictive gun control policies of the United Kingdom and Liberia controlled access to firearms as an element of its elite management political structure. The casual violence that betokens arms saturated societies was absent in these two West African states and in many ways this makes their metamorphosis into Kalashnikov cultures that much more difficult to explain. The evolution of gun culture into Kalashnikov culture is a fundamentally logical trend; the transition from seemingly passive unarmed state to what some commentators consider to be harbingers of a new anarchy is more opaque. However, what occurred in Liberia and Sierra Leone does indeed have its own logic. Within the structure and traditions of both societies were tensions and fault lines that included rituals of violence as an element of substate identity and cohesion. Sublimated by the primacy of the state, it took the decay of the instruments of centralized authority to amplify such rituals to a national and then regional level. Combined with an infusion of arms from outside of the two countries, Liberia and Sierra Leone had, by the early 1990s, the binary precursors necessary for what only appeared to be a spontaneous metamorphosis into Kalashnikov cultures.

The Liberian civil war began in 1989, and that of Sierra Leone in 1991. During the same period the wider world was absorbed with the collapse of communism and the conflict in the Gulf and the events in West Africa were principally remarkable for the images that were broadcast from the conflicts. Combatants, many in their teens or even younger, were filmed and photographed in bizarre masks, wearing women's clothing or with their features smeared with mud. To many Western observers these displays were symptomatic of a degeneration into barbarism, a position that was reinforced by accounts of cannibalism and mutilation that emerged from the battlefronts in the two countries. The U.S. journalist, Robert Kaplan, identified the region with a "coming anarchy" on a global scale and this perception was given added weight when his viewpoint was proliferated amongst the American diplomatic service as a viable explanation for seemingly uncategorizable conflicts in the Balkans, the Caucasus, and sub-Saharan Africa. But other, more specifically knowledgeable experts demurred from this Conradian, Malthusian perspective.

Although neighbors, Liberia and Sierra Leone have different roots as modern states. Liberia was a territory composed of lineage societies, many conforming more to the definition of clans than tribes, when freed American slaves arrived in the area in 1822. Some of these societies were linked by secretive organizations, such as the Poro and Sande, which served to broaden out the clans beyond the traditional lines of kinship that usually provided the bonding for such groups. When the Americans arrived they therefore added a new element to this extant structure and in its own way this intrusion was as impository as had been the arrival of British colonists in Sierra Leone some two decades earlier. They brought with them the twin concepts of a European-style state architecture and the notion of American-style democracy, both of which required centralized authority to reach fruition. In order to achieve such "stability," the immigrants, operating from their enclave on the coast, were forced to engage in the same strategy of conquest and co-optation that was the hallmark of the colonial powers in Africa. In attempting to create a state, the Americo-Liberians would, therefore, tear the fabric of the delicate political ecology of the region and help lay the foundations for conflict within their country.

The British also attempted in their own fashion to impose political homogeneity upon Sierra Leone and by using the blueprint applied throughout the British empire they had some success. At independence in 1961 Sierra Leone was considered to have successfully absorbed the rationales behind European political and judicial structure and to have enough self-identity to qualify as a nation-state. But such judgements were premature and the postcolonial period evolved into confrontational politics within seven years of independence. Between 1968 and 1985 under the leadership of Siaka Stevens the country became a single-party state, with most of the power vested in the chief executive and with an economy beholden to him under a patronage system. All institutions that might threaten the primacy of Stevens, including local government and the army, were reduced to rump entities and any emergent political challengers were discouraged through intimidation and physical duress. By the time that he was replaced by a military regime in 1985, Stevens had established the precedent of centralized authority as being primarily concerned with trickle-down kleptocratic economics rather than service to the population. This perception increased under the government of General Momoh, which so reduced fiscal outlay that the education system ceased to function and most civil servants only performed their appointed tasks for financial inducement from their customers.

In Liberia the centralization of authority and the extent of the patronage system had, under the presidencies of William Tubman (1944–1971) and William Tolbert (1971–1980), become highly refined. Under Tubman no government payment of more than $250 could be made without the president's approval and through a complex association between government and nongovernment institutions virtually all upward mobility within the Liberian economy was linked to the Americo-Liberian elite. With the military and police dominated by officers from the elite class, suppression of the hinterland, which took place bloodily up until the 1930s, became another bone of contention between the predominantly coastal-dwelling Americo-Liberian elite (never more than 4 percent of the total population) and the seventeen ethnically identifiable groups in the interior. By1980, a century and a half of rule by the Americo-Liberians had created such pressure for change that the inevitable final straw, in this case rioting over an increase in the price of the staple of rice, brought representatives of the hinterland to power through the vehicle of a military coup staged by the lower ranks. But instead of eliminating or at least broadening the recipient base of the patronage system, the military regime of Samuel Doe (1980–1990) simply transferred power from the Americo-Liberians to Doe's own ethnic group, the Krahn, while at the same time using the managerial skills of the former group to consolidate and maintain his position as head of state. With the army's loyalty maintained through personal and fiscal linkages and with the external support of the United States, Samuel Doe used applied violence against any element that might oppose him and, as with Sierra Leone, this created reservoirs of deeply resentful opposition.

The Americo-Liberians had not been identified with any clan or ethnic group in Liberia and therefore the tensions within that country prior to 1980 were not, unlike in many parts of Africa, identifiable as tribal in nature. But Samuel Doe, in changing the patronage system from elite based to tribal or ethnic, introduced an element of schism that unbalanced the delicate interrelationship between Liberian clans. In response, two of the principal groups, the Gio and Mano, assisted rebels in an abortive coup in 1985 and as a result these tribes were subjected to major depradations by Doe's Armed Forces of Liberia (AFL). When, in 1989, Charles Taylor's National Patriotic Front for Liberia (NPFL) made an incursion into Liberia from the Ivory Coast, he used the rallying call of tribal identity to gather forces and to identify the Doe regime with the president's tribe, the Krahn. The Gio and Mano, amongst other ethnic groups, readily responded to such an impetus and this allowed Taylor (ironically from an Americo-Liberian family himself) to inflate his forces from the small (perhaps 500 men under arms) group that he brought with him over the border to the thousands that he needed to seize the 90 percent of the country that he controlled by July 1990.[1]

Both Liberia and Sierra Leone are primarily rural societies, with associations and traditions that reflect the concerns of rural people in general. Much of the spiritual sense was derived from threats posed by forests (leopards are a favored image of threat and power) and of the need to protect crops and herds from de-struction and disease. This spirituality was, for more than 40 percent of the overall population, expressed in terms of traditional beliefs, many of which revolved around elaborate protective measures, including ritual sacrifice.[2] The Poro and Sande societies (which predated colonialism in Sierra Leone and the arrival of the Americo-Liberians in that country) helped to proliferate such beliefs and in Liberia particularly these groupings had a profound, apolitical influence upon the populace. Much of the seemingly bizarre behavior of combatants in both conflicts can be traced to residual elements of traditional faith (the wearing of women's clothing, for example, is a form of shape-shifting). But more importantly, as the wars in both countries progressed, the role that the societies played in the educa-tion and disciplining of young men and women as they emerged into adulthood was lost. In countries where formal education was almost nonexistent, groups such as the Poro and Sande provided guidance on behavior and accountability that were otherwise lacking in the society as a whole. When the forest became too dangerous for such educational exercises and when the lure of war became too much of an alternative attraction to restive youth, groups such as the NPFL and the Revolutionary United Front (RUF) in Sierra Leone adopted a degenerated form of the rules and beliefs of Poro and Sande as their spiritual (and ideological) underpinning.[3]

Although the bulk of the two populations were rural, there was one group of urbanites in both Liberia and Sierra Leone who, despite the repressive nature of both societies, had been able to cultivate a reputation as rebellious and noncon-formist. These were the groups of undereducated, unemployed young people (but principally males) who gathered in the open spaces of major towns and cities, abused alcohol and drugs, and felt alienated from the "system." Often placed un-der the umbrella concept of the lumpen, in Sierra Leone this group, beginning as the "*rarray* boys" in the 1940s, began to evolve as a distinct subculture, with a language and an attitude that, in its defiance of authority, has obvious echoes in the attitudes of such groups as the West Side Boys some fifty years later.[4] Initially simply concerned with social interaction (including the use of marijuana and the ingestion of large amounts of spirits), in the 1960s and 1970s the rarray boys began to change into a political force, allowing themselves to be used by Siaka Stevens to terrorize his opponents and gaining, through the induction of college students, a rudimentary knowledge of political ideology. It was during this period that the lumpen of Freetown, now called "service men," began to gravitate from criticizing the system to believing that they might be able to change it to benefit themselves.

One of the galvanizing elements that facilitated the transition from social interaction to political awareness was music and most particularly Jamaican reg-gae. Bob Marley and other voices of alienated, angry, and marijuana-influenced Caribbean youth found a ready audience at the "debel" or carnivals in Freetown. And the reflective mirror was not restricted to comparative social conditions. In both Sierra Leone and Jamaica the lumpen youth had become tools of politicians who encouraged them to make physical attacks upon rivals and rewarded them for their participation in such activities. In Sierra Leone such rewards were limited to police indulgence over the use of marijuana and the excesses of the debel. In Jamaica, the rewards included access to power, the creation of a drug-based "gangsta" economy, and guns. The "service men" of Freetown were not to achieve such bounties until the RUF recruited many of their members in the late 1980s but by then the influence of Western cultural sounds and images, including those that glorified physical force as a way to resolve complex issues, had helped to create a doctrine that was a melange of Gadaffism, Fanonism, Alvin Toffler, and Hollywood.

Several observers of the West African wars have commented upon the confusion of imagery that one called the "Liberianization of war."[5] In many ways this was the local response to Frances Fukuyama's "end of history"; a world beyond ideologies where icons of Western culture (John Wayne, Sylvester Stallone, Chuck Norris, et al.) were substitutes for traditional leaders and traditional cultural norms.[6] The militias in Liberia, Sierra Leone, and Cote d'Ivoire, particularly those comprised of children and teenagers, were acting in their own movies and videos, mimicking the violence that they interpreted as a contributing element to the strength of western, and most particularly American, cultures. This "contagion by media" helped to create a social bond among and between militias in West Africa that allowed them to sublimate the horror of their actions and instead to see themselves as the inheritors of the mantle of their media heroes.[7] Fetishism had always been a part of West African society and the action figures of movies and television were fetishes for the psyche, in which the young people became "big men" through the power of the Kalashnikov.

The rarray boys were the local equivalents of the media heroes that galvanized the West African militias. They were not commanders of violence but they were independent and rebellious and it is the independence and antiauthoritarian attitudes of the insolent heroes of the silver screen that was attractive to the youth. The image of the bad-boy trickster who flaunts his antisocialism as a badge of distinction and individualism is common throughout many of the Kalashnikov cultures. This image of rebellious child was particularly potent in societies such as Liberia where violence and intimidation by adults against children was a part of the parenting and educational process.[8] The association of violence with power and independence and the seeming reinforcement of this association through the actions of John Rambo and Bruce Lee did not require intellectuals to interpret the dialectic or political leaders to inculcate their followers with doctrine. If the militia members could not all become wealthy they could, with the assistance of drugs and alcohol, appear to themselves and their peers as heroic figures. But some, a very few, could also aspire to wealth out of the chaos of West Africa and the rush to control the diamond wealth of the region helped fuel the process of Kalashnikov enculturation.

Before the description "conflict diamonds" was placed into general use, diamonds were at the core of a fundamental conflict within African society. It revolved around concepts of ownership of natural resources, exploitation of those resources by mining companies, and the image of the illegal diamond miner as bandit and rebel. Not restricted to Africa (for example, the alluvial gold miners or "pork knockers" of Guyana are surrounded by the same mystique), this idea of a lumpen mass of bush "pirates" helping to redistribute wealth through social banditry is, in places where entrepreneurialism and opportunity are controlled by external factors, a potent image. The possibility of finding wealth in the soil is in itself seminal, creating a credible analogy with the ganja farmers and traders of Jamaica. Add the outlaw element of local youth pitted against corrupt officialdom and foreign mining companies, then there is something universally recognizable and even appealing about the scenario. However, the dark side of this image is one in which the spirit of independence becomes subservient to forces that would use the physicality of the miners and the proceeds of their labors to help pursue political ambitions.

A study of a diamond rebel group in Lesotho, the Liphokojoe (foxes), indicates that there is an almost inevitable political dimension to such activity.[9] What may begin as a nonconformist way to make a living develops into a lifestyle that encourages resistance to authority that in turn is often rationalized in ideological or philosophical terms. The leader of the Liphokojoe, a young man named Nyemotsa, had been a miner in South Africa, where he was the member of a gang called the Marashea or Russians. Mirroring the activities of the "service men" and the Jamaican "crews," the Marashea engaged in criminal activities amongst the expatriate mining communities in South Africa, fought the police, and allowed themselves to be used as strike breakers by the mine owners and their political allies. Nyemotsa then became an illegal diamond miner in Lesotho, where he organized other miners into a type of cooperative of resistance. The culmination of this effort was an open revolt against the Lesotho government in 1970 in which Nyemotsa and many of his followers were killed.

Originally definable as apolitical, the Marashea became politicized as they began to see themselves as economic nationalists, waging war against a government that allowed foreign mining companies to exploit Lesotho's (and Africa's) natural resources. When they rose up in 1970 it was with a declared mission to "cleanse the country of . . . carelessness" that is to stop it from devolving into a dialog between domestic and foreign elites in which the average citizen was marginalized. But in reality the Liphokojoe was engaging in a rationalization for banditry that was quite traditional in much of Africa. The forces of centralized authority had to confront the illegal diamond miners because they were disrupting a trade that relied upon a tightly controlled, monopolistic approach in order to maintain the artificial scarcity of the product. The illegal miners had to resist the police and military because they felt that they had no choice if they were to maintain their lifestyle. But the imagery, of free-spirits making a hard living from the earth, harassed by officialdom and eventually rising up, only to die in a cathartic spasm of violence, is potent.[10] What was required to transform this image into a useful instrument of political rebellion was a framework that reinforced in the minds of the illegal miners that they were truly rebels with a cause. With their talk of overthrowing the "system," Foday Sankoh in Sierra Leone and Charles Taylor in Liberia struck a distinct chord. They also brought the necessary weapons to ensure that, unlike the Liphokojoe, they would defeat the agents of the "system."

The illegal diamond miners, or tributors, in Sierra Leone were the rural equivalent of the "service men." The harsh conditions of the bush ensured that the majority of the tributors were young men and indeed a number of them were former "service men" hoping to achieve wealth in remote areas of the alluvial diamond territory in the south of the country. Ironically, their existence was dependant upon a network of supply and support that was as restrictive as the hierarchy of power to be found in the cities. The freedom was largely illusory and by the 1980s few became tributors if there was any credible alternative. Even when miners found diamonds they were trapped by a purchasing system (Lebanese buyers at the fields, Selection Trust/De Beers at the wholesale level) that imposed severe limits on their ability to break free of what was, at best, a subsistence activity.

The physical demands of mining and the frustrations inherent in the activity drove many tributors to alcohol, drugs, and violence. The admixture was given further potency by one of the few forms of entertainment available to the miners, that of American and Chinese action videotapes. Using gas generators, the tributors amused themselves with martial arts sagas and with Hollywood products such as the "Rambo" series.[11] The latter, with its theme of the independent warrior in confrontation with a corrupt system, was particularly appealing to the miners. Later, during the civil war, the original of the series, "First Blood", would be used as a military training device by many of the field commanders. In this manner the recruits to the RUF were indoctrinated to view themselves as heroic figures in a universal mould, rather than as an angry and undisciplined adjunct to corrupted political power.

The mining pits at Kono in Sierra Leone would provide both a disaffected component from which the RUF and others could recruit and, perhaps more importantly, a prize of wealth that sustained, practically and psychologically, the conflict in both Sierra Leone and Liberia. During the Liberian civil war, Charles Taylor's NPFL maintained a political strategy in which the destabilization of Sierra Leone was an integral element of a plan that relied upon the Kono diamonds to help support his force. After the end of the Liberian civil war, now-President Taylor continued to support the RUF in order to facilitate the continued flow of Sierra Leone's diamonds to support the Liberian exchequer. In a classic countertrade, the RUF held the diamond fields with arms that were brokered through Liberia, which took payment in diamonds that were then partially used to defray debts accrued by the Liberians for arms shipped to Charles Taylor during the Liberian civil war.[12] In this way, the president of Liberia had become dependent upon Foday Sankoh and the RUF to maintain a civil conflict in Sierra Leone in order to provide the Liberians with the necessary hard currency to maintain his regime.

Neither Liberia nor Sierra Leone was a traditional gun culture.[13] Although hunting clans existed in both countries, they were most often armed with traditional weapons (bows and arrows and single-shot firearms) and were anomalous. As in Jamaica and other British colonies, Sierra Leone was subject to an imperialist perspective that considered the private ownership of arms to be a potentially destabilizing activity and this attitude continued after independence. In Doe's Liberia, even the troops of the national army were restricted in their access to arms. When, therefore, Charles Taylor and his 150-man guerrilla army invaded Liberia on Christmas eve 1989, they represented not just opposition to the regime in Monrovia but, through the arms they carried and later dispensed to anti-Doe tribesmen, they were to provide the catalysts that transformed social disaffection among the alienated lumpen masses of Liberia and Sierra Leone into waves of remarkable violence.

Charles Taylor had himself received arms from Libya and from Burkina Faso. The former state had provided training for both Taylor and Foday Sankoh during the 1980s as part of a strategy by Colonel Khaddafi in which he moved his external policy interests from the Middle East to sub-Saharan Africa. The majority of the arms that Charles Taylor dispensed to anti-Doe factions in Nimba County, however, were provided by the administration of Blaise Campaore in Burkina Faso. This tripartite relationship between Burkina Faso, Charles Taylor, and the RUF was to become an enduring facet of the West African conflict. The role of the Burkinabe was crucial to Taylor in the formative stages of his own war with Monrovia and later became equally important as they acted as brokers for arms acquired by Taylor and destined for the RUF. Having a legitimate state acting as an expeditor for arms transactions is, for non-state actors or pariah regimes, virtually a necessity and Burkina Faso has fulfilled that role in respect of Liberia and Sierra Leone. Indeed, prior to the coup that placed Blaise Campaore in the presidency, Burkina Faso had contributed to the weaponisation of the region when President Sankara had, in mimicry of Samora Machel in Mozambique, dispensed arms to his people as an act of revolutionary theater. Most of these arms were to disappear into the black market, eventually to emerge in Liberia and Sierra Leone, where they were traded for diamonds or other loot from the conflicts.

The conflict in West Africa came at a time when access to arms on the international market was facilitated by a number of factors. The end of the Cold War had de-ideologized the trade in arms so that interest in arms shipments to fractious parts of the world was no longer predicated around concerns of ideological shifts in the balance between West and East. There was concern over inflating violence in places such as the Middle East or in the Balkans but transferring arms as an instrument of Cold War polity no longer dominated the concerns of Europe and the United States. The end of the Cold War had also thrown states such as Romania and Bulgaria into the world of competing economies and their stock of Warsaw Pact weaponry was one of the few competitive products available to underwrite the formative years of their participation in capitalism. The civil wars in Lebanon and the Balkans had also schooled and encouraged a new generation of arms brokers and shippers who were available to service clients who could pay in cash or kind. The natural resource wealth of West Africa, combined with the political marginality of the region, allowed enough arms to flow into the area to achieve Kalashnikov enculturation within three countries in a short period of time.

In 2001 it was estimated that there were 77,000 small arms held by insurgent groups in West Africa.[14] Many of these weapons had been captured from government troops but others had been imported into the region through gray and black market channels. As an example of the spillover effect from one civil war to another, the United Nations tracked six flights by an Ilyushin aircraft between June and September 2002, with all flights originating in Belgrade and terminating in Liberia.[15] The cargo on these six flights, amounting to more than 200 tonnes in weight, was comprised of more than 4,600 Kalashnikov-type rifles, 4,500 grenades, 5 million rounds of ammunition, sniper rifles, handguns, rocket-propelled grenade launchers, and landmines.[16] The Ilyushin was based in Ukraine, the documents (not an end-use certificate) were forgeries indicating that Nigeria was the end user and the supplier of the arms was a company based in Belgrade. A complicated dual-track documentation approach was used to disguise the true destination of the arms, with the authorities in Belgrade apparently duped into believing that Nigeria was in fact the final destination of the arms shipments. As is commonplace in these types of transactions, false flight plans and lading documents were used and the actual buyer of the arms remained a mystery.

Liberia had been under UN arms embargo since November 1992 and in 1999 in a highly publicized event 19,000 weapons were publicly destroyed in Monrovia. Despite attempts by the government of Charles Taylor to have the sanctions removed, the embargo remained and this forced Liberia to be creative in its attempts to find weapons. Among the many brokers that assisted Liberia (including the omnipresent Victor Bout) was Leonid Minin, who had already achieved a certain notoriety before he was arrested in Italy in 2000. An Israeli citizen of Ukrainian origin, Minin is representative of an opportunistic and entrepreneurial criminal class that gained prominence after the fall of the Soviet Union. Trading in anything that might prove profitable (including used clothing and oil) Minin, using multiple passports and operating through offshore front companies, became aware of the opportunities provided by a close association with Charles Taylor in the late 1990s.[17] In return for access to Sierra Leonean diamonds and to Liberian hardwoods, Minin found weapons for the Liberian regime and shipped them, often in his private jet aircraft, into Liberia. Much of the weaponry was from his homeland of Ukraine and was from the stockpiles maintained by the Ukrainian military after the devolution of the Soviet Union. Operating on a personal level with Taylor and his son, Minin was typical of the sanctions busters that were able to achieve profits through resource stripping in conflict zones while fueling the same conflict through trafficking in arms.

One of the reasons that Kalashnikov cultures endure is that few of the principals who are responsible for promoting or prolonging the insecurity and conflicts that attend the culture are ever called to account for their actions. Indeed, the very insecurity that is the hallmark of Kalashnikov cultures militates against the likelihood of rule of law being used against them. The capture and trial of Leonid Minin in Italy was an exception rather than the rule and the fact that nobody was imprisoned or even tried over the Wazan affair is indicative of how difficult it is to apply inexact laws against individuals and corporate entities. When Kalashnikov cultures reach the point of supplanting laws and legal authority with their own versions of ad hoc justice then the concept of accountability becomes moot. But if the laws of states might be a victim of Kalashnikov enculturation it is still possible to employ international law to punish the lords of chaos and others who have taken advantage of chronic insecurity.

The fact that Charles Taylor was brought to trial on matters relating to the civil war in Sierra Leone, together with trials over the Rwandan genocide and the Balkans conflict, could give certain promoters of Kalashnikov enculturation pause for thought. The notion that the conditions of conflict, insecurity, lack of authority, and absence of written record all act as camouflage to hide the malpractices within Kalashnikov cultures is for the most part supported by the evidence. The traffickers into and out of the cultures use confusion and credible deniability to protect themselves and even when evidence is collected, such as in the United Nations reports on West Africa, the Great Lakes region, and Somalia, it is either incomplete or the lines of accountability are so complex as to be open to doubt. But even if there are not always survivors from massacres, there are usually enough witnesses to provide the basis for a case to be brought before an independent court.

One of the crimes laid to Charles Taylor was that of encouraging and using child soldiers in the conflict in Liberia and Sierra Leone. Indeed, the enduring image of the West African conflicts is of children as both perpetrators and victims of violence. The youthfulness of combatants is a hallmark of all Kalashnikov cultures but there is also a subset of "warriors" in the age range of low teens to preteen whose existence within a Kalashnikov culture is an indicator of a particular metamorphosis. When Charles Taylor established the notorious Small Boys Units (SBU), he was indicating that childhood was not a sacrosanct or even identifiable aspect of his war society. After the ubiquitous machete, the weapon most often found in the hands of the SBU soldiers was the AK rifle and the combination proved to be highly volatile and extremely lethal.[18]

The phenomenon of child soldiery is not limited to modern warfare but what was once an isolated and circumstantial activity has now become commonplace. In Southeast Asia, Africa, and Latin America the recruitment (mostly forced) of children into irregular forces (and sometimes into regular forces) became a facet of conflicts in those regions during the 1990s and as a result garnered an interest in Kalashnikov cultures that was tantamount to that achieved during the antilandmines campaign. The imagery of armed children, often as young as eight or nine, that emerged from the Liberian and Sierra Leonean civil conflicts touched upon a widely held taboo against the use of children as soldiers and these images, together with those of the amputation atrocities that were often committed by children, raised consciousness to a level that encouraged external intervention within the region, firstly by regional actors and then by the United Kingdom and France.

Child soldiers might not be the "last taboo" but, particularly in Western societies, they do generate a level of concern that other elements of Kalashnikov enculturation (rapine, resource stripping, civilian casualties, etcetera) do not achieve. This concern in part emanates from an empathy with the children but it also taps into concern over adults maintaining primacy over their offspring. In West African societies, deference to parents and elders is one of the social ties that bind together tribes, clans, and family groups and, although children are encouraged to become economically useful at an early age, they are still, often in a brutal and violent manner, made to acknowledge the primacy of their parents.[19] When child soldiers were encouraged to mutilate and kill adults, this primacy was overridden by the law of the gun. Indeed, one of the longest-lasting effects of the West African conflicts is likely to be from the break in deference to authority that occurred amongst the youth of that region. The pseudo-empowerment that they were accorded by their militia leadership (the children were always aware of their vulnerability to the capriciousness of their own leaders) was most often directed against adults and this severed the ties of authority that had existed previously. With children spending their formative years in militias, the "education" that they received inevitably resulted in a distorted perception of what constituted authority and in how to conduct oneself in a society bounded not by fear but by laws.[20]

The concept of "gun law" is inherent within Kalashnikov cultures. It is the assumption that authority and enforcement capability are embodied within the weapon and that legitimacy (and survival) is not achieved through normative and positive actions but rather through possessing the means and ability to take life. Child soldiers are inculcated with the values of threat, intimidation, and death as demonstrations of power, rather than power through education, positive acclaim, and useful labor. To reeducate child soldiers into acceptance of the subtleties of politics, law, and socially acceptable behavior is, under the best of circumstances, a daunting task. Where Kalashnikov enculturation has dominated within a society for decades (as in the case of the Lord's Resistance Army and Northern Uganda), it might not be possible to retrieve a generation that grew from preteen years to maturity with Kalashnikov law being their only frame of reference on matters of authority. Even when societies attempt, as in Yemen and NWFP, to meld gun law into clan and tribal traditions in order to exert control over a weaponized community, the rules are always predicated upon an acceptance of a level of violence that accommodates the use of the gun to settle disputes. A community that contains large numbers of former child soldiers is one in which the blunt trauma effect of years of gun law is inevitably going to demonstrate itself in terms of armed crime, domestic violence, and continual challenges to the authority of the state.

West Africa would not have been the first choice if, at the end of the Cold War, most observers of wars and conflicts had been asked to nominate those places that would be overwhelmed by Kalashnikov enculturation. There had been few armed liberation movements in the area, most countries had enjoyed a degree of economic and political stability, and the level of social violence was not excessive. It is true that gerontocracy was the abiding political framework and that concomitantly corruption and stagnation were prevalent but there was no pedigree of violence and reservoirs of arms that could account for the speedy metamorphosis from relative quiescence to Kalashnikov culture. Part of this acceleration can be laid at the doors of external actors. Libya underwrote, in an apparently casual way, the rise of the Taylor phenomenon in Liberia and then arms traffickers and asset strippers fueled the expansion of the conflict in order to enrich themselves as entrepreneurs of chaos. But much of the devolution toward Kalashnikov enculturation was homegrown and was a combination of greed, anger, and despair. The greed was shared amongst the leadership within the region who saw personal enrichment as the primary rationale behind obtaining and maintaining political power through force of arms. The anger had been present through the colonial era and was exacerbated when the underclass became aware that in the modern era their opportunities to participate in governance and the economy were not going to be realized. It is true that Liberia did not have a colonial past but domination by the Americo-Liberian elite served the same depressive function as had colonial administrations. The fuel of the despair was the lack of government support for basic services such as health care and education and this was then reinvigorated by the complete collapse of traditional values, hierarchies of control and access to food and water that took place during the time of war.

It is tempting to state that if Kalashnikov enculturation could take place so quickly in West Africa then it could happen anywhere. There are still sponsors in the international system who might provide the same type of low-order, seed-corn support that was provided to the West African insurgents. The number of weapons that were required to turn a nonweaponized region into a Kalashnikov culture was not great and could certainly be accommodated by the existing peripatetic global inventory of arms. The prize of arms, mostly in the form of diamonds and hardwoods, can be replicated in terms of value and ease of liquidation in many parts of Africa and elsewhere. If children are factored into the manpower equation, then there is no shortage, particularly in the less developed countries, of soldiers to provide the fodder for armies and militias. But West Africa is also the beneficiary of post-Cold War marginality, in which triage takes place based upon discernible interest versus minimal investment. For most of the developed world West Africa (with the exception of oil-rich Nigeria) was a somewhat quiescent backwater of a globalized economy. With the end of ideology as a determinant of interest, West Africa could not parlay its geopolitical position (during the Cold War the region was of interest in respect to maritime operations in the north and south Atlantic) to retain the attention of the major powers. As a result of these exigencies, West Africa slipped into conflict and into Kalashnikov enculturation partly due to benign neglect but mostly through disinterest. (Some interest was belatedly created when intelligence indicated that al Qaeda was involving itself in the diamond trade.)[21] When Britain intervened in Sierra Leone in 2000 and

France into Cote d'Ivoire in 2002 it was partly triggered by ex-colonial angst and partly by the imagery that global media outlets proliferated throughout the twenty-four-hour news cycle. And while these interventions might have had an impact upon the Kalashnikov eras within those two states, the weaponry itself migrated to create issues elsewhere.

A Tradition of Arms: Yemen

In many ways the North West Frontier Province of Pakistan and the political entity that is called Yemen are quite alike. Both are partly tribal in structure and Islamic in faith. Each was affected by the interruption of colonialism. And neither has been quite comfortable with the concept of the supremacy of the state. But there are also certain cogent differences and one of the most important of these concerns the role of the personal firearm in the conduct of daily life. In Pakistan the gun performs the dual role of tool and symbol. In Yemen the firearm assumes both these roles but it is also the dominant element in an elaborate and complex honor code that both encourages systemic violence and attempts to mitigate it. There is, in a very real sense, a cult of the gun in Yemen and in a perverse manner this has resulted in perhaps one of the most refined of all Kalashnikov cultures.

Yemen is both physically isolated and yet strategically significant. Its position at the southern end of the Arabian peninsula has kept it distant from both the Arab-Israeli conflict and from direct involvement in the crises of the Gulf (although it did align itself with Iraq in 1990). But its adjacency to Saudi Arabia, with implications related to both oil and to the Islamic holy places, and its role as a Red Sea littoral state have served to elevate its regional importance. However, within the context of the Middle East as a whole, Yemen has tended to be marginalized in much the same manner as was Afghanistan before the Soviet invasion or Albania under Enver Hoxha. Often denigrated in reportage as a "medieval" curiosity, Yemen's reputation in the wider world (including within the Middle East itself) has for the most part been attached to observations concerning systemic violence, tribal structure and, in the case of the former People's Democratic Republic of Yemen (PDRY), an idiosyncratic blending of Islam and Marxism. Out-of-region concerns have tended to center upon Yemen's role in the support and training of radical groups whose members have played roles in Afghanistan, Chechnya, Bosnia, and other areas of conflict.

As with most reputations, that of Yemen is somewhat deserved but it is also derived from simplistic extrapolations relating to an extremely complex society. For those who are dedicated to the concept of the primacy of the state, the role of the tribes in northern Yemen is confusing and counter to the notion of effective governance. Certainly the national government of President Saleh (in office since 1978) considered the northern tribes to be in competition with the state and has fought an almost continuous battle, literally and figuratively, with them for nearly a quarter century. But the omnipotent role of the state is not now as firmly fixed within the political firmament as it was for most of the twentieth century. The devolution of power down to levels of more personal affinity does not necessarily equate with incipient anarchy in the international system but may relate to a structure that is less distant and more relevant to the lives of individuals. This is the position of the tribal adherents within Yemen and it cannot be dismissed as simply either reactionary or rejectionist. However, the coda that binds the tribal societies is, in comparison to expectations relating to the conduct of states, contrary to many of the universalist tenets that have evolved over the past century. Tribal law and codes of conduct do not fit comfortably within the context of human and civil rights. The single statistic of the 400 "honor killings" of women that took place in Yemen during 1997 is, to many who espouse the belief that the sanctity of life is universal, an affront. Similarly, the fifty public executions that took place during the period 1998–1999 is also, to many, an indicator of social primitivism.

Violent death is an inarguable facet of Yemeni society. Grenades are used to settle disputes between buyer and seller in the marketplace, explosions are punctuative reminders of rivalries between political parties and assassinations of religious leaders on the steps of the mosque are characterized as professions of faith. During the twentieth century Yemen was, to a greater or lesser extent, involved in a war every seven years. The two civil wars of 1962–1970 and 1994 were brutal by any standard, with the former particularly notable for the use of poison gas in combat. Given this litany of prolonged conflict and violence, it is arguable that prior to the introduction of modern automatic weapons Yemen was simply a "Kalashnikov-culture-in-waiting" and that the introduction of those arms made little difference to the basic dynamic of the society. While this may be true it is also fundamentally irrelevant. The "Kalashnikov" in Kalashnikov culture relates less to the weapon than it does to the manifestations of violent interaction that are exemplified by weaponized societies. What is important in relation to Yemen was that a set of rules designed to control the nature and extent of such violent interaction was already in place within much of Yemen by the time that modern light weapons proliferated within the society. The case of Yemen, therefore, is an important test as to whether societies can be weaponized to a very high level (there are an estimated three firearms for every person within Yemen) and still retain an element of human security through adaptation to such a level of saturation.

Yemen was an armed society before it became weaponized with firearms. The curved dagger or janbiyyah remains an important symbol of personal power in Yemen and the level of decoration indicates wealth and prominence. But it is the rifle that is the true discriminator. Since the nineteenth century the type, quality, and number of rifles that a man owned has been the measure of his stature within the tribe and in the society as a whole.[1] The gun is concomitant with personal power and, in numbers, with the power of the tribe. It betokens resolve, induces respect, and is the instrument of its own law. It is a portable emblem of responsibility and security having devolved down to the level of the individual. The code that dictates how the rifle may be used and the penalties for abuse are the focus of *sharaf*, which defines honor and, in the concept of *ayb*, dishonor or disgrace.[2] Penalties are also paid in rifles, with the weapons sometimes being held "hostage" until conflicts are resolved.[3] Blood debts, or compensation to victims, are also either paid with rifles or the guns are used as a form of currency with which to judge adequate payment (even sometimes down to the "half of a rifle").

Anecdotal material can be notoriously unreliable as purported evidence of a general phenomenon. But in certain cases an incident can encapsulate the essence of a broader set of problems. Such an incident took place in the port city of Hodeidah, in northern Yemen, on an evening in late April 1999.[4] A businessman from the Redaa tribal grouping drove his automobile into a place where picnics were held. He parked close to a vehicle in which a man and several women were seated. The man in the second vehicle remonstrated with the businessman for parking too close to a car occupied by women. The businessman traded words with the owner of the parked car, who then drove away, only to return some time later, accompanied by two more cars "loaded with armed tribal compatriots."

The "tribal compatriots" were from the Hashed tribal group and they proceeded to assault the Redaa businessman, breaking an arm and some ribs. As the Hashed men walked away the beaten man produced a gun and fatally shot one of his assailants. The authorities then arrested the businessman and placed him in the Central Hodeidah Prison. The facility was then surrounded by 250 armed Hashedis, demanding that the prisoner be executed. Men from the Redaa tribe then arrived at the prison and confronted the Hashedis, demanding that their compatriot have a fair and just trial. They also proposed that the matter be settled with a "tribal solution" but the Hashedis refused, saying that nothing short of the death of the Redaa businessman would satisfy them. The Redaa tribesmen, who had recently been engaged in a major clash with government troops, threatened to fight both the Hashedi and the state authorities if their man was hanged. Prospective judges that might be called upon to try the case were quoted as saying that whatever the verdict might be, they feared for their lives. Since there had been thirty-two separate shooting incidents between tribes in the previous ten days, their concerns were probably valid.

This incident is indicative of a form of escalation that is prevalent in all Kalashnikov cultures. Seemingly trivial disputes become deadly confrontations within a very short period of time. This form of accelerated conflict also occurs within gun cultures but the movement up to the level of mass confrontation and to the implicit challenge of the lawful authority is quite normative in Kalashnikov cultures and rare (urban riots are probably the most obvious exception) in gun cultures. The element of "honor" in this incident is also redolent of an omnipresent aspect of the psychological underpinning of Kalashnikov cultures. What was a matter of personal honor (parking a car too close to one in which women were passengers) became a matter of tribal honor very rapidly. Under the code of honor prevailing within the tribes of northern Yemen such a confrontation might be an expected and accepted occurrence. Only the shooting of the Hashedi assailant as he walked away fell outside of the code of honor. In Kalashnikov cultures, very often it is the manner of killing rather than the death itself that predicates the level and extent of future conflict.

A highly developed sense of honor is often to be found in societies in which most people have little else to claim as their own. It is also a binding agent within a community in which group cohesion is the best protection against being victimized. In Yemen, the obverse of sharaf is ayb, meaning disgrace.[5] Such disgrace is a moderating influence in conflict between tribes and also codifies what actions may be taken against nontribal outsiders (killing an outsider who is considered lower in status is considered to be a dishonorable act). The rules governing the definition of honorable and dishonorable behavior are complex, extensive, and in many ways a suitable substitute for state-based law and regulation. But in Yemen, as with many Kalashnikov cultures, when the code of honor is breached or fails then such failure is often catastrophic, with violence being done to individuals and to the system alike. In a society where killing in the defense of honor is an acceptable practice and where guns are an extension of the honor code, it is natural that the one should be used as an instrument in support of the other. The problem with such a system in a society that is weaponized with modern arms is that indiscriminate killing and collateral damage are an inevitable by-product of any failed attempt at arbitration and such killing of innocents are themselves the fuel of blood feuds and vendettas that can last for decades.[6]

States such as Yemen provide a distinct problem on the matter of statistical data. The central authority in the capital Sana'a does collect data on crime (and such data indicates an annual increase in the national crime rate of more than 10 percent per annum between 1994 and 1998) but this material does not comprehensively cover activities between tribes.[7] Therefore much of the evidence on tribal conflicts is the result of reportage rather than from primary source statistical databases. Nevertheless, it is possible to discern patterns from the available data.[8] In the two years 1998–1999 one source cataloged 198 violent events in a noncomprehensive survey. Of these, 25 percent were identifiable as tribal in nature, 30 percent were related to religious or ideological disputes, and the rest were either purely criminal in nature, were accidents, or were for unknown reasons. There were fifty-two incidents in which firearms were the principal instrument used during the event and there were seventy-four incidents involving explosives in the form of bombs. There were also six incidents involving rocket-propelled grenade launchers and five involving hand grenades. One assassination was by knife. Twenty-five percent of all the explosions related to tribes sabotaging oil pipelines. In one case a bomb was delivered under the saddle of a donkey.[9]

None of these incidents was trivial and all contributed to human insecurity within Yemen. But certain of the incidents were more symptomatic of a Kalashnikov culture than were others. In the realm of tribe versus the state, the constant interruption of oil through sabotage of the pipeline network is indicative of a deliberate campaign to weaken the authority of the central government in Sana'a. By the late 1990s oil revenue was one of the few hard currency earners available to the government of Yemen and its relationship with the oil companies was one of the few external linkages left after Yemen had become alienated within the region by siding with Saddam Hussein in 1990. Similarly, the assassination and attempted assassination of military and political leaders (during the period 1998–1999, seven such leaders, including the prime minister and president, came under armed attack) is an indicator of both the capacity and will to injure the body of the state.

The series of bombings that took place in southern Yemen during this time were not the result of intertribal or tribal/state conflicts. They were instead the overt manifestations of competition amongst religious groups and between political organizations such as the Yemen Socialist Party (YSP) and the General People's Congress Party. In respect of the former, mosques were a favored target, with Friday prayers being the preferred time of detonation. In the latter cases, the political parties not only campaigned against each other but also, particularly in the case of the YSP, against government targets. The government itself saw the hand of "foreign" governments or radical groups behind many of the actions, with nationals from Sudan, Iraq, Eritrea, Egypt, Spain, Algeria, Tunisia, and Ethiopia being individually identified.

Many of the armed confrontations between the tribes and the government and amongst the tribes themselves were in the form of protracted battles, often lasting for days and with the expenditure of large amounts of ammunition from a wide variety of weaponry. Such weaponry had been acquired over the previous thirty years and from a number of sources. In the civil war that began in 1962 both sides, the Republicans and Royalists, were armed by external sponsors. The Republicans were supplied with weapons by Egypt, China, the Soviet Union, Bulgaria, and Czechoslovakia. The Royalists depended primarily upon Saudi Arabia for their munitions. The Royalists also offered a bounty on arms to the tribes, who obtained them by ambushing Republican units and occasionally by attacking Saudi arms convoys and ransoming the weapons to the Royalists.[10] In this manner the tribes began to acquire battle rifles, submachine guns, machine guns, and mortars and to establish inventories that would allow them to challenge centralized government. Indeed, the British found themselves under attack in Aden during this period and there was no shortage of rifles, grenades, and explosives that the principal guerilla group, FLOSY, employed against the colonial authorities. The end result of the eight years of fighting between 1962 and 1970 was a weakening of the sovereignty of the national governments (at the end of the war Yemen was divided into two states), a strengthening of the armed tribes, and a quantum increase in the commerce of arms.

Yemen does not produce its own arms, therefore all weapons that are sold within the country are either residual arms from major internal conflicts or are the result of black market trading. The marketing of many of these arms is directed through the souks at such towns as Jihana, south of Sana'a, and at Al-Talh, which is a central collection point for arms up to the size of heavy machine guns, mortars, and light artillery.[11] By the early 1980s Al-Talh was the retail outlet of a sophisticated arms smuggling activity that included arms hidden in trucks coming from as far as Syria and Lebanon, from Djibouti across the Red Sea by dhow, and from across the ill-defined border with Saudi Arabia.[12] Apart from those that were remaindered from the civil war of 1962–1970, the arms were of Chinese, Russian, U.S., British, Polish, North Korean, Belgian, Italian, and Czech origin, with the AK (given the appellation "Ali" by the Yemenis) and its variants being the preferred personal weapon.[13] Prices for new weapons were high during the 1980s, indicating that demand outpaced supply. An AK, depending on variant, sold for between $800 and $2,400, while the same weapon was available for $200 in 1999, indicating that the market was somewhat saturated by that time (most authorities quote a number of 50–65 million firearms in private hands within Yemen post-1994.)[14]

The trade in arms in Yemen is not as comprehensive as that in the North West Frontier of Pakistan (for example, it lacks the manufacturing element to be found in Darra) but, nevertheless, it is an integral element in a significant "black" economy in Yemen. The tribes sell used firearms through nontribal intermediaries to raise capital and arms are themselves considered to be convertible wealth.[15] As with all commerce, the black market in arms is linked to the overall health of the economy. If, as in the late 1990s, the economy was in recession, then fewer arms are bought by the tribes and dealers are forced into such promotional exercises as renting arms for use at wedding ceremonies. The arms sellers in Jihana also diversified in the 1990s, selling foodstuffs and other household requisites that had been smuggled from many of the same sources as the guns.[16] But as with Pakistan, Colombia, and many other Kalashnikov cultures, it was the economic relationship between drugs and arms that has proven to be the most enduring in Yemen.

Authorities within Yemen estimate that 80 percent of the male population over 18, 50 percent of the female population in that age group, and between 15 and 20 percent of children under the age of 12 habitually use the drug known as qat.[17] This habit, comprised of chewing the leaves of a low shrub-like plant in the company of others, is a centuries-old activity that is defended in Yemen (and in the Horn of Africa where it is also pervasive) and is tantamount to drinking beer in a social setting. But while the physiological effects may be mild (alertness and volubility, followed by lassitude and headaches), the social and economic effects of the qat habit upon Yemen are extensive.

The leaves that are the basis of the qat experience are best used when fresh, preferably within hours of being picked. The morning harvest must therefore be consumed during the early afternoon hours. Most commercial business and even government activity is terminated at this time, with a concomitant effect upon productivity and the functioning of the state. Such was not always the case. Until the latter quarter of the twentieth century the chewing of qat was restricted to the wealthy and used only on special occasions. But the popularization of qat, coinciding with lessening of control over the tribal areas after the 1962 civil war, has served to turn an elite activity into a dominant aspect of Yemeni life and to make the leaf into the lynchpin of both tribal and national economies.

Most production of qat is undertaken by small farmers operating within the tribal areas, with middlemen in the towns operating markets catering specifically to qat users. The average qat farmer can earn $30 to $40,000 per annum, more than eight times as much as can be earned from the cultivation of coffee, the only competitive cash crop.[18] The agricultural impact of this differential has been to create a monoculture in the north of Yemen, with the subsequent effect of depletion of the aquifers and diminution of the acreage dedicated to subsistence farming.[19] The cultivation and commerce in qat had, by the 1990s, become the single largest economic activity within Yemen, accounting for 30 percent of the gross domestic product (GDP) and absorbing more than 20 percent of the average income of each user household.[20] And while qat may, arguably, not be classifiable as a narcotic drug (although the United States and several other countries do classify it so), the imperative to obtain access to the leaf bears many of the hallmarks of addictive behavior. Certainly, its cultivation has become economically addictive, with attempts by the government in Sana'a to restrict consumption or sale having been defeated by expressions of popular will and by the political power exercised by those that benefit from the commerce.[21]

The consumption of qat does not in itself exacerbate the climate of violence in Yemen, although a combination of drug-induced boastfulness and automatic weapons is potentially lethal. However, the most direct link between the qat economy and violence in Yemeni life is to be found in the need by the farmers to protect their harvest and the need of the users to find the 20 percent of their income that is expended on qat.[22] In respect of the latter it is worth quoting one Yemeni youth on the subject: "We do nothing. We get money from selling qat . . . But you know we need ($3.50 to $7.00) per day to pay for qat. So we carry out raids, for example stopping passing cars and asking people for money."[23] The unconscious irony of being both producer and consumer may not have been appreciated but the addict's need to feed the habit would be recognizable on the streets of Karachi or Bogota or New York.

Qat farmers have two forms of protection. They themselves provide localized security, often by using unemployed youths from the vicinity of the farm. A more general form of support is provided by the tribe, who consider the qat harvest to be part of the communal wealth.[24] Although it is unusual for qat plants to be stolen during cultivation, the journey to the marketplace is fraught with problems, ranging from "taxes" imposed by local shaykhs along the route to the hijacking of cargoes. Often such occurrences are accompanied by gunfire, with the consequent initiation of a blood feud. On the occasions that government forces attempt to intercept such convoys (either to "tax" them or as part of one of the desultory control campaigns) there are also exchanges of fire, which again can escalate to the level of major confrontation between the military and the tribes.

The association between drug cultures and Kalashnikov cultures will be addressed elsewhere but the level of cohabitation between the two in Yemen is useful because of the clarity of the linkage. The guns help the producers maintain the sanctity of their crop and the gun also helps the consumer raise funds for the acquisition of the product. In turn, certain of the profits accrued from the commerce in qat are used to acquire arms to protect the harvest. The trade in the drug and in the arms, in combination, is symptomatic of a subeconomy that is in itself a direct challenge to any centralized authority.

At this juncture it might be useful to deconstruct the elements that established Yemen as a prototypical Kalashnikov culture. In the realm of the sociopsychological, the linkage of arms with personal honor (often spoken of in terms of manhood in the Yemeni media) and with the honor of the tribe provides the almost unassailable emotional underpinning of Yemen as a weaponized society. The comments by Yemenis on the potency of the symbolism of bearing arms (". . . many Yemenis consider arms a part of their costumes and the symbol of manhood." ". . . men, especially from tribal backgrounds, know their weapons as their honor.") are indicative of an emotional attachment that transcends the traditional utilitarian rationale of possession of arms solely for self-defense.[25]

When stripped of the rhetoric, however, the function of the personal weapon is as much about defining identity as it is about characterizing the societal phenomenon of honor. It is an advertisement of knowledge (the type and design of the weapon carried indicates an understanding of arms technology), wealth (the cost of an average rifle and the annual per capita income are almost exactly the same), and individuality (much of the wealth of the tribes is in the form of corporate possessions but the rifle belongs to its owner).[26] It is also, en masse and in the context of relations between tribe and state, a manifestation of self-determination and sovereignty. Consequently, when the government in Sana'a issues its annual edict calling for the surrender of personal weapons, this is interpreted by the tribes as an attack upon their autonomy rather than as an attempt to achieve a civil society.[27]

Tribal autonomy and the right of self-defense are interdependent in the minds of those that defend their need for arms. This perceived need is comprehensively addressed by Shaykh Abdullah Mohammed Taoiman, chief of the largest tribe in the Mareb governorate, the Dahm, in reference to a proposed national law to disarm individuals: "Weapons are a tribal tradition that tribesmen keep to defend themselves in case of aggression. Tribes can not comply with this law because they need to protect themselves against other tribes. I . . . stress that tribes have become more aware of consequences of conflicts. What they need is more security and stability. When they feel that they can travel to any place in Yemen with no fears about their safety, they will be the first people to disarm themselves. They are even ready to put aside the janbiyyah which is part of the Yemeni tradition. Otherwise, I strongly object to disarming tribesmen under the current conditions. Some tribesmen work in the army. If a military man sees an unarmed enemy from another tribe, that military man may not hesitate in using his army weapon against that enemy."[28]

Within this statement is embedded the spectrum of arguments for the retention of personal arms in Yemen and for the rejection of any attempt to disarm the tribes by the government in Sana'a. The shaykh argues for the primacy of tradition over national law but then, by implication, expects Sana'a to provide the "security and stability" that makes the carrying of arms necessary. However, the major agency that might ensure such security, the national army, is suspect because it is perceived as a vehicle of intertribal conflict. These rationales would appear to create an impasse between the national authorities and the tribes on the issue of arms and indeed there has been very little movement on the matter over the past forty years. At an interpersonal and intertribal level this has led to a climate of chronic insecurity, albeit managed to a certain extent by the code of honor. But at an intertribal-intergovernmental level the competition between armed tribes and the modernizing national government of President Saleh in Sana'a has created not only conflict between the two political entities, tribe and state, but has exacerbated difficulties between the two states of Yemen and Saudi Arabia and, through the tribal practice of kidnapping non-Yemeni nationals, has jeopardized relations between Yemen and the wider world.

Most of the border between Yemen and Saudi Arabia has been in dispute since before the two entities became nation states. In areas in the north and east where rainfall may occur only once in two years and where one well serves 50,000 people, competition between tribes for any land with water or cultivatable possibilities is intense. When Yemen and Saudi Arabia became states this competition took on the additional dimension of a border dispute. Even when both state entities were at odds with their own tribes, they still supported the tribes in their cross-border raiding and land expropriations. In addition, the Saudi government also provided cash payments to tribes within Yemen to pacify shaykhs who might otherwise create problems along the borderline. But the immutable realities of living in such a hostile physical environment ensured that major tribal clashes over territory and land would dominate relations between states and tribes.

In June 2000 the states of Yemen and Saudi Arabia signed an agreement that delineated the territory of each country in disputed areas. This agreement, termed the Jeddah treaty, was designed to mitigate a situation that, during the previous forty years, had led to a series of deadly incidents between the two countries.[29] However, tribes in the disputed area, most notably the Wa'elah in Yemen, rejected the treaty on the basis that they possessed a 240-year-old document that gave them and the Yaam tribe on the Saudi side of the border sovereignty over areas now claimed by the states of Yemen and Saudi Arabia.[30] To support their position the

Wa'elah fortified the area with twenty-two strongpoints, artillery, and thousands of armed tribesmen. They then came into confrontation with Yemeni forces that were attempting to enforce the treaty. Parenthetically, Yemeni and Saudi border guards also clashed and the Wa'elah fought artillery duels with rival tribes who occupied the land now ceded to the Saudis. In this way intertribal conflict and interstate conflict merged to create an environment of blurred political loyalties and multiple layers of confrontation. The tribes, as substate actors, had, in the confused environment of a state-level contest over sovereignty and territory, the power to abrogate decisions made in the capital cities of two states. It is this capability to inject "Kalashnikov diplomacy" into the arena of formal statecraft that elevates Kalashnikov culture from the level of a localized phenomenon to that of a distinctive player in international relations.

The geographical and political isolation of many Kalashnikov cultures allows the wider world to either ignore them or to treat them with prurient interest. Even confrontations that escalate to the level of civil war or to crises between state entities can be ignored by those governments and peoples who are remote, in culture and by distance, from the zone of conflict. Empathy and interest require subjective involvement in the affairs of distant lands and such subjectivity often requires a recognizable human face to help create and sustain such interest. This is the rationale behind the strategy of kidnapping foreigners as an element of Kalashnikov diplomacy. The drama of the act of kidnapping, amplified by a ubiquitous media, gives the perpetrators of such an act the ability to raise their parochial demands to the level of global interest and concern. In this way their opponent, often a susceptible state government, can be coerced, under threat of adverse world reaction, to give into demands that might otherwise be rejected. This is why, during the last two decades of the twentieth century, the kidnapping of foreign nationals by dissident substate actors became a pro forma tool of resistance and propaganda.

Kidnapping is most often undertaken for financial gain. It is a form of coercion, using the physical bodies of abducted individuals as the point of leverage and to be successful certain conditions must prevail. The opportunity to physically seize the person or people must prevail, the hostages must be held in a secure place while negotiations take place, and the threat to do them harm must be credible. In addition, if financial gain is the objective, then the demands must relate to the capacity of the families, friends, or employers to pay the ransom. In most advanced industrial societies the response of law enforcement to this type of crime ensures that it is a high-risk activity. In urbanized societies it is also difficult to keep an individual or individuals under clandestine circumstances for long periods of time. But where the mandate of law enforcement is restricted by the level of the threat posed by the criminal community or by armed competitors such as militias or tribes, kidnapping is a low-risk and potentially high-reward activity.

In 1999 more than 2,700 people were kidnapped in Colombia, yielding $625 million to the insurgent groups and criminal gangs that held them.[31] These statistics indicate that the fiat of national and local law enforcement did not extend to the physical protection of much of the citizenry of Colombia. The amount of money demanded and raised also indicates that the primary rationale for such kidnappings was financial gain, with political embarrassment and the creation of a climate of insecurity the ancillary objectives. As often occurs in kidnap-prone areas of the world, political motivation and the possibility of personal enrichment become blurred as the leaders of kidnapping groups rationalize the latter in respect of the former. Evidence from experiences in the Philippines, South Asia, and the Caucasus indicates that political demands can be moderated by a sufficient monetary inducement.[32] However, if the kidnap victims are nonnationals then there is the added international dimension that both increases pressures for a speedy resolution of the situation but also complicates negotiations. When, as in the case of nearly all of the kidnapping of foreigners in Yemen, the demands are almost entirely of a political nature, the domestic political ramifications of acceding to the kidnappers and the foreign policy demands for a speedy resolution of the crisis are difficult to resolve.

Hostage taking is an established element within the coda of intertribal law in Yemen. At its most formalized, hostages are offered by a tribe or clan until a bone of contention with another tribe is resolved. In one such case, eight members from Haraz were held by the Joham tribe because a girl from the latter had eloped with an individual from the former. The hostages were to be held until the girl was returned to her tribe and a "ransom" (100 rifles and two automobiles) was paid.[33] To hold such hostages, the tribes established private prisons within their domains, a practice that proliferated when various institutions (including the main university in Sana'a) took it upon themselves to incarcerate employees, students, and others whom they deemed troublesome or threatening.[34] This concept of a parallel prison system is indicative of a high level of confidence by hostage takers that their activities would not be interrupted by organs of the state and indeed only in one instance involving foreigners (or when the tribes took government personnel hostage) did the authorities react forcefully.

In the context of Yemen, a distinction must be made between hostage taking and kidnapping. In intertribal conflicts, certain shaykhs and other personages were taken and held against their will. But for the most part hostage taking was as much about confidence building during dispute negotiation as it was about formal kidnapping. In the case of the taking of foreigners, however, the practice, while in itself highly stylized, was closer to normative kidnapping. Tribal law places severe restrictions on interrupting the passage of travelers through tribal territory but few precise penalties are attached to such behavior. In contrast, national law prescribes heavy penalties, including the possibility of the death sentence, upon kidnappers. Therefore, when the tribes kidnapped foreigners they were directly challenging the authority of the government in Sana'a as well as calling attention to their grievances.

Between 1996 and mid-2000 there were a total of forty incidents of foreigners being kidnapped in Yemen.[35] A total of 149 individuals were seized, with citizens of Italy (thirty-eight), France (twenty-six), Germany (twenty-two), and the United

Kingdom (twenty) being the largest numbers of kidnapped by national representation. Among those kidnapped were the Polish ambassador, oil workers, teachers, and tourists. In respect of the latter grouping, more than 80 percent of the total numbers of foreigners kidnapped were categorized as tourists. Nearly all of those taken were kidnapped in transit or at tourist destinations (one oil worker was taken from within a company compound). All but one of the kidnappings resulted in the freeing of victims without any physical harm being rendered. More than 90 percent of the perpetrators were tribally associated, with the remainder being from ideologically motivated groups in the south of Yemen.

The rationales behind the kidnappings were varied but most revolved around perceptions of government malfeasance or unresolved issues relating to government treatment of the tribes. On three occasions members of the al-Hada tribe kidnapped foreigners (including the wife of the South Korean consul) to try to pressure the government to execute three rapists. Other kidnappings centered on demands for new roads in tribal areas, concerns over school closures, and for the release of compatriots held in Yemeni state prisons. In some cases demands were made for money (and cars and guns) but most kidnappings appear to have emanated from frustrations in dealing with the government and particularly in relations between the tribes and the judicial and security branches. Such justifications were valid enough for liberal Yemeni media to consider the demands "legitimate" and to characterize the kidnappings as an inevitable consequence of the neglect of the infrastructure, political and concrete, by the Sana'a government.[36]

Most of the kidnap victims were treated well by their captors and some (perhaps subject to the Stockholm syndrome) became sympathetic to the concerns of the kidnappers.[37] One kidnapped German, interviewed in the Yemeni media, commented that she "felt sorry to see young children carrying AK-47 rifles and hand grenades" instead of being in school. In order to foster such attitudes, a language of politesse emerged to define the kidnappings, in which the abductees were termed "guests," the kidnappers were "hosts" and the whole experience was a matter of "forced hospitality." Naturally, however, the number of tourists visiting Yemen began to drop precipitately after the kidnappings increased in the mid-1990s, with only a few "adventure tourists" willing to risk kidnapping or to defy bans, such as that imposed by the European Union, on travel to Yemen.[38]

The government's response to the kidnapping of foreigners was, for the most part, acquiescent. In 1991, when the kidnappings began, the government gave incentives, in the form of cars or money, to achieve "sobrah" or guarantees for future behavior from the tribes. Later, at a minimum the government gave a commitment to listen to grievances if the kidnappers released their hostages. But in one case, in December 1998, the government felt impelled to attempt to mount a rescue and the result was not auspicious. Sixteen tourists (twelve Britons, two Americans, and two Australians) were taken hostage in Abyan province by a group of ideologically motivated kidnappers. If the kidnappers had been tribesmen making traditional demands it is possible that, even with the abnormally large numbers of victims involved, the situation could have been resolved peacefully.

However, the Yemeni government, despite concerns voiced by British authorities, instructed security forces to attack the kidnappers' camp. In the ensuing firefight four hostages were killed and most of the kidnappers escaped.[39]

The negative publicity surrounding the outcome of the rescue attempt further encouraged the Yemeni government to avoid confrontation with kidnappers and to give in to their demands. But when government officials were taken, and especially when military or police personnel were kidnapped, the Yemeni government reacted violently. Units of the armed forces made use of artillery and tanks against villages suspected of harboring the kidnappers, houses were destroyed with explosives, and in at least one case President Saleh was forced to intervene personally in order to stop the destruction.[40] Relations between the military and the tribes further deteriorated as a result of these actions and in turn this led to revenge attacks by the tribes on military convoys, which encouraged further retaliation by the military.[41] The level of tension under such circumstances was high enough to affect attempts at mediation even at the presidential level. One group of sixty-five tribal representatives who remonstrated with President Saleh in the presidential palace was arrested and thrown into a military prison, as were those who came to inquire about the fate of the group.[42] Such actions tended to reinforce the belief of the tribes that they were in conflict with the state and such actions as the kidnapping of government officers was indeed justifiable.

At the most basic level, the question raised by the weaponized condition of Yemen is whether the presence of 65 million firearms in the hands of the general populace has perpetuated endemic insecurity within the society. Such insecurity can be characterized as having regional, or extraterritorial, manifestations; as being systemic, with ramifications for relations between the state and substate actors; and as affecting the human security of the individual Yemeni. In the case of the latter category, some differentiation must be made between the in-group, comprised mostly of tribes and of politicians and government officials, and out-groups, comprising those who have no tribal affiliation or who are categorized as being of the professional or middle class. In many ways this latter group is the most vulnerable to activities such as kidnapping or extortion, since the tribes are self-protecting and the poor have nothing to give. It is also this group of professionals or tradesmen that, of course, provide the managerial infrastructure of the country.

Deterrence prevails in Yemen until it fails. This is not quite as paradoxical as it might appear. Tribal law and intertribal conflict management do help to mitigate some of the tensions between tribes and to reduce the potential level of mortality. But the honor code only works if it is honored and oftentimes it is not. As in the case of the incident at the picnic area, confrontations can escalate to the level of deadly force with very little warning and with seemingly little rational forethought. Similarly, the relationship between the tribes and the state is bound by tacit understandings that are breached by both sides on a regular basis. After a bloodletting the actors return to the status quo ante but property has been damaged, lives have been lost (including in many cases those of innocents), and distrust has been exacerbated. It is natural that the forces of the state would become nervous for their physical security in such a climate of tension and to feel that they are under siege in the very society that they are attempting to police. It is a small step from such nervousness to the taking of preemptive action and thence to the exercise of arrogant and aggressive power by the military and police, which in turn creates a climate of grievance between tribe and state. This cycle of conflict, once established, becomes almost impossible to break, given that neither side has sufficient numbers or firepower to overwhelm the other.

Even nondeliberate, nonpolitical violence within Yemen bears the imprimatur of a Kalashnikov culture. The casual display of grenades attached to belts or other articles of clothing results in accidents whereby the grenade is shaken loose from its pin in a jostling crowd and six people are killed and dozens are wounded.[43] Minor traffic accidents become battles between armed men and stray rounds kill women and children. Guests firing into the air during a wedding ceremony are mistaken for assailants by a military unit who fire upon the wedding group and use tanks to break through a wall to close with the celebrants.[44] And a dispute over the price of a watch leads to a grenade and shooting spree in a marketplace that left four dead and a number of injured. In addition, there is the usual litany of children who are killed and injured as they play with arms and explosives that have been left available in a casual manner.

The social impact of the consequences of this violence is demonstrable. Military spending averaged more than 8 percent of the gross domestic product (GDP) over the ten years from 1989 to 1998 (the United States expended less than 4 percent of its GDP on defense over the same period).[45] Life expectancy in Yemen is a combined (male and female) 55 years, one of the shortest in the world. Less than 30 percent of the population are schooled beyond two years of primary education, at least partly because funds are being expended on arms acquisitions and because the disruption caused by the conflicts inhibits teachers from working outside of the major urban areas.[46] Yemen also lacks doctors, engineers, and has one police officer per 100,000 citizens.

Certainly factors other than the violence contribute to these deficiencies but the human insecurity of living in an armed and conflict-prone society does play a major role in the overall dysfunctionalism. Most observers, from the president through the shaykhs to journalists and academics, recognize the link between the level of violence and the overall underdevelopment of Yemen, but each tend to blame the other for maintaining or emphasizing the schisms that encourage the resolution of problems through the use of the bomb and the gun. Even though the codes and conventions that are established within Yemen are perhaps the most highly developed in any of the traditional weaponized cultures, these laws-of-the-gun do not appear to be able to overcome "gun law" in that country.

Kalashnikov Islands: Favelas, Yards, and Raskols

There are a group of Kalashnikov cultures that have evolved in relative isolation from the mainstream. Some of these are quite literally islands and others, such as that typified by the armed gangs of Brazil's favelas, are isolated in a social and economic sense. In the case of Papua New Guinea (PNG) the isolation has resulted in an acceleration of development that has spanned from Stone Age to Space Age within three generations. The isolation of Jamaica is redolent of many states undergoing postcolonial development; problems associated with the search for national identity were compounded by benign neglect from the outside and political opportunism on the inside. When arms were injected into these places the result was a new form of collective anomie that stressed violence and insecurity over a normative evolution toward rule of law and respected governance.

As with the term "small arms" the use of the word "gangs" does not do justice to the new tribalism of these particular Kalashnikov cultures. Gangs are usually identified with outlaw activity, in which groups of alienated and desperate deviants are inevitably overcome by the overwhelming power of the state. But in the case of urban Brazil, Jamaica, and PNG gangs have become the new vehicles of social and economic mobility. They have supplanted either the old tribal system (Papua New Guinea), or a class system (Jamaica, Brazil) that is no longer relevant to the conditions obtaining in those societies. At the most fanciful level they are revolutionaries but without a political agenda. At the most literal level they are armies that directly and systematically threaten the primacy of the state. As such they are not gangs per se but instead are a hybrid somewhere between urban guerrillas and Hobsbawm's bandit rebels.[1] Unlike traditional gangs their strategy is not one of clandestinity. Instead they arm and organize themselves to a level that intimidates the state. Behind this cofferdam of intimidation they conduct the activities of a parallel legal system and parallel economy. And they do so while waging a two-front war.

The gangs are constantly engaged in confrontation with the state. At the level of arms to be found in Rio, Kingston, and Port Moresby, this conflict has often migrated from the level of gang-police interaction to that of gang-military confrontation. On both sides the tactics, operational goals, and strategic objectives mirror those to be found in the conduct of nontraditional warfare anywhere in the world. The instruments of the state attempt to isolate and contain the "insurgents," with the objective being to maintain the violence at an acceptable minimal level. The gangs themselves attempt to hold a perimeter behind which they have a guarantee of security and freedom to conduct their economic activities. Each side may make sallies into the other's territory but their mutual strategies usually result in some form of armed stalemate. This modern equivalent of trench warfare does, of course, include an attritional element. In Jamaica during the two years 2002–2003 the local police forces killed 274 suspects and lost twenty-nine of their own number.[2]

Behind the front lines of the gang-versus-state war there is another conflict that is the civil war between the gangs. In Nicaragua pandilla gangs engage in semiritualized civil warfare that escalates in steps from sticks and stones through to AKs and mortars and costs the organizations between 3 and 5 percent of their manpower each year, a mortality rate that would be unacceptable for an army conducting full-scale conventional war. Demarcation in the favelas of Rio and the yards of Kingston are attempts to minimize such conflicts but when agreements fail, which they do on a regular basis, the resultant urban warfare is often protracted and bloody. In Rio, Kingston, and Port Moresby revenge killing (known as payback in PNG) helps perpetuate a constantly high level of insecurity and turf warfare over the illegal economies of drugs and robbery is unremitting. In order to survive in all three communities the citizenry is forced to choose protectors from amongst the warring factions and this creates an environment in which the terminology of war (front line, no-man's land, free-fire zone) is used to define the local geopolitics. Perhaps nowhere is this better exemplified than in the "garrison" communities of Jamaica.

In some places criminal activity achieves political power and influence. The Sicilian Mafia metamorphosed into a political animal by dint of corruption and intimidation. But the reverse can also be true; what begins as political organization and activity can mutate into criminal enterprise. In both PNG and Jamaica such was the case. In Jamaica the concept of "garrisons" originated in political competition in the postcolonial phase of governance during the 1960s. Only later, in the 1970s and 1980s, did the "garrison" structure become a vehicle for an impressively complex criminal subculture. In effect the political elite of Jamaica laid the foundations for their principal competitors for power on the island. The original intent, however, was to mobilize, through patronage and preference, core elements within the poor areas of Kingston that could be used as reliable bastions of support, or garrisons, by the extant political parties. It was a model that could be recognized in Boston or Glasgow but what was different in the Jamaican context was that in Kingston the political parties did not simply recruit and train their adherents; they also armed them.

In 1962 Jamaica achieved independence from the United Kingdom and from the inception of the new state two political parties, the People's National Party (PNP) and the Jamaica Labour Party (JLP), operated in aggressive competition with each other. This competition, however, was not initially violent. The two parties were led by cousins Alexander Bustamante and Norman Manley and politesse prevailed. But when, in 1972, the second generation of Jamaican political leaders ascended to power the structure and dynamic of political alignment became the order of battle of a new politics. The emphasis of the new order was on armed confrontation rather than on pointed rhetoric and the political base of this change was less to be found in the rolls of constituency supporters but rather in the very concrete structures of the garrisons.

Edward Seaga, later to become a JLP prime minister, is credited with the invention of the "garrison."[3] Faced with rapid urbanization, the JLP government of the early postindependence period committed itself to a slum clearance and re-building campaign in the poorest areas of Kingston. Although using money from the public purse Seaga and the JLP promoted the new concrete block communities as a visible commitment to the poor and of the power of patronage. In reality they were establishing enclaves of rabid commitment, controlled by the party faithful and owing allegiance to either the JLP or PNP leadership. As the parties alternated in control of the Jamaican government they extended these blocks, or garrisons, until they formed a map of political tribalism across Kingston. With names such as Tivoli Gardens and Arnett Gardens they initially promised a protective tran-sition for rural Jamaicans. Unfortunately, these garrison communities proved to be urban traps whose chronic insecurity militated against economic growth and social stability.

It is not clear as to when the guns started arriving. One observer identifies the early 1970s as the watershed between old style political rivalry and the rise of political gangsterism.[4] It is certain that by the time of the 1980 election Jamaica's party politics had deteriorated into a series of skirmishes and pitched battles. Communal violence was also a manifestation during this period. PNP and JLP mobs burned the apartments of their rivals (20,000 were made homeless) and political sectarianism was behind many of the 800 deaths that occurred during the election period.[5] The majority of the deaths were from gunfire and the origin of the weapons was the subject of much speculation and accusation. Some placed a Cold War connotation on the buildup of weapons, with implications that the left-of-center PNP was receiving arms and training from Cuba and the United States was balancing this with arms shipments to the JLP. Others were of the opinion that the Jamaican community in the United States was purchasing arms in that country and shipping them to friends and relatives in the besieged garrisons. Whatever was the origin of the arms, by 1974 the level of armaments had prompted Prime Minister Michael Manley to constitute a mechanism specifically designed to counter the arms buildup. This was the establishment of a unique judicial entity know as the "Gun Court."[6]

Manley, the PNP leader in the 1970s and 1980s, had come to the conclusion that the guns being provided by the political parties were placing the political elite themselves at risk. Also, by giving the garrison "soldiers" arms they were empowering them to a point whereby they might achieve independence away from their political roots. The Gun Court, therefore, was an attempt to reexert control over the garrisons and to contain the gun violence. To this end the Gun Court had jurisdiction over anybody found with a firearm or anyone who used a firearm in the commission of a crime. Complete with its own prison, the court handed down mandatory life sentences (lesser sentences were allowed by the 1990s) and conducted itself apart from the main judicial system. However, the Court itself was subject to politicization and even by the mid-1970s the measures, no matter how draconian, were insufficient. In less than a decade political factionalism and firearms had transformed Jamaica into a siege state. The metamorphosis into criminal enterprise state would take even less time and only required an economic incentive to fuel the engine of mutation. In the tradition of heroin in Pakistan and qat in Yemen, that incentive came in the form of the drug trade.

During the period of the political wars a genuine idiosyncratic culture had emerged out of the garrisons. Part religious, in the form of Rastafarianism, and part outlaw poetry, in the guise of reggae and ska, it had created its own heroes, villains, and social mores. The heroes were the dons, or garrison leaders. The villains were the police and their informers. The social mores included drug consumption, the abuse of women and children, and the elevation of the gun to totemic status. Abetted by a diaspora centered in the eastern United States and in the United Kingdom, this culture had gone global in the 1970s. But apart from a few superstars such as Jimmy Cliff and Bob Marley few Jamaicans had been able to capitalize on the Jamaican outlaw lifestyle. However, an aspect of that lifestyle, marijuana or ganja, had positioned Jamaica to become an important island of origin and transit at the onset of the drug decade, the 1980s.

By the 1980s the garrison communities had spawned their own coda of behavior.[7] In the ghettoes of Jungle, Payne Land, Tel Aviv, and Tivoli the law of the outside very rarely intruded into the lives of the inhabitants. Garrison behavior included obeisance to the "top ranking" members of the gangs, with the gang leader or "don" being recognized as lawgiver, law enforcer, and community leader. So comprehensive is the power of the don that many of the inhabitants of the garrisons transfer their loyalty and fealty from the state to the gangs and to their leaders. When the "don" system fails, as it does when wars of succession occur after the death of a don or when a don appears weak and is susceptible to challenge, the violence increases. A strong don can enhance the security of his garrison and, through acts of philanthropy, might be the only obvious manifestation of economic prosperity. Naturally, such an aberrant leadership structure leads to an aberrant social framework and a perverse economic environment. In Jamaica the lords of insecurity might consider themselves to be masters of their domain but the very insecurity that allows them to exercise their control also creates and fosters a nervous society of chronic and immobile victims.

The victims of violence in the Kerio Valley of Kenya moved to the lip of the escarpment to escape the depredations of the cattle rustlers and this placed environmental stress upon the local ecology. The stress on the local ecology of Kingston is social rather than environmental but it is quite as disruptive and perhaps even more difficult for the populace to control. The concept of childhood is truncated and distorted in the garrisons and ghettoes. Communications, transportation, medical care, and utilities are all affected by the level of insecurity in and around the garrisons. Gangs destroy telephone lines and street lighting in order isolate their garrisons from the outside world. Water and electricity companies are reluctant to send employees into the ghettoes to check meters and bus companies will not route vehicles into the more violent areas. In Kingston, fully one third of the population are squatters, paying no rent and undermining any confidence in housing investment. Schools are closed because teachers are intimidated by the level of violence in the neighborhoods.

Compounding these problems was the reality that employment opportunities outside of the ghettoes were restricted by area stigma. Two growth industries, street selling or higglering and private security companies, are indicators of a siege economy, with the former indicating a parasitic survival occupation within the walls of the garrisons and the latter being a combination of police substitute and extortion racket.[8] With unemployment amongst the young male population (15–24) chronically in double digits the only real opportunities were through flight to Britain or the United States or through participation in the drug trade. In certain cases these two opportunities merged, with some in the Jamaican diaspora providing an export link for island drugs.

The "tools" or guns that protected turf and commerce in the drug trade were enough in number and type to challenge the authority of the Jamaican constabulary. Beginning with M1 rifles in the 1970s, the arsenal soon included M16s (and their semiautomatic variant the AR-15), submachine guns (some of which were Sterlings bought from Jamaican Defence Force soldiers), and latterly AKs.[9] This level of weaponry had provided the security necessary to carve out landing strips in the hinterland from which quality ganja was exported in tons during the 1970s. It also, when the cocaine period began in the following decade, ensured that when the inevitable gang wars broke out that they would be extraordinarily violent.

The cocaine trade was entrepot trafficking, with Jamaica acting as a transshipment point between Colombia and the United States. Unavoidably, some of the drugs remained in Jamaica, helping to create a dependency population that in the 1990s graduated to crack cocaine. Numerate high school dropouts became the dealers in this domestic trade and they themselves recruited runners in the 12- to 15-year-old age group.[10] While "donmanship" still existed, instead of garrisons being under the patronage of a single don, youthful "micro-gangs" came into prominence, with urban child soldiers employing the same violent and immature practices that are the hallmark of these psychologically damaged recruits throughout the world. These impressionables, lacking the rudimentary code of the ganja generation, indulged in what became known as "pure killing," where any inhibition in the use of arms was withdrawn and where the use of guns was linked to "respect." The contemporary anthem of "No gun, no girl" typifies the adolescent philosophy of the gangs. It also, by linking the instrument of violence with that of sexual attraction, is an indicator that another element of Kalashnikov cultures, that of sexual abuse and rapine, is present in Jamaica.

In 1993 Jamaica reported 1,100 rapes.[11] Half of this total were children under the age of sixteen. Thirteen percent of eighth grade females had been subjected to attempted rapes, 4 percent had been raped. Rape and the threat of rape is used to send messages on issues such as territory and revenge and the possibility of gang rape and retaliatory rape was a constant concern for women in the garrisons. Although not at the levels of "pack rape" in PNG, the obvious vulnerability of women in the garrisons forces them into protective relationships with men at an early age, the result of which is often early pregnancy (25-year-old grandmothers are not unusual) and spousal abuse. The children of these relationships are often themselves subject to beatings (70 percent of parents admit to having used corporal punishment on their children), with the adults often using the "toughening" argument to support their use of "wicked licks." Governed by the fear of being branded an informer most of those who suffered these abuses never reported them to the authorities. As with all reportage from Kalashnikov cultures the real figures for rape and child abuse in Kingston's garrison communities will remain incomplete.

As in Karachi the law enforcement authorities in Kingston are considered by many observers to be part of the problem rather than part of the solution. Over a period of time beginning in the 1970s and extending to date the Jamaican constabulary has been condemned by a number of human rights organizations on the basis of corruption, partisanship, overzealousness and extrajudicial killing. Notorious cases such as the police raid into Denham town in July 2001, which resulted in the deaths of twenty-seven people, have tended to support the belief amongst many that the police treat the garrisons as occupied territory and attack them as an army would assault the stronghold of the enemy.[12] Units such as the Anti-Crime Investigation Detachment (ACID) certainly had a reputation for heavy-handed tactics bordering on systemic vigilantism and their raids into the garrisons often resulted in multiple casualties. However, the Jamaican police force is also like that in Karachi in that it is almost always outnumbered and very often outgunned in its confrontations with the garrison gangs. During the Denham township raid gangs used AKs, M16s, submachine guns, sniper rifles, and rocket launchers against the police. Casualties among the police force run into the hundreds of injuries and include thirteen police deaths in 2003 and eleven in 2004. Many gangsters specifically acquire AKs (at $1500–2,500 apiece at 2005 prices) in order to outgun the police and ambushing police units and attacking police stations have become a regular facet of the gangster-police confrontations.[13]

During the Denham operation the Jamaican government resorted to calling upon the Jamaican Defence Force (JDF) to supplement the constabulary. Although using the military to quell civil unrest would appear to be a desperate measure, it is in many ways a more realistic use of these resources by the governments of less developed states than preparing them for external invasion.[14] Internal defense in all its forms is the most likely contingency for the use of the military in these states and preparations for such contingencies would seem to be auspicious. But the use of heavily armed troops in street warfare raises the condition from that of banditry to insurgency, with a concomitant rise in the stakes on both sides. If the gangs can beat the military on the streets of the garrisons and ghettos then there is no further recourse than for the state to surrender or to solicit foreign intervention. It was to the latter that PNG resorted when confronted by its own inability to control the gangs of Port Moresby.

Some comment must be made regarding the export variant of Jamaican gangsterism. Whether termed "posses" in the United States or "yardies" (from the yards behind the garrison blocks) in the United Kingdom, they have come to represent the darkly negative aspect of the Jamaican diaspora. In Britain they have become inextricably interlinked with a gun culture that has been traditionally alien in the United Kingdom and in the United States they are associated with the hypperviolence that accompanied the cocaine and crack epidemics of the last two decades of the twentieth century.[15] The tools of intimidation and violence that allowed the gangs to control the garrisons in Kingston have also been transferred to London and New York and drugs remain the economic incentive behind much of posse and yardie activity. By tarring the reputation of an entire community these groups have also exacerbated racial tensions between their ethnic group and the host states and in this way they have threatened relations between Jamaica and other countries. At a more mundane level, when Jamaican gang members are arrested in the United Kingdom and United States and are deported back to the motherland (more than 1,000 per year are sent back from the United States and United Kingdom), they serve both as new recruits into the garrison gangs and as plenipotentiaries from the gangs in Britain and the United States.

In the early months of 2005 the JDF was again patrolling the streets of Kingston.[16] The Jungle 12 and Judgment Yard gangs were at war with each other, as were the One Order and Klansman crews. Four hundred people had been murdered in the first three months of the year. Joint JDF-constabulary patrols had been fired upon in the center of the city and the Denham Police Station had been assaulted again. In Spanish Town groups of armed men with AKs and M16s openly confronted the police and conducted running firefights. Residents fled neighborhoods and became internally displaced persons; entire areas of the city were deserted. One Jamaican newspaper described the gangs as "para-military" and the language of the media was less that traditionally used to describe criminal activity and more closer to that used to define military actions.[17]

What has and is occurring in Jamaica is clearly a hybrid between banditry, organized crime, and insurgency. The political conflict between the PNP and the JLP weakened the state and reduced its capacity to provide services and security. The dons and the garrison gangs, taking advantage of both the weakness of the state and the PNP/JLP rivalry, established themselves as a third force that itself provided the hierarchy, structure, and economic opportunity that the state was failing to offer. By arming themselves to a level of weaponization that challenged the authority of the state, the gangs moved beyond criminal outcasts and became a competitor of the legal authority. By accumulating wealth and constituents the dons and micro-gang leaders were able to literally corrupt the system and figuratively were able to undermine the legitimacy of the police and the judicial system. The weaknesses of the state and the inherent strengths of the criminal community have created a plateau of conflict in which neither side can win an outright victory against the other. The internecine warfare between the gangs, however, has created such a level of insecurity within the state that the government must engage in a constant campaign of containment. The conflict in Jamaica is beyond crime versus state and its level of violence, insecurity, and dislocation should not be classified as a "law enforcement" problem. It is obviously as much a state survival scenario as that faced by countries confronting guerrilla movements or those in the thrall of terrorist threats. In many ways it is more dangerous than either of these, since there are contingencies with which to confront such exigencies. There are few if any precedents for the war on the streets of Kingston but in the favelas of Rio and in Port Moresby, Papua New Guinea, there are variations of garrison culture that are closely analogous.

Papua New Guinea and Jamaica share a colonial heritage but not the same colonial experience. Jamaica was a long-term colonial possession with strategic importance and a slave-fueled economy. Papua New Guinea was an imperial afterthought that was only important in the context of nineteenth-century cartographic neatness. The Dutch had taken control of the western half of the island in 1848 and the Germans arrived in 1884, to be followed, three days later, by the raising of the Union Jack at Port Moresby. Berlin and London divided the eastern part of the island precisely in two and the Germans began to organize their portion as a profit-making commercial enterprise. The British passed the administration of their area to the Australians in 1906 and for the next seventy years PNG was in essence an Australian territory. Unlike the Germans, the British and Australians had illusions of benevolent management and modernization for their part of the island.[18]

In the Highlands of PNG "first contact" with the outside world had occurred later than in other parts of the island. Some of the tribes in the Highlands had only been contacted during the 1940s and very few had been subject to the direct control of the colonial powers. The concept of the state was alien to these groups and the subtleties of democratic, representative government were a philosophical irrelevance. The benefits of development were attractive to many of the clans but consumerism and capital were also largely unknown within these communities. Conflict did occur between 750 tribes and clans but over successive millennia a complex system of conflict management and mitigation had evolved. It would be anthropologically inexact to state that violence and premature death was not a facet of Highland life but it was subject to rules that were understood and accepted by most of the participants in conflicts, including amongst the youth. The weapons might have been Stone Age but the regimes of control that bounded conflict in the Highlands were sophisticated, if fragile.

Although Australia was conscious of the problems associated with framing a state from a collection of subnational entities, the administering power did attempt to impose a degree of centralized authority and order upon PNG. Australian multiroled civil servants (kiaps) spread the civilizing word in the hinterland, proliferating their view of law and order through a network of constables, magistrates and "native" administrators. Economic development, in the form of copra harvesting, coffee growing, and mining was attempted with varying degrees of success but the principal benefit to most Papuans came in the form of a subsidy from the Australian government. In the order of colonial administrations this was, given the isolated nature of the communities involved, an intrusive presence with a marginally instructive effect. Only in the twenty years prior to independence did Australia concentrate upon putting into place the structure of a modern, centralized state in PNG, and when they did so they came into confrontation with many local traditions that pulled against the concept of responsive, balanced, and objective government.

Wantokism was and remains one of the inhibitants to nation building in PNG.[19] At its crudest it is a form of networking in which tribes, clans, and others with a shared affinity belong to a collective of responsibility and mutual assistance. In its inclusionary form it performs the function of social safety net, defense alliance, and marriage bureau. In its exclusionary guise wantokism is the basis of a system of cronyism, discrimination, and a constant undercurrent of intergroup tension. Plausibly, wantoks are "garrisons without walls." They are power at a tangible, meaningful level with the promise of security at the expense of limitations in the breadth and extent of associations outside the wantok. One aspect of wantokism, in which any member of the group has the right to demand the goods of another member, is a form of entitlement that is also contrary to the work ethic demanded in a capitalist-based society. In many ways the philosophy of wantok primacy runs directly contrary to the concept of the corporate state.

Compounding the counter-state elements of wantokism is the "big man" approach to authority that is held by many in PNG.[20] A "don" by any other name, the "big man" is one who takes on the responsibility of leadership in exchange for the absolute support of his followers. The status of big man is usually achieved through a succession of acts of leadership, prowess, and benevolence. The big man is part warrior and part paternalist, binding others to him through dependency and submission. In its traditional context it has often worked well, reducing tensions and inequities through the use of interpersonal skills. But the move toward centralization both undermined the "big man" concept and mutated it into the center of an abusive political system. Members of parliament became the new "big men," with the national exchequer being interpreted not as a general fund for the general good but rather as fount of spoils to be seized upon and dispensed according to the whims of the big men. Becoming one of the 109 members of the PNG parliament is an opportunity for personal enrichment and instant elevation in status. In a system where wantokism and big man-ism are already accepted practices, the concept of *korapsen* (corruption) is almost moot. Taking money and giving a part of it to ones followers is arguably the correct practice according to the prevailing ethic. Unfortunately it means that projects that require a state-based approach, such as long-term investment in roads, communications, and economic development, are never achieved. It also means that the general populace, watching the kleptocratic example of the elite, is encouraged to mimic the big man and wantok arrangements in their own way.

The origins of raskolism are to be found in the last decade before PNG achieved independence in 1975.[21] The move toward centralized government had attracted many rural inhabitants to the cities and particularly to the capital, Port Moresby. There was a general expectation that modernization would bring jobs and that most of those jobs would be centered in the towns. When that expectation was unfulfilled the squatter camps of the poor became bases from which groups affiliated by wantok, ethnicity, or linguistic ties conducted their criminal activities and to which they retreated when challenged by the police. In the early period there were perhaps fifty raskol groups but attrition and incorporation reduced their number to a dozen in the late1980s. By that time the weaknesses of the new state of PNG had become apparent and the relative strength of raskol organization placed them in a position to openly challenge the security forces.

Equally as well organized and innovative as Kingston's garrison gangs, the raskols specialized in armed robbery, carjacking, and drug dealing. Raskol hierarchy was predicated upon a family tree, with the "father" above "elder brothers" who administered "younger brothers."[22] As with the "big man" system, the "father" achieved rank through prowess as a criminal and forcefulness of command tempered by largesse and philanthropy. The raskols patrolled their own areas, providing security from casual street crime and meting out community justice. Their networks included affiliations with rural raskol units (85 percent of the population still lived in the countryside) and also relationships with politicians, who used them as enforcers during political campaigns. Although this affiliation with the political "big men" did not assure the raskols the same level of protection afforded to their Jamaican counterparts, it did reduce their vulnerability during the states of emergency that were declared when crime became intolerable.

The rise of the raskols was facilitated by a judicial and law enforcement system that was unprepared for a rapid deterioration in social order. Although warrants were signed they often took months to serve. Bail jumping was pervasive, as was the intimidation of witnesses. Even when convicted and imprisoned the gang members could take advantage of the many prison breaks that seemed to be a facet of the PNG penal system. With a police force numbering just 3,000 officers to serve a population of 5 million and with raskols willing to engage in gun battles with police patrols, it was perhaps inevitable that in Port Moresby in particular the law enforcement authorities would fall into the same kind of siege mentality that affected the Jamaican constabulary.[23] During the early 1980s the police conducted frequent and heavy raids into the squatter settlements, sweeping up suspects and building dossiers on the raskols. Not trusting many of the senior community leaders, they failed to coordinate their activities with politically connected individuals and this eventually redounded on the police. Aggressive policing did not end in the 1980s but it was severely curtailed, allowing the raskol groups to consolidate their control over the myriad squatter settlements in the capital.

As mentioned before, one of the most identifiable elements of crime in PNG is "pack rape."[24] This activity, in which women are raped by multiple assailants, is closely linked to rite-of-passage behavior and to the payback system of revenge activity. When the rural and Highland tribes and clans moved into the towns of PNG they became isolated from many of the traditions that provided the transitional waypoints in their lives. Abuse of the women of enemy tribes had been a traditional aspect of Melanesian warfare and it was one of the weapons of payback that made the journey from country to city. Exacerbated by a high consumption of alcohol (the colonial powers had banned alcohol sales, which were resumed in 1962) and cloaked in a code of silence that ensured gross underreporting, rape became an instrument of terror that the raskol groups used to intimidate opponents and initiate their own membership. Children were not spared this violence and as is often the case those who were raped became twice victims as they were shunned within their own communities. The introduction of HIV/AIDS into the island in the 1980s added another dimension to the assaults and helped hasten the island to a 1 percent infection rate by 2005.[25]

If raskolism had been the only conflict confronting the nascent state of PNG, it is possible that the concept of state-based authority might gradually have displaced competing traditional associations. But at the same time as the urban groups began to develop two additional struggles were diverting the attention and resources of PNG. One, the attempt at separatism on the PNG incorporated island of Bougainville, tested the capabilities of the PNG defence forces and finally undermined the authority of the civil power. The other conflict was an outgrowth and evolution of traditional warfare in the Highlands. The former issue touched upon issues of sovereignty and territoriality and related directly to PNG as a state. The latter problem, that of tribe and clan in almost constant conflict, was a challenge to the concept of nationhood. Between them they served as twin assaults upon the fundamentals of the nation-state.

If the police were tested by the raskol phenomenon then the Papua New Guinea Defence Force (PNGDF) was thoroughly debilitated by the insurgency in Bougainville.[26] Beginning in 1988 and continuing for the next sixteen years, the Bougainville Revolutionary Army (BRA) fought a continuous campaign against the PNGDF in an attempt to gain independence for the island that had been included as a somewhat careless adjunct in the division of spoils in 1884. But the issue was not simply that of contested sovereignty; Bougainville was also the site of arguably the richest copper mine in the world and the authorities in Port Moresby were unwilling to allow this asset to be lost. The mine at Panguna, as in the Highlands of PNG proper, was itself a major part of the conflict. Those landowners who had been dispossessed by the excavations had received little or no compensation for their displacement and this fed a general sense that Bougainville was being exploited by a rapacious PNG (the mine was an early casualty of the conflict when it was closed for security reasons in 1989). It was this sense of alienation that allowed BRA, which rarely had more than a few hundred fighters, to conduct a successful long-term guerrilla campaign against the PNGDF. Such conflicts are difficult for a military to prosecute under the best of circumstances and the PNGDF was not well prepared for such a war.

An integrated, disciplined, and nonpartisan military is considered to be an indicator of a mature state. Obversely, a military that is a reflection of all the tensions and insecurities within a state becomes a net contributor to the weaknesses of the state. For much of its existence the PNGDF has exhibited most of the insecurities and fragmentational aspects of the wider society while at the same time isolating its members away from their traditional roots. In a society where wantokism provides the basis for individual security, any person who appears to transfer that association to a state-based organization is making a deal with the state that passes beyond that of simple service. The expectations that are raised by this type of contract are hard to fulfill and in PNG the military has made its disappointment known on a number of occasions. In 1997, when the government of Prime Minister Chan enlisted the support of a private military company, Sandline, to try to decapitate the BRA leadership on Bougainville, the PNGDF openly revolted and forced the government to reverse its position. Similarly, in 2001 when a proposal was made to halve the PNGDF some of the soldiers seized equipment and premises and again forced the government to make concessions.[27] While not necessarily precursors of a coup these types of incidents indicate that the PNGDF is an unreliable partner in the process of nation-building. This unreliability, when compounded by a paucity of equipment and resources that has reduced the PNGDF to a role in which its own force protection is its paramount concern, undermined any prospects of containing the third conflict in PNG, that of intertribal warfare in the Highlands.

The highlands of PNG have been fertile ground for study by cultural anthropologists for more than a century. Much of the subject of that study has centered on the highly evolved, subtle, and complex conduct of warfare that exists among the mountain tribes and clans. The rules and conventions that bound these conflicts were designed to provide a balance of forces and weapons in such a manner that contests were won through individual prowess rather than by superior numbers or firepower. Mastering the rules was as important as understanding the nature of applied force. Killing was an element of the game but warrior prowess was as much about cunning and finesse as it was about taking of life. With bows and spears as their weapons, the highland tribes engaged in a highly personal, close-quarters conflict that, as with the traditional pastoralists of East Africa, was fragile in its balance between coercion and catastrophic attrition. Insecurity may have been a consistent element in the lives of the highland tribes, but until the postindependence period it was maintained at a level and in a fashion that allowed the tribes to coexist within a bounded universe. After that time the intrusion of the state and of modern weapons turned what had been a finely balanced and stylized form of combat into a series of lethal skirmishes and revenge raids.

In the Highlands democratic government brought a new form of cyclical violence. The wantok and big-man elements of the culture reduced electioneering to the equivalent of traditional tribal warfare but without the constraining aspects of the traditional subculture. Before and after each election the highland tribes contested the involvement and tactics of their opponents. In 1986 the violence included rioting, destruction of property, mass arrests, arson, and murder. One incident, however, indicates that this particular election predated the "modern" era of PNG politics. Tribesmen who besieged a group in the Southern Highlands capital of Mount Hagen used spears and arrows against the barricaded party. By the early 1990s the political competitors had equipped their adherents with firearms and "quaint" Stone Age warfare had been eclipsed by Jamaican-style political gunfighting.[28]

The Kalashnikov cultures of Yemen and northwest Pakistan are the result of a saturation of arms. In Karamajong and the other pastoralist communities of East Africa the impact was less in terms of numbers of firearms than of the mutation of traditional conflict into modern destructive warfare. The number of arms taken from the garrison at Marakwet pale in the context of the millions of arms available in Yemen but the quantum increase in lethality destroyed an equilibrium that had been nurtured across centuries. Such also was the case in the Highlands of PNG. The number of modern factory arms available in the region is in the thousands rather than millions but that fact is largely irrelevant. The force multiplier effect of even a small number of arms when they were injected into the framework of tribal and clan warfare was exponential. In the province of the Southern Highlands it is estimated that there might be as few as 2,000 factory-made firearms but that was enough to fuel a five-year-long war between two tribes, the Ujamap and Wogia, which took hundreds of lives and created a profound level of destruction and insecurity within the province.[29]

The origin of the modern arms that transformed the Highlands has been the matter of some debate. As with Jamaica, PNG is the point of origin for high-potency marijuana that is much valued outside of the country. There is some indication of arms-for-drugs dealing, with the narrow and largely unmonitored Torres Strait between PNG and Australia encouraging such speculation.[30] There is also evidence that mining companies have provided firearms to groups in exchange for security guarantees. Arms may also have transited across the border from the Indonesian state of Irian Jaya, where separatists have been conducting their own campaign. But most evidence indicates that the majority of the arms in the hands of the Highlands tribes (and the raskols) were not clandestinely imported into PNG but rather that they were acquired from the arsenals of the PNG police forces and from the PNGDF.[31]

In 2004 semiautomatic assault rifles sold for $1,500 to $2,500 in the Highlands of PNG. A selective-fire assault rifle, such as the M16, cost for $2,500 to $3,000.

Medium machine guns, such as the M60, cost $7,500 to $8,000.[32] Average pay in the police and defense forces is less than $250 per month.[33] The police in the Highlands often are restricted to patrolling on foot because they are not provided with sufficient funds to buy fuel for their vehicles. Constrained by insufficient budgets, undermined by big-man politics, and under constant threat in a highly insecure environment, it is perhaps understandable that certain members of the PNG police sell their arms to participants in the tribal wars. These transfers, however, have a twofold effect upon the Highlands region. The firepower of the tribes is increased and the power and legitimacy of law enforcement is undermined. In addition, many of the arms were acquired by itinerant gunmen who sold their services to the tribes and clans on a mercenary basis, thereby further reducing the traditional control mechanisms that relied upon kinship bonds.

As the "strong guns" (military weapons) began to gain prominence in both the Highlands and raskol conflicts, the overall security situation deteriorated significantly. The PNGDF and the police force went through phases of belligerence alternating with demoralization. In the Highlands a Rapid Deployment Unit was mobilized in the 1990s to help provide protection for the foreign-owned mines in the hinterland but the initiative failed after accusations that mining interests were being afforded protection, while the population at large remained vulnerable.[34] Arms amnesty programs were attempted but the arms that were retrieved were mostly nonfactory weapons and in very small quantities. In addition to these failed attempts to halt the deterioration in security, by the onset of the new millennium international media began to focus upon the level of violence in PNG, and in Australia the academic and NGO communities became concerned about the prospect of having a failed state as a northern neighbor. By 2004 what had been an intransigent domestic issue had metamorphosed into a regional problem.

External intervention into a Kalashnikov culture is obviously problematic. The concept of sovereignty still pertains, even if the state itself is no longer capable of fulfilling its obligation as protector of its citizens. By the time intervention has been contemplated it is axiomatic that at least one, and in the case of PNG multiple, armed actors have become powerful enough to challenge the primacy of the state. The external actor, which in the case of PNG was Australia, must attempt the resurrection of the state and at the same time diminish the threat from competing armed interests. It must accomplish these two tasks while conducting its operations with great sensitivity and with demonstrable humility. When the interventionist state is a former colonial power, as has been the case in West Africa and in PNG, the level of sensitivity and humility must be proportionately higher. Australia accepted these challenges when it announced its five-year Enhanced Cooperation Program for PNG in 2004.[35]

The concept of regional hegemons has, particularly since the end of the Cold War, been a contentious issue when considering viable future security architectures. For the global superpower, the emergence of competent and willing local powers who could help share the burden of maintaining order in the international system is an attractive prospect. However, such a regional power cannot be relied upon either to remain "regional" or to retain the priorities of the superpower. Nevertheless, in the case of Australia the emergence of that state as a regional power, first through its intervention in East Timor and then in Bougainville and PNG, has created a new dynamic in Southeast Asia. But the intervention in PNG was not akin to those in Bougainville and East Timor. In the latter two cases Australia intervened as a participant in a sanctioned peace process. In the case of PNG the Australian intervention was in many respects a mea culpa for the state of unpreparedness in which Australia had left PNG thirty years previously. In the context of the post-9/11 and Bali bombing environment the Australian move was also designed to minimize the risk of PNG being used as a base of operations for terrorists and others that might use it to attack Australian interests.

The Enhanced Cooperation Program for PNG was designed to provide both short-term and long-term support for increased security in PNG. In the short term Australia was to send 275 policemen to PNG, along with lawyers and others who were recruited as an anticorruption task force. The police were to concentrate their efforts on achieving control over the raskol gangs and the anticorruption elements were to attempt to control the hemorrhaging of public monies (Australia itself sent more than $1 billion Australian in aid to PNG every year). The longer-term efforts included a reappraisal of the centralization of power in PNG that had begun under Australian tutelage fifty years before. The rationale behind the latter initiative was a tacit recognition that democratic governance through centralized organs of power and administration had failed in PNG. Raskolism, the separatist war in Bougainville, and the violent mutation of the Highlands conflicts had successfully challenged a centralized authority that had weakened itself through corruption and big-manism. The "strong guns," literal and figurative, had triumphed over the attempt to transfer the fragile elements of democracy and law to an unprepared and rejectionist culture.

In 1997 homicide became the principal cause of premature death in Brazil.[36] In 1999 in the state of Rio de Janeiro firearms-related deaths were 44 percent of all deaths recorded in the 15- to 19-year-old male age group. During the 1990s some 266,000 Brazilians died from gunshot wounds, with 218,000 of these deaths attributed to homicide.[37] The majority of these lethal encounters took place within the favelas or slums of major Brazilian cities and the 600 favelas of Rio are some of the most violent of these shanty-towns. Structurally and in terms of their conduct the bandido gangs of the favelas are remarkably akin to the garrison gangs of Kingston or to the raskols of Port Moresby. But while Brazil may be weakened by the corrosive violence of its urban gangs the primacy of the state is not directly challenged by the power of the bandidos. Instead, Brazil has been forced to accommodate a permanent parallel society within the broader confines of the state.

Between 1964 and 1985 Brazil was governed by successive military admin-istrations. As might be expected, these years were marked by controlling and repressive measures that were principally aimed at maintaining social stability within Brazil. The principal target of such measures was left-wing organizations and individuals who were assumed to be preparing for a radical shift in the Brazilian politics, following on the lead of the Cuban revolution. With the exception of a minor urban guerrilla movement that specialized in bank robberies, the expected radicalization of the Brazilian population did not take place, due in part to the comprehensiveness of the suppressive aspects of the military regime. However, while a radical ideological shift did not occur within Brazil, an existing aspect of the society, namely the rapid and uncontrolled urbanization of the country, accelerated throughout the last four decades of the twentieth century.

Although the favelas originated in the nineteenth century it was not until post-1945 that they began to emerge as an iconic aspect of Brazilian culture. Romanticized and magnified through the lens of such works as the film *Black Orpheus* existence in the favelas became linked to both the desperation of the slum dwellers and to their spirit of independence.[38] Life "beyond the asphalt," with its negligible services and location stigma, encouraged a neo-separatist attitude amongst the favelados. A criminal economy, initially predicated upon armed robbery and kidnapping, was established, as was a rudimentary form of favela law enforcement and justice. Most of these activities were contained or controlled during the years of military rule and their impact was localized. But the end of military rule coincided with the emergence of the drug economy in the favelas in the 1980s and the thin membrane that separated life in the squatter townships from the rest of Brazil became breached.

During the period of armed robberies the favelados were imprisoned with politically driven urban guerrillas who were engaging in the same practices but toward ideological rather than economic goals. The imprisoned guerrillas schooled the criminals in methods of organization and armed action against the police, using many of the tenets to be found in Carlos Marighella's *Minimanual of the Urban Guerrilla*.[39] The organizational end result of this commingling of teacher and criminal was the Comando Vermelho (Red Commando). Originally intended as a self-help group for imprisoned favelados it metamorphosed into a disciplined criminal organization that melded the tactics of the urban guerrilla with the objectives of organized crime. Comando Vermelho continued to dominate the evolution of the economy of the favelas during the transition from traditional crime to that of the drug economy of the 1980s, although it had to share the wealth with such rivals as Terceiro Comando and Amigos dos Amigos during this period.[40]

The organization of the favela gangs helped them to manage the drug distribution network that was required when the cocaine trade became the dominant element in the 1980s. Headed by a *dono*, who might control a number of favelas but usually did not live in one, the structure mimicked military, corporate, and mafia managerial elements, with general managers, soldiers, lookouts and bodyguards. With the most humble operator earning more than five times the national wage and with many providing the sole support for their families, the members of Comando Vermelho and the other gangs promoted themselves as an alternative to a corrupt and unresponsive Brazilian body politic. Inevitably this brought them into conflict with the agents of that body politic, namely the police and military forces. In order to contain the favela gangs the police adopted tactics and weaponry that were more closely akin to that of an occupying army than to law enforcement, with the concomitant effect of helping to create a siege mentality within the favelas and encouraging an arms race. During the 1990s confrontations between the gangs and the police took the form of raids, ambushes, and firefights, with the police armed with battle rifles, assault rifles, and submachine guns and the gangs responding with handguns and a selection of rifles. Comando Vermelho and the other gangs made re-arming a core goal during this period, with the intent on intimidating the police from entering the favelas but with the peripheral effect of raising the mortality rate in intra-favela gang fighting.

The arming of the favelas is divisible into two distinct phases. The initial phase, beginning in the 1960s and ending in the 1980s, might best be described as the ".38 Special" period.[41] During this time most of the favela gangs were armed with Brazilian revolvers in .38 Special caliber, the same handgun used by the Brazilian police forces. The fact that concealable revolvers were the principal firearm indicates that there was still a requirement to hide weapons from the presence of the authorities. By the 1990s, however, the favela gangs were so pervasive and their control over their territory so assured that there was no longer a need to conceal their weapons. Assault rifles and battle rifles came into prominence, particularly in the hands of the *soldados* (soldiers) who were tasked with maintaining security for the drug traffickers. Initially U.S.-made arms (Ruger and Colt semiautomatic versions of their assault rifles) predominated, to be followed later by such military weapons as the G3, FAL, and the AK.[42] Submachine guns and hand-grenades also came into use. As with the Highlands tribes of PNG, the numbers of such weapons were relatively small but their impact was magnified both within and outside of the favelas.

The guns came from many sources. Brazil has a well-developed small arms industry and many of the handguns are traceable to the two major Brazilian manufacturers, Rossi and Taurus. These revolvers and pistols leak out into the community through theft (Brazil has some 7 million registered firearms in circulation) and through a curious circular trade in which Brazilian arms are exported into the Iguacu Triangle, principally to Paraguay, and are then smuggled back into Brazil by arms traffickers.[43] The military weapons are from U.S. commercial sources and are bought or stolen from the Brazilian police and military. Some of the more esoteric weapons (grenades, rocket launchers, high-priced automatic weapons) may have been bought from the drug traffickers who supply the cocaine for the Brazilian market.[44]

The military-style weapons were designed both to deter the police and to conduct campaigns against rival drug factions. They were also used to equip the *bonde* or armed convoys that the gangs used when they had to move drugs or arms between favelas.[45] The calibers of these weapons allowed them to defeat the body armor of the police and to place distance between the soldados and the officers of the law. As they were openly carried in the favelas they also served as badges of office for the gangs and to indicate their control over the slums. Some 5,000 to 10,000 armed gang members controlled the favelas by the end of the twentieth century and apart from their drug activities they also administered their own social discipline (*as leis do trafico*).[46] With virtually no official law enforcement or judicial oversight within the favela a rudimentary and often brutal form of rough law was enforced by the gangs with punishments ranging from beatings to execution for such crimes as theft, wife beating, and communicating with the police. Movement between gang territories is strictly controlled and "poaching" of drug clientele by one faction over another is a casus belli.

Although the gangs might appear to have usurped the presence of the central authorities within the favelas the rationale behind their control is one of economics rather than part of a political agenda. A stable environment allows the gangs to market their drugs without interruption and even when the police do make occasional raids on the slums they are very often allowed to proceed without interference as long as they do not threaten the drug commerce. Market expansion, however, often requires gangs to make physical moves upon the territory of a rival and sometimes protracted wars ensue. When such conflicts overflow the favelas the authorities are forced to act and often they do so by engaging in extrajudicial activities. An extensive review of police practices in Brazil in 1997 indicated that they participated in torture, beatings, wrongful arrests, and even murder.[47] During Operation Rio in 1994–1995 the police and military coordinated in an effort to break the control of the favela gangs and the operation was conducted with little regard for human rights or civil liberties. As a result of this and successive operations the inhabitants of the favelas came to consider the police as the enemy and this allowed the gangs to consolidate their control over the slums. Further frustrated, the police began to average a thousand shooting victims per year in the state of Rio, with only such singular incidents as the killing of thirty people by the police in one day in March 2005 raising any alarums within the wider public.[48]

The drug bandidos of Rio's slums could, under certain conditions, become a political rival of the state but there is no indication that they wish to do so. Comando Vermelho is a power in Brazil but it limits most of its activities to the welfare of its members in prison and to the administration of its drug domains. The power that it has already achieved is enough to protect its drug consumption and distribution base in the favelas. Its confrontations with the police are about maintaining their primacy within the slums rather than about challenging the government in their primacy over the state. However, the level of general insecurity that is maintained within Rio and other major Brazilian cities as a result of the activities of the gangs is no different in its effects than would be that of ideologically motivated urban guerrillas. The gangs, with their intelligence apparatus, guns, support network, and financial underpinnings, are quite analogous to an insurgent force, with the only difference being their more limited objectives. Their perverse investment in a relative status quo cannot mask the reality that the state tolerates their activities because it cannot find a way to defeat them.

The garrison gangs of Kingston, the raskols of Port Moresby and the bandidos of Rio defy easy analysis. Much of their activities are criminal in nature but their innate and sometimes realized power is far greater than simply that of a criminal association. Their ability to confront, frustrate, and cow the agents of the state make them a threat but their capacity to provide a certain security, livelihood, and identity to those behind their *cordon criminalle* also makes them an alternative to the state. Their weapons are those of an army but their conduct is that of guerrillas without a cause. The majority of their victims are from their own support base, particularly when the drug trade provides the basis of their wealth. They selectively abstract elements of traditional culture to support their control structures but at the same time they destroy the traditions that have helped maintain identity and order across generations. They also distort such basic definitions as childhood, social consciousness, democracy, and life itself.

In Jamaica and PNG the process of democratization was partly responsible for the evolution of the gangs. By using the garrisons and the tribes as election gangsters the political machines of these two countries undermined the delicate validity of the ballot box and helped to create a rival to any elected authority. In Brazil political and economic neglect of the urban poor allowed them to construct an entity that by the late twentieth century could not be dismantled or even controlled by the state. Although the military dictatorships in Brazil were able to contain the favelas, all that this achieved was to allow them to develop structure and confidence that in the postdictatorship period blossomed into almost unassailable socioeconomic contrarians.

The weaponization of all three communities is an important aspect of their evolution toward permanent phenomena. Although in literal terms the "Kalashnikov" is a minor player in Kingston, Port Moresby, and Rio de Janeiro, the level and extent of availability of arms served to remove the activities of the gangs from their outlaw roots and allowed them to become a fixed and maturing element within their host societies. Sufficient numbers of particular types of weapons, most notably assault and battle rifles, raised the level of conflict from that of traditional banditry to one of unconventional warfare. Aided and abetted by ill-funded, poorly trained, and often corrupt police and militaries, the casual insurgents of Jamaica, PNG, and Brazil were able to debilitate the state to the point whereby it was forced to either quarantine the criminal communities or to accept external intervention. Even if these places cannot be truly termed Kalashnikov cultures, they were manifestly subjected to "kalashnikov enculturation."

Kalashnikov Counterculture: Control and Disarmament

To reiterate, Kalashnikov cultures are more than the gun but the gun is an intrinsic element in all the Kalashnikov cultures. It is not surprising, therefore, that many of the attempts to control the evolution and continuation of Kalashnikov cultures have concentrated upon controlling the spread and availability of weapons. The logic that drives this approach is predicated upon the belief that without the "Kalashnikov" there can be no "culture" and that therefore the control of small arms and light weapons is the most economical way of addressing the issue. But even if the Kalashnikov was the lynchpin of the culture that bears its name, any illusion that the control of small arms was an easy shortcut to stabilization and peace would be disabused at the onset of the new century.

Attempts to control the spread and effects of small arms have varied from the globally macro to the village-level micro. The spectrum of actors runs from the United Nations to sculptors fashioning antiproliferation messages from the weapons and lethal detritus of Kalashnikov cultures. At one level discussions centered upon the primacy of sovereign states in the international system and at another level it was simply about parents attempting to protect their children from the casual violence within Kalashnikov cultures. The curative elements ranged from attempts to formulate international laws to control and punish dealers in illicit arms to intervention by external actors to bring order to failing states. Given the diverse nature of these approaches, it is perhaps not surprising that a high degree of confusion reigned over the "counterculture" community and that this confusion has resulted in lost opportunities and failed prescriptions.

In the late 1990s many of those who were involved in efforts to counter the proliferation of Small Arms and Light Weapons (SALW) saw an opportunity to harness what was perceived to be a popular global movement against indiscriminate casualties amongst civilian populations. This movement had been responsible for the largely successful campaign to control landmines and it was believed by many that the momentum provided by the antimines campaign could be used to push through international laws and conventions that would provide the framework for a small arms control regime. To this end the proponents of control proposed that the UN should sponsor a conference in July 2001 that would consider the "illicit trade in small arms and light weapons in all its aspects."[1]

That the conference should narrow its considerations to the "illicit trade" was an important stipulation. With many in the IGO and NGO community concerned with arms exports as a whole, including government-to-government transfers, there was a sense amongst some, particularly in the U.S. government, that the UN conference would turn into a "peace conference," with all that implied for constraining the national policies of the last remaining superpower. This concern remained undiminished throughout the preparations for the conference and when, on July 9, John Bolton, then U.S. Under Secretary for Arms Control and International Security Affairs and later U.S. ambassador to the UN, rose to make his statement to the conference it became clear that the United States saw a "diffusion of focus" in the conference agenda that precluded U.S. support.[2] For Bolton, who tended to view the UN as a competitor to state sovereignty, many of the proposals laid before the conference were an affront to "the exercise of popular sovereignty by participating governments" and in his statement he iterated those proposals that he felt impinged particularly upon U.S. sovereignty.[3]

Bolton's statement is worth considering in some detail since in it he represents multiple constituencies and positions that mirror many of the narrower issues inherent in Kalashnikov cultures. He makes an economic argument that imposing any rules that "would constrain legal trade and legal manufacturing of small arms and light weapons" would be discriminatory and anyway that such traders were not part of the problem. Such an argument echoes the position taken by the traders of Darra Adamkhel and to a lesser extent those in the arms markets of Somalia and Yemen. Inherent in this position is an element of dissociation, in which the supplier is operating within a bubble of commerce that isolates them from the consequences of their actions. This problem is compounded when Kalashnikov cultures devolve into communities where rule of law is supplanted with rule of the gun. Under such conditions the term "legal" is made moot by the very instruments that at some point in their manufacture and ownership have been part of "legal trade" but which have passed beyond the ability of states to control them.

In his statement John Bolton also took the domestic U.S. issue of the "right to bear arms" and extrapolated it into a global right.[4] Having already made the distinction, as seen by the U.S. delegation, between small arms as strictly military arms and firearms such as hunting rifles and pistols, Bolton then states that "we do not support measures that prohibit civilian possession of small arms." He appeared, therefore, to be explicitly in favor of civilian ownership of automatic rifles, machine guns, shoulder-fired missiles, and light mortars. The Second Amendment to the U.S. constitution has always been open to interpretation but "shoulder-fired missiles" have not often found a constituency of support for ownership in the United States, even from the National Rifle Association, whose members were on the U.S. delegation to the UN small arms conference.

As stated above, this author believes that the distinction between the United States as a gun culture and those that have been identified as Kalashnikov cultures is real and not simply semantics. The law enforcement, legal, political, and social framework can absorb the 30,000 deaths from firearms every year in the United States by placing it in the broader context of individual rights in relation to the responsibility of the state. The primacy of the state is not threatened by the negative effects of 200 million firearms in private hands, even when such negative manifestations include riots, massacres, and armed insurrections by extremist groups. But this primacy is only maintained through constant vigilance, an evolving legal process and a fundamental commitment by the society as a whole to abide within a system of laws. In true Kalashnikov cultures these elements have either not been present or they have been eroded by the insecurity created by high levels of weaponization in relation to a weak state system. The concept of a global "Second Amendment" belies the reality that in many places the primacy of the state cannot be taken for granted and that in such places a "right to keep and bear arms" would equate to a devolution of power down to street level.

In respect to the primacy of the state, in his statement to the UN conference John Bolton made another comment that was a reflection of U.S. foreign policy concerns. The United States, Bolton stated, could "not support measures limiting trade in small arms and light weapons solely to governments . . . most important [-ly] this proposal would preclude assistance to an oppressed non-state group defending itself from a genocidal government. Distinctions between governments and non-governments are irrelevant in determining responsible and irresponsible end-users of arms."[5] In a clear reference to U.S. support for the contras in Nicaragua and the mujahedin in Afghanistan, this position was historically understandable (the United States itself had emerged due to the actions of armed non-state actors) but it was fraught with foreseeable and unforeseeable implications. In terms of the foreseeable, it would not be possible to control the arms once they had been delivered to the non-state groups and many, such as in the case of U.S. arms sent to Afghanistan during the Soviet period, would end up in the hands of those who would not only challenge the primacy of the targeted state but would also spread the contagion of violence regionally or even extra-regionally. Unforeseeable consequences might include state actors who supplied arms to non-state groups who would not serve the interests of the democratic powers and who could create pools of insecurity in such places as the South Caucasus.

The opposition of John Bolton and the U.S. delegation was not the only reason that the UN conference on illicit weapons failed. The analogy of small arms with landmines was in many ways simplistic and the emotion-fuelled atmosphere that had sustained the genesis of the UN small arms conference was not enough to overcome the complexities of SALW control. Landmines were a niche issue, well suited to the recruitment of public sentiment. But the very extent of small arms proliferation militated against a ban-them-all solution. Few people outside of the specialists in the field were educated to the complexities of the gray and black market trade in arms, and although there was some prurient popular interest in arms trafficking (the film *Lord of War* exemplifies this level of interest), it was not enough to maintain a groundswell of support for a global effort to restrict the trade in small arms and light weapons. But many of the NGOs and IGOs who had observed and contributed to the UN conference did not desert the issue and they reverted to their missions to inform policymakers, educate the public, and embarrass the transgressors.

In the wake of the failure of the UN conference on small arms (and of its equally fruitless follow-up in 2006), the efforts to prevent or reduce the effects of Kalashnikov enculturation diversified and evolved. The United Nation itself did not completely withdraw from experimenting with attempts to control the flow of illicit arms into zones of conflict or to diminish the effects of arms once they had become resident in such zones.

One of the more creative and potentially successful experiments took place in arms-saturated Albania. After the collapse of the government of that country in 1998 the national armies were sacked and small arms disappeared onto the open market and into the homes of Albanian citizenry.[6] At the behest of the Albanian government the United Nations, through its Development Programme, began a weapons collection pilot program centered on the Albanian town of Gramsh. Later replicated in other parts of Albania, the approach was one that concentrated upon exchanging weapons for assistance with development projects and for the completion of public works. The results were mixed (in Gramsh the number of weapons recovered was less than 6,000 and the cost per weapon of the overall project was $207) and the efforts did not equate to a national program but attempts to tie arms recovery to social welfare rather than to individual recompense was a useful experiment.[7]

Buyback programs can be large and expensive (a 1997 buyback program in Australia cost more than $A304 million to acquire 640,000 firearms) or less ambitious and less expensive (in the seventeen rounds of buyback programs in El Salvador 8,000 weapons were collected in exchange for vouchers that could be cashed at supermarkets, pharmacies, and shoe stores).[8] For some countries the exchange or barter approach is more practical and in the long term more positive in respect to encouraging development, however it may not always be the most cost-effective. In Mozambique the Transformation of Arms into Ploughshares (TAE) project costs $350,000 a year to collect 1,000 weapons and 40,000 rounds of ammunition. Individuals are paid with barter goods such as bicycles and sewing machines, while larger caches of weapons are exchanged for cash.[9] Given the literally countless numbers of weapons in Mozambique this was more a symbolic display of concern and of grassroots response than it was a genuine attempt to significantly diminish the threat posed by the weapons themselves.

Excepting buyback programs in generally pacific societies such as the UK and Australia, this type of response to Kalashnikov enculturation is fraught with difficulties. Black market prices can drive costs for buyback weapons into the realms of the prohibitive (in 2007 the humble Glock handgun, available on the U.S. open market for $500, could be sold on the illegal Turkish market for $3,500).[10] When the weapon represents life and livelihood it is difficult, especially when personal security cannot be guaranteed by the state, to relinquish that security blanket in exchange for a bicycle, a sewing machine, or cash. And often those weapons that are bought in are either nonfunctioning or of low quality and their removal from the society will have little or no effect upon the level or frequency of violence. Even when weapons have been successfully retrieved, they must be destroyed quickly before they can leech back through the hands of corrupt and venal officials. However, even with all these caveats buyback programs can provide an incentive to disarm, particularly for those who feel sufficiently safe and for whom the retention of the weapon poses more problems than it might solve.

Mozambique was also the venue for two other approaches to the problem of uncontrolled small arms proliferation, one of which was concerned with the retrieval of arms and the other concentrated upon the issue of raising awareness of the problem. This latter activity centered upon how to make small arms proliferation into a cause celebre in much the same way that Princess Diana had achieved in respect to the landmines issue. In Mozambique a collective of artists chose to forge sculptures out of AK rifles and other weapons and to display them as tangible representations of problems associated with Kalashnikov enculturation. Many of these sculptures were exhibited outside of Mozambique, including one that was shown at the British Museum in London.[11] This activity, together with attempts to rally celebrities to the cause, certainly raised awareness but small arms proliferation never reached the level of a global issue in the manner that landmines had done so. This might have been because at the onset of the new century a certain amount of cause fatigue (world hunger, natural disasters, Africa, global warming) may have set in but the major issue related to both the size of the problem and to the lack of a single or obvious solution to small arms proliferation. A heightened state of awareness could not easily be turned into clear policies and tangible results, and this lack of progress robbed the SALW movement of any momentum that it might have gained from the successes of the landmines campaign.

It was left to NGOs and to the academic community to keep the issue of Kalashnikov enculturation alive. They did so by establishing networks and internet sites, by engaging in field research, publishing monographs and books, and by funding regional and local initiatives. The impact of this effort might have been less than the sum of its parts, but in many ways it represented an alternative to the high profile "great issues" approach to world problems. The academic community, through research and analysis, placed Kalashnikov enculturation within a disciplined framework that could service policymakers and activists with the necessary data to make useful decisions. The NGOs, while sometimes more proselytic and less objective than the academics in their analysis of Kalashnikov cultures, often undertook research in dangerous places and collected information where others might fear to tread. The combination of these two streams of information and analysis resulted in a coherent picture of both SALW proliferation and of the phenomenon of Kalashnikov enculturation.

Such works as the annual Small Arms Survey from the Graduate Institute of International Studies, Geneva, and the pioneering work undertaken by Ed Laurance at the Monterey Institute in California added a gravitas to the study of SALW proliferation that had hitherto been reserved for the study of WMD. Field work conducted by organizations such as the Institute for Security Studies in South Africa and by Viva Rio in Brazil, apart from adding a certain edgy frisson to the subject area, provided much needed analysis of the manner in which Kalashnikov cultures developed and how they were perpetuated. When combined with material on poverty and armed conflict collected by the World Bank and intelligence on arms trafficking by the United Nations sanctions committees, most of the elements that helped form Kalashnikov cultures were available for serious study by the turn of the new century. What had been at best a minor chord of arms control studies and at worst a source of prurient interest in colorful "merchants of death" was now a full canon of work that could be used as the basis for policymaking.

The policy that emerged immediately before and then after the failed UN conference was a mix of regional, national, and parochial efforts. Regional efforts included the moratorium on importation, exportation, and manufacture of light weapons in West Africa, adopted by the Economic Community of West African States (ECOWAS) in 1998 and extended every three years thereafter. This approach, born out of Malian concerns over the arming of Tuareg tribes in the 1990s, was given impetus as Kalashnikov enculturation migrated from Liberia to Sierra Leone to Cote d'Ivoire and to the Delta Region of Nigeria.[12] The 6 million small arms in private hands in West Africa posed a clear danger to the weak governments of the region and the porous nature of area borders ensured that SALW could not be addressed as simply a national problem. The moratorium was judged by some to have been a successful first step but others felt that it had been either ignored or was a subject of ignorance within West Africa as a whole.[13] In 2006 the heads of state of the West African countries adopted a convention to regulate the importation and manufacture of SALW, and it was hoped that this would add strength and permanency to the regional counter-proliferation efforts.[14]

Regional agreements such as the West African moratorium and convention are noble efforts, but they are often eroded by a lack of political will, mutual suspicion over motives, and an inability to enforce such regulations that emerge from any agreement. In the case of Mozambique, however, such problems were addressed through a unique bilateral association between that country and South Africa. The long-running "Rachel" program is an example of two states forced into joint action by a common threat, in this case posed by the uncontrolled weapons within Mozambique. After the end of the apartheid regime in 1994 South Africa was confronted with a practical and psychological dilemma. Part of the strategy of the African National Congress in its confrontation with the white minority regime had been to use violence and the gun as tools to destabilize the South African state. A clandestine community of violence had been established that was adept at acquiring and transferring weapons and in waging an insurgency against the authorities. South Africa was not a Kalashnikov culture by the time of the transfer of power but it was in a weakened state and uncontrolled criminal violence threatened to derail prospects for economic and social growth. Psychologically, the postapartheid government had to reverse the public perception that the man with the gun was a freedom fighter and to move the population, and in particular young males, to the rejection of violence in respect to conflict resolution. What made this strategy particularly difficult was the easy availability of small arms within South Africa in the mid-1990s and the fact that the supply of arms could easily and cheaply be replenished from the uncontrolled stocks held in Mozambique.[15]

In the early 1990s Mozambique, with the best will in the world, was unable to police its own borders or to disarm its own population. The TAE initiative was more symbolic than it was a significant disarmament program and arms were used as an item of currency and exchange both within Mozambique and across borders into neighboring countries. South Africa was one of the major destinations for black market Mozambican arms and the South African Police Service (SAPS) became increasingly alarmed as rifles, machine guns, RPGs, and even man-portable air defense weapons made their way into South Africa.[16] Recognizing that the security forces of Mozambique were not trained or equipped to stop the flow of weaponry the South African government, through the vehicle of SAPS, proposed a joint bilateral program to identify, seek, and destroy weapons within Mozambique, using the resources of SAPS in conjunction with those of Mozambican security forces. Finding arms caches would be an intelligence-driven activity and the Mozambicans would provide that capability. The South Africans provided manpower, transportation, communications, and initial financing. The first operation, codenamed "Rachel," took place in October 1995 in an area along the shared Mozambique–South African border and it was deemed enough of a success to spawn an annual series.[17]

During the period 1995–2006 the Rachel operations achieved the destruction of more than 45,000 small arms and over 24 million rounds of ammunition.[18] The estimations of small arms in private hands in Mozambique varied from 1.5 to 6 million.[19] Therefore, conservatively Rachel operations resulted in the depletion of these stocks by 3.5 percent. But the relatively small numbers of weapons retrieved belies the importance of the Rachel operations. Two states were able to maintain a practical arms control initiative over more than a decade based upon a pragmatic shared interest and with each maximizing their own capabilities and complementing each other. The South Africans provided a technological edge that enhanced the Mozambicans' knowledge of the area (as an example, informants were provided with GPS receivers to identify the exact locations of arms caches), and even when funding became an issue (European states began to subsidize the operations at an early stage), there was enough political will in Mozambique and South Africa to continue the series. The Rachel operations were also important in terms of the practice of destruction; as they were discovered weapons were destroyed in place, therefore minimizing the possibility of the arms being recycled through the hands of corrupt officials.

Retrieving arms once they have proliferated into the hands of private citizens is an arduous process that requires a consistent, well-funded effort over a prolonged period of time. It also requires that a sense of security be established so that the populace will feel comfortable in divesting themselves of their own Kalashnikov security blanket. In places such as Yemen, where arms have a deep psychological hold upon the populace, any attempt at arms retrieval also had to take into account the role that weapons play in the maintenance of group independence and in the establishment of individual identity. Indeed, in Yemen the arms control debate did not so much center upon the ownership of arms but rather upon the right to carry and display arms in public and upon the right of tribes to deploy artillery and rocket launchers (the United States helped to diminish stocks of heavy weapons by contributing $32 million to a buyback program).[20] During the first five years of the twenty-first century the "bearing of arms" was banned within the confines of Yemeni cities as not only a public order issue but also to ensure that intertribal conflict was not perpetuated beyond the limits of tribal areas. The public display of arms was considered by the government in Sana'a to be an affront to its authority and to encourage the type of behavior that would fuel blood feuds. But a 1999 draft law to regulate the possession rather than the display of arms was still not the law of the land by 2007, principally because of resistance by the tribal elders.[21]

The government in Sana'a also attempted to curb open sales at the al-Talh and Jihana souks and by 2005 much of the trading had become more circumspect and less obvious.[22] The impetus for this crackdown was not the result of a general concern for public welfare but rather because of pressures relating to global terrorism and to extreme elements operating within Yemen and in the Horn of Africa. In 2004 a Shiite religious group, Shabab al-Mu'minoon, under the leadership of Hussein al-Houthi, staged a revolt that threatened the cohesion of the state and although al-Houthi himself died in the uprising the movement refused to be extinguished.[23] The arms bazaars had provided the weapons to the insurgents and for this reason the state attempted to close them. However, the dealers would not easily relinquish their trade and the business continued in a clandestine manner.[24] In respect to the Horn of Africa, the UN team monitoring the arms sanctions applied to Somalia was able to link, to their satisfaction, the arms traders of Yemen to the inexhaustible demands of the various Somali factions and this in turn placed pressure on the Sana'a government to try to exert a constraining influence on the arms dealers within Yemen.[25]

Before the year 2000 the issue of Yemeni arms had been, for the most part, a local phenomenon. It was not until the attack on the *USS Cole* in October 2000 and later the events of September 11, 2001 that the chronic insecurity of the Yemeni state became of broader regional and global concern. The preternaturally weakened state of Yemen's central government and the ability of armed factions to exploit that weakness allowed groups to form and to exist within enclaves inside the territory of Yemen. This was of great concern to the United States and to others that felt threatened by such groups and thus what had been a matter of distant curiosity became an issue under close scrutiny. The United States positioned military and intelligence elements in Djibouti to specifically monitor events in Yemen and Somalia and part of the surveillance mission inevitably concerned itself with arms entering and leaving Yemen. In addition, U.S. security assistance to Yemen increased dramatically after 2001, with much of the effort aimed at strengthening Yemeni security forces and tightening border surveillance.[26]

It remains to be seen whether global concerns over the threat of terrorism will prevail over tradition in respect to Yemen's Kalashnikov culture. Even while government forces fought against the al-Houthi rebellion, the wars between tribes and clans continued unabated within Yemen.[27] During the period 2004–2006 more than 23,000 violent deaths were officially recorded in Yemen, with more than 85 percent of the fatalities being from the use of firearms.[28] Most of the incidents were over the traditional issues of blood feuds, land ownership, and the business of *qat* and most of them were beyond the will and capability of the Yemeni authorities to resolve.

In East Africa attempts to control the Kalashnikov culture amongst the pastoralists was less overlain by world events than in Yemen but nevertheless it was affected by certain wider events. The end of the civil war in southern Sudan and the gradual marginalization of the Lord's Resistance Army (LRA) allowed the Ugandan authorities to concentrate upon disarming the Karimojong and establishing primacy over the pastoralists. Beginning in 2001 the attempts to de-Kalashnikov the Karimojong oscillated between promises of greater economic and social support by the Ugandan government and the use of the Ugandan military to conduct armed interventions into Karamoja in order to seize arms.[29]

As with all central governments within Kalashnikov cultures, the Ugandan authorities were in a weakened state at the onset of the new century. The depredations of successive corrupt and brutalizing regimes, the impact of the AIDS epidemic and the actions of Joseph Kony and the LRA had all undermined the capacity of the state to control the substate elements within its boundaries. In Karamoja the authority of the government in Kampala was perceived as marginal and negative and its attempts to halt the neo-modernist style of raiding were perceived as ineffective and unwelcome. Therefore when, in 2001, the Ugandan authorities requested that the Karimojong voluntarily disarm, this request was met with silent opposition and resistance (during the two tranches of the voluntary disarmament program only 3,300 of the estimated tens of thousands of weapons in Karimoja were handed in).[30] Confronted with this failure, the Ugandan government decided upon a program of forceful or involuntary disarmament and inevitably this led to armed conflict with the pastoralists.

The Uganda People's Defence Forces (UPDF) had always been treated as an alien and occupying force in Karamoja and when in 2002 they began their "interventions" in search of arms, the pastoralists reacted as they would toward an invading army. In some cases the resistance was active and army patrols were ambushed and in other cases the Karimojong simply refused to comply with the demands for disarmament. In its turn the UPDF began a campaign that emphasized "cordon and search," in which the military sequestered whole villagers within an armed circle and then conducted searches for firearms. As with all such campaigns there were inevitable abuses of power and human rights and by 2006 these issues had become a matter of international concern.[31]

Conducting operations against armed groups within a hostile environment is always a test of discipline. There is an impetus to punish the available population when the armed fighters cannot be engaged and with an undisciplined and nervous military the opportunity for rape, pillage, and destruction is always present. Investigations conducted by the UN indicated that the UPDF engaged in all such practices in Karamoja, sometimes casually and sometimes in an organized fashion.[32] In "cordon and search"-type operations frustrations over failure to find arms are often vented against the most vulnerable in the target area and, as with Karamoja, the elderly, women, and children become victims. If the military force itself has been attacked, there is also a wellspring of anger and fear that encourages reprisals against the civilian population. The end result is that what began as an action to disarm a population becomes an armed intervention by an occupying army with civilians as victims and hostages. It is an irony that in most cases the armed males have removed themselves from the search area and few weapons are left to be found through the "cordon and search" technique. In some cases when the UPDF arrested and held villagers hostage until guns were produced, the villagers had to sell cattle and buy guns in order to give them to the soldiers.[33]

There is a perennial issue when states have failed to exert sovereignty within their borders for a prolonged period of time. De facto partition takes place and reassertion of sovereignty often requires the agents of sovereignty (the military and other security forces) to in essence reconquer from within. In the case of Kalashnikov cultures this intervention, almost by definition, will be resisted. This resistance might be fuelled by a spirit of independence, but more likely resistance will be stiffened by the belief that opportunities afforded by being beyond governance will disappear once dominance by the state is reestablished. Kalashnikov enclaves are nations without statehood and this allows them to engage in practices that the international system abhors in respect to states. These practices, which in the case of the Karimojong include the metamorphosis of cattle raiding from warrior ethic to commercial enterprise, can have a deleterious effect upon economies and societies beyond their parochial borders, and in many ways the state authority has an obligation to bring the challengers back within the boundaries of sovereignty. The process of reclamation, however, is rarely, if ever, easy or pleasant.

Sometimes the sovereign power is not able to summon enough authority to confront the agents of the Kalashnikov culture and in that case intervention by an external entity may be required. The Enhanced Cooperation Programme between Australia and Papua New Guinea was declared unconstitutional by the PNG supreme court in 2005 and the Australian police officers left the country after eighteen months. This somewhat low-level intervention was trumped by the issue of sovereignty, even when the control over that sovereignty was threatened by tribal warfare and raskolism. Whether 230 Australian police officers could have succeeded in containing or defeating the raskol gangs is open to question but the PNG police were arguably unable to achieve that effect on their own. When the balance between weakened state and strengthening armed groups tips toward the latter, it is difficult to redress the balance without somehow adding weight to the side of the state. This can take the form of strengthened leadership, perhaps even dictatorship, or in the form of an external actor intervening for benevolent or self-interested reasons. That such intervention is fraught with dangers for all parties is obvious but so is the laissez-faire alternative.

Making the case for intervention is easier if Kalashnikov cultures are considered as "crises in the making" that demand attention from the international community. In the case of PNG the motivation for Australian intervention was partly that of a concerned former administrator, but it was also that of a neighbor who considered a failed state to its immediate north as a security issue. If the raskols were to predominate then drugs, arms, uncontrolled immigration, piracy, and even terrorists could flow unchecked from the island into Australia. The relationship also needed supporting in order to protect Australian mining interests in PNG and Bougainville, as well as to ensure that Australian financial aid was not squandered. In the context of Australian intervention in East Timor, the effort in PNG was minor but it did signal that the Canberra government was willing to play an active role in stabilizing its neighborhood. Whether such interventions, benevolently motivated or not, can succeed when a Kalashnikov culture has gone beyond the tipping point is unclear.

In regard to the favelas of Rio de Janeiro, the Brazilian Kalashnikov counterculture was one that embraced both the disarmament approach and that of intervention-from-within. In December 2003 the "Statute of Disarmament" passed through the National Congress, providing for the most stringent arms control in modern Brazilian history.[34] This law raised the age for purchasing firearms from 21 to 25, prohibited the carrying of firearms, allowed for psychological and proficiency testing, and required that a national referendum take place on a complete ban on firearms sales to civilians. The law itself was the result of pressure from such groups as Viva Rio that, through demonstrations, published research, and contact with the media had raised awareness on the topic of gun deaths. A flurry of legislative proposals had preceded the Statute of Disarmament and in the climate of increasing urban violence some sort of political response was inevitable. The law that resulted was designed to control the availability of arms, but it also contained punitive elements such as minimum sentencing for illegal possession of guns, defining arms trafficking as a distinct and separate crime, and identifying trading in the Kalashnikov and other like weapons as worthy of harsh sentencing.

The referendum on the complete ban on civilian ownership of firearms took place in October 2005 and the proposal was soundly defeated.[35] A well-orchestrated and managed campaign against the proposal, together with a series of political scandals that undermined faith in the national government of Brazil, overwhelmed the antigun movement that had given birth to the Statute of Disarmament just two years earlier. Those against an outright ban used many of the traditional arguments of arms control oppositionists: criminals would still be able to acquire arms, civilians would be more vulnerable to criminal activities, the Brazilian firearms industry would be unfairly victimized, people in rural areas who needed firearms in pursuit of a livelihood would be disproportionately affected. Placed within the context of a persuasive media campaign, these arguments resonated with enough Brazilians to overwhelm the less well organized and less well funded groups that favored the ban. As with disarmament programs elsewhere, the citizens of Brazil were unwilling to give up the comfort provided by the individual ownership of firearms and to cede their personal security to the state. This is a further indicator that when insecurity becomes chronic and constant it is difficult for authorities to retrieve the confidence of the populace.

As part of the Statute of Disarmament approach to gang violence the Brazilians also engaged in a gun buyback program. More than 450,000 firearms were bought in and in consequence the value of black market arms increased considerably.[36] But although the availability of arms was impacted by the Statute, the level of gang violence itself was not diminished and the military was called upon to intervene on a number of occasions. The Brazilian army had intervened against the gangs during the period 1994–1995 and Operation Rio had become notorious for examples of human rights abuses by the military.[37] The army moved against the favela gangs again in 2004 and in 2006 and 2007.[38] In a country where the military had staged coups in the past there was a potential danger in the civil power admitting that it had lost control of the security situation in the largest Brazilian cities. In addition, the army's rules of engagement when patrolling the favelas were always unclear. Although the military were called upon to "police" the slum areas, by implication the police themselves were outgunned and outnumbered and therefore there was an expectation that the military should use overwhelming force to control the gangs. But the military was constrained by political sensitivities related to the period of the military dictatorship and there was some confusion as to what was allowable and what was not.[39]

The essential messiness of Kalashnikov cultures ensures that any solutions to the problem of Kalashnikov enculturation are themselves messy and amorphous. Even if disarmament is a key to controlling or minimizing the effects of Kalashnikov enculturation, at what level and in what manner disarmament should take place will be circumstantial. The prospect of a comprehensive and enforceable global control regime targeting SALW appeared, after the failure of the 2001 conference, unlikely in the foreseeable future and local disarmament efforts, such as those practiced in Mozambique, rarely had an impact upon the climate of insecurity. Similarly, intervention was often stymied by ambiguities over the role of the military or heavily armed police, especially when such intervention came from outside of the country. In places such as Somalia, even forceful intervention by a large neighbor (Ethiopia) could not confront the extant Kalashnikov culture without itself becoming enmeshed in the political and economic complexities of that culture.

Stopping arms reaching the Kalashnikov cultures or from leaving the cultures and infecting neighboring states is one area in which the international community might appear to have a greater level of common concern. Regulating and controlling arms brokers would also appear to be one activity that might pay dividends but history does not indicate that such controls have inhibited the gray and black marketeers. Countries such as Canada, Sweden, and the United States have laws and regulations that require registration by arms brokers and they even extend their mandate beyond their shores, but lack of political will and of resources necessary to monitor the activities of arms brokers has undermined enforcement practices.[40] The Wazan case illustrated the deliberate complexity of many arms transactions and how difficult it can be to allocate accountability for actions taken by individuals who may never have direct contact with the weapons. Even when individuals are identified and international warrants are issued, as in the case of Viktor Bout, the protection afforded by governments to such persons allows them to continue with their activities.[41] This protection might be afforded through the corruption of government officials or it might be that such individuals can be useful when governments themselves need to avail themselves of the services offered by the gray market, as was the case with the Iran-Contra affair and in the supply of arms to the mujahedin in Afghanistan.

When political pressure is applied to states that are shipping arms into conflict zones the result can be positive. In the case of Bulgaria it was the prospect of entry into the North Atlantic Treaty Organization (NATO) and into the European Union that led to tighter controls being placed upon Bulgarian arms exporters.[42] In respect to East Africa the pressure came from the realization by the regional states that arms traffickers were exploiting the lack of coordination between the states and that uncontrolled arms posed a threat to them all. The result of this realization was the Nairobi Protocol for the Prevention, Control and Reduction of Small Arms and Light Weapons in the Great Lakes Region and the Horn of Africa, which was achieved in 2000.[43] The protocol, sometimes called the Nairobi Declaration, called upon the states of the region to cooperate on cross-border operations, to police the arms trade in their own countries and to aid the United Nations and other intergovernmental organizations in their exposure of arms traffickers. Like other well-intentioned regional initiatives (there were similar declarations on the trade in small arms in West Africa, Europe, South Asia, and the Americas in the year 2000), the objectives of the Nairobi Declaration were laudable but they proved difficult to implement. The fact that the declaration itself emanated from one of the most corrupt countries in the world (Kenya) was not auspicious and indeed in the years following the signing of the protocol the United Nations was able to tie most of the countries in the region to arms trafficking into Somalia, southern Sudan, and the Great Lakes area.[44]

If regional agreements are supported by political will then there are activities that could be curtailed by committed governments. Standardization of end user certificates, which has been discussed since the 1960s, could avoid the confusion over what is a valid request for a government-to-government transfer and what is a false or fake transfer request. Similarly, the standardization of transport and transit documentation might constrain shippers from participating in sanctions busting or other illegal transfer activities. Requiring all arms and ammunition manufacturers to clearly stamp their products with identifying codes would also be useful in the forensic determination of the origin of weapons. Identifying and monitoring ships and aircraft that are used by illicit and illegal arms traffickers could also be regularized in such a way as to overcome the problem of constantly changing tail numbers and names of vessels. Additional radar coverage, particularly in relation to the movement of arms in African air space, would also be helpful, if only to supply more evidence that could be used in name-and-shame United Nations reports.

A step beyond naming-and-shaming is arrest and prosecution under international law and, while arms traffickers have traditionally had little to fear in this respect, the overlords of Kalashnikov cultures could be more vulnerable. The constitution of the Sierra Leone war crimes tribunal, following that of the Balkans war crimes trials, indicated that the lords of chaos within Kalashnikov cultures could not escape retribution in perpetuity. The arrest and trial of the former president of Liberia, Charles Taylor, in respect to events in neighboring Sierra Leone appeared to extend culpability for depredations beyond the immediate territory under his direct control, and this example could have a salutary effect upon those of like habits. But the effect could also be one in which, with the example of Taylor and Serbia's Milosevic before them, the warlords become intransigent and unwilling to give up power lest they too become plaintiffs before the bar of international justice. At worst this could ensure the prolongation of conflict within Kalashnikov cultures and at best it could result in amnesty being granted to the leaders of armed groups within the cultures.

At the risk of being crass, there is no "magic bullet" in terms of arresting the proliferation or digression of Kalashnikov cultures. Even when, as with Northern Ireland, the number of armed men is small and the central authority is strong, it can take decades of conflict before there is movement toward permanent peace and disarmament. In most Kalashnikov cultures the central authority weakens over time and those who are under arms achieve de facto devolution. The strength of this devolution can be seen in the neighboring countries of Afghanistan and Pakistan, where even intervention by powerful external forces and the presence of a military regime cannot overwhelm the fragmented but aggressive armed tribes and clans. It is also an unfortunate truism that the economic opportunities provided by Kalashnikov enculturation are often more tangible and reach down further into the social strata than do the formal economies of traditional states. Poppies or qat, grown within the enclaves of Kalashnikov cultures, may be dangerous and debilitating exports but the return on investment eclipses anything that might be viable in the uncertain soil, literal and figurative, of Afghanistan and Yemen. Any formula that would address the problems that accompany Kalashnikov enculturation must also solve the issues that have proven to be beyond the wit of communism and capitalism to solve.

Kalashnikov Future

There is no evidence that Kalashnikov cultures are a transient phenomenon. The conditions that have fostered and encouraged the issue remain in place and attempts to overcome or mitigate the effects do not appear to be having an impact upon extant Kalashnikov cultures or on stemming the creation of new ones. There are, however, lessons that can be learned from the evolution of the first generation of Kalashnikov cultures that could be useful in understanding how and why they develop and in attempting to control the worst excesses of these societies.

Places such as Yemen, Afghanistan, East Africa, and the tribal areas of Pakistan easily morphed from weapons cultures into Kalashnikov cultures. The laws and understandings that were able to keep violence in check in the pre-Kalashnikov era were not robust enough to withstand the vulgarization of violence that occurred with the proliferation of the Kalashnikov and the RPG. Warrior codes that had prevailed for generations were made moot by the availability of weapons that did not require the prowess of the warrior in order to kill or intimidate. What might appear at first sight to be an incremental change in weapons capability became, through the numbers available and the technological variant, the street-level equivalent of the shift that occurred after the American civil war. As the latter betokened the beginning of war in the industrial age at the state level so did the instruments of the Kalashnikov era at the social level. The clumsy firepower of the "people's weapon" allowed men, women, and children to participate in battle in a manner that their stature, education, or discipline would have disallowed them in earlier times.

When the Soviet Union, China, and the other Second World powers proliferated the Kalashnikov at least part of their motivation lay in the belief that they were also proliferating an ideology and facilitating the liberation of peoples. Similarly, when the United States sent arms to the Afghan mujahedin it also foresaw an end-state that was positive. As articulated by John Bolton, the transfer of small arms and light weapons should not be restricted to deals between governments because such transfers could also be an instrument of freedom against tyranny. But the iron law of second- and third-order consequences and effects was always at play during the gestation period of Kalashnikov cultures. In a political environment in which weak, postcolonial states were attempting to define their national identities and in which armies and police forces were metamorphosing from instruments of imperial enforcement to useful guarantors of national security, the millions of weapons that ebbed and flowed around the world always threatened to derail the nascent states. The promoters of socialism, of course, hoped that this would be the case but the guns lasted longer than the ideology, and for the peoples living where the arms had been cast ashore the prospect of liberation through force of arms became the reality of imprisonment through Kalashnikov enculturation.

Part of the problem is the perception that "small" arms equals small problem. Arms transfers have always been recognized as having an inherently political element attached to them and as such they have been placed in a special category of commerce. Sometimes, when this knowledge was forgotten or displaced by seemingly more important contingencies (as in the case of U.S. arms transfers to Iran under the late Shah), the consequences were dire. But for the most part the transfer of aircraft, ships, and tanks have been conducted with a concern for the transfer of power that ensues. But the transfer of small arms, even in large numbers, has not received the same level of scrutiny and concern. While it is true that most developed countries do place small arms on their export control lists, at the policy level small arms are still in the allowable category when dealing with states that are known human rights abusers but which are useful friends. It is also true that where weapons of mass destruction command an extraordinary level of interest and expenditure in terms of constraining their proliferation, the same cannot be said of efforts to constrain the illicit and illegal trade in small arms. Even when the catalog of Kalashnikov cultures encompasses such incubators of terrorism as Pakistan, Yemen, and Somalia the dotted line of association is not made solid. Perhaps, in these times of irregular warfare, where the weapons of choice are small but the effects are cumulative, it might not be inappropriate to consider a modified view of the threat of small arms in the same way that, post-9/11, we have reconsidered the threat of terrorism.

If such a reconsideration included at least some element of interventionism, then some attention must be given to Kalashnikov cultures as operating environments for modern militaries. As Operation Iraqi Freedom (OIF) and Operation Enduring Freedom (OEF) have moved beyond the conventional phase there has emerged an interest in understanding the cultural context that sustains and encourages the local fighters. Arguably somewhat belatedly, the wisdom of "knowing the enemy" became part of the evolving strategy in Iraq and Afghanistan. Much of the cultural context is specific to the unique social environment of each country but there are also some generic elements of Kalashnikov cultures that can be studied and that could prove useful in future interventions. Perhaps first and foremost is the knowledge that preventing Kalashnikov enculturation is always preferable to confronting a heavily weaponized society. Even if, at first sight, it might appear auspicious to arm a populace in support of a military strategy, the inability to re-trieve those weapons is an invitation to lawlessness at best and insurgency at worst. Similarly, small arms control and destruction should be placed at the same level as the control of major weapons. Soldiers should be taught how to de-commission weapons in the field (removing bolts, bending barrels), special operators should target arsenals so that they are not looted ahead of an advancing force and penalties for carrying or owning personal weapons should be made clear to the populace and enforced. This latter, however, does create a variation on the (in-)security dilemma that must be addressed whenever arms control and Kalashnikov cultures are considered together.

A sub-element within all Kalashnikov cultures is the ownership of arms as an instrument of self-protection. An explicit aspect of all Kalashnikov cultures is that the ability of the host state to provide law and enforcement is undermined or completely negated by the armed groups (tribes, clans, militias, gangs) who control their territory. The rule of law is either supplanted by the security provided through membership of the armed group or it is a case of each individual providing for their own security. To encourage or enact the disarmament of the individual is, without being in a position to guarantee them physical security or protecting them with laws, to place them at the mercy of those that remain armed. However, to allow individuals to remain armed is to allow latent insurgents and other substate elements to retain the very instruments that rob the state of the ability to enforce law and order in the first place. Indeed, as individuals learn that in the context of Kalashnikov cultures the individual, armed or not, is still a victim-in-waiting, they will either gravitate toward militias and other groups for protection or will establish their own group, which might in turn become vigilantist or predatory in nature. For commanders in the field, this is a difficult dilemma and is yet one more reason why as many instruments of state authority as possible should be allowed to remain in place during the transitional or, as it is known within the U.S. military, Phase Four period between the end of open hostilities and the beginning of reconstruction. It might be distasteful to allow judges, policemen, and military officers to retain their authority after the regime that they served has been overthrown but the violence that fills a vacuum of power is just as distasteful and its implications for the society as a whole are even more morally fraught than is cohabitation with a former enemy.

A conventional military that must fight its way into a Kalashnikov culture, and then hold what it has "won," is confronted with a set of problems and options that are daunting and often not soluble through conventional means. The battlespace is less a physical environment than it is one of competing interests, complex relationships, and hyperviolence. The population as a whole will be either numbed or inured to violence and threats of physical retribution by the conventional force will not have the same impact as they would in a normative society. The use of weapons to resolve disputes, some of which might appear trivial to the occupiers or that might (in the case of honor killings, for example) not equate to any aspect of their own societies, will increase the likelihood of firefights, polarization, and lethal misunderstandings. Children and young people carrying weapons will also create confusion among the soldiery, as will the displaced persons who will congregate near military installations for the security they offer. The lack of law, which may or may not denote lawlessness, will not allow the occupiers to hand off problems to a civil authority but at the same time they must endeavor to master the complexities of tribal, clan, and militia "laws" in order to utilize them in place of state law.

Modern armies can approach and confront Kalashnikov cultures successfully, particularly since not all such societies are created equal. Displays of weapons technology (aircraft, armored vehicles, artillery) that might not succeed in one place (Somalia) might have a chastening effect in another (Sierra Leone). Kalashnikov cultures that are demonstrating manifestations of conflict fatigue (spontaneous street demonstrations against violence, the fragmentation of armed groups, the emergence of peace parties or movements) might also welcome intervention. But acquiescence can quickly turn to hostility if the imposition of order threatens the livelihoods of those whose economic activities relied upon the autonomy of the culture. If, as with the arms manufacturers of Darra in NWFP and the arms bazaars in Yemen and Somalia, these economic activities are a direct contributing factor to the level of insecurity in the area, then a choice has to be made as to whether to grasp the nettle or to turn a blind eye.

The militaries of advanced postindustrial countries most often prepare to fight the wars that they want to fight rather than the wars that are most likely. The preferred war is one in which technology, training, and professionalism can be leveraged against a less well prepared but like enemy. In many ways Kalashnikov cultures are the antithesis of this preferred battleground because in nearly all dimensions they lack the clarity that is inherent with conventional state-on-state wars. When confronting Kalashnikov cultures the fog of war is replaced with an environment that is a parallel universe in which criminality, superstition, random death, and opaque chains of authority cohabit within a soup of chronic insecurity and constant uncertainty. Conventional armies may train and prepare to be practitioners of applied violence but in the context of Kalashnikov cultures, where everyday violence is the norm and its application is unvarying, such armies can easily become disoriented by the alien habitat. However, simply to declare Kalashnikov cultures as no-go zones for conventional militaries is to allow those cultures to become bases for anyone who might need a refuge and protection within these parallel universes. It will also allow them to become nodes of infection that could create Kalashnikov meta-cultures, such has occurred in sub-Saharan Africa. Conventional militaries, therefore, should organize, train, and equip to confront these parallel universes with a permanent activity that itself parallels that of preparation for conventional war.

Controlling the movement of weapons as they pass within and between regions can slow the inception of a new Kalashnikov culture or the prolongation of an existing one. As is evidenced by such incidents as those outlined in the Cameron Report, laws and regulations to control the movement of small arms do exist, but they are often either not followed or are undermined by the inexactitude of the regulations or by venal officials. The regularization of documents such as end user certificates and cargo manifests would make the task of enforcement officials that much easier, as would rules requiring the correct certification and identification of ships and aircraft. Identification markings on weapons and ammunition would also allow investigators to trace the point of origin of the basic currency of Kalashnikov cultures and perhaps even to prepare prosecutions against the proliferators themselves.

Other steps might be taken against the lords of chaos who exploit the idiosyncrasies of Kalashnikov cultures. If there are no markets for conflict diamonds, hardwoods, and charcoal from depleted forests, seafood from uncontrolled fishing grounds, and people trafficked for their labor, then much of what makes Kalashnikov cultures attractive to gray and black market entrepreneurs would disappear. The successful demonization of conflict diamonds and the trial of Charles Taylor served to popularize the issue but this was offset by activities elsewhere in Africa and Asia. The omnipresence of drug production and distribution in Kalashnikov cultures is an entire subset of the economic dimension of the cultures and can be so overwhelming in its profitability that it alone can be the creative and nurturing force behind a Kalashnikov culture.

The moral crusade against small arms and light weapons proliferation was, perhaps, one of the casualties of 9/11 and its aftermath. Great events tend to overwhelm complex matters on which there is not a consensus. The failure to achieve that consensus, as typified by the U.S. stand taken at the UN conference in 2001, did not allow the momentum built up by the landmines campaign to result in any meaningful global strategy on arms transfers. In many ways, however, the stable door had, by 2001, remained open too long for any closing to have had a profound impact on the evolution of the first generation of Kalashnikov cultures. The weapons were already proliferated, either during the Cold War or during the years when the likes of Bulgaria exported weapons in an uncontrolled manner. Areas whose precariousness would have been cause for concern by both sides in the balance-of-power world of the Cold War could now be allowed to metamorphose into errant quasi-state entities like Abkhazia or Waziristan. Even when, as in Afghanistan, a Kalashnikov culture morphed into a repressive theocracy, this was deprecated but not seen as having ramifications beyond the immediate region. It was convenient to cast Kalashnikov cultures as manifestations of an anarchy that had already come and to use them as examples of the newly discovered category known as failed states. But Kalashnikov cultures have their own dynamic, their own raison d'etre, their own structures and their own strengths and vulnerabilities. Since they cannot be cast adrift they must be studied and understood in all their post-Westphalian complexities and inconsistencies. If nothing else, one of the lessons of 9/11 should be that bad things come out of dangerous and neglected places and Kalashnikov cultures, in their prickly remoteness, are good examples of where bad things may lie.

Notes

Chapter 1

1. "Due to the long tradition and the special organization of the Swiss armed forces as a militia army, special rules are applicable to army weapons.... Swiss soldiers and officers keep their personal weapons at home. After they have left the army, they may keep those arms in order to continue practicing..." Fact Sheet, Gun Ownership in Switzerland, Embassy of Switzerland in Washington, DC. Available at www.eda.admin.ch/washington_emb/e/home/legaff/Factgunown.html.

2. The second amendment to the United States Constitution reads: A well-regulated militia, being necessary to the security of a free state, the right of the people to keep and bear arms, shall not be infringed.

3. Oskar Verkaaik, *Migrants and Militants: Fun and Urban Violence in Pakistan* (Princeton, NJ: Princeton University Press, 2004), p. 128.

4. "... the tradition of karo kari was mostly practiced for property and revenge," Statement of the Governor of Sindh Province, Pakistan, June 21, 2003, Press Release, Sindh Governor House, Pakistan.

5. See, for example, Paul Jackson, "The March of the Lord's Resistance Army," *Small Wars and Insurgencies*, Vol. 13, No. 3 (Autumn 2002); Oxfam, "Conflict's Children: The Human Cost of Small Arms in Kitgum and Kotido, Uganda," January 2001; Human Rights Watch, "The Scars of Death: Children Abducted by the Lord's Resistance Army in Uganda," London, September 1997.

6. Stephen Ellis, *The Mask of Anarchy* (New York: New York University Press, 1999).

7. William Fowler, *Operation Barras: The SAS Rescue Mission Sierra Leone 2000* (London: Weidenfeld and Nicholson, 2004).

8. David Keen, *The Economic Functions of Violence in Civil Wars* (London: International Institute for Strategic Studies/ Oxford University Press, 1998).

9. Rachel Monaghan, "One Merchant, One Bullet: The Rise and Fall of PAGAD," *Low Intensity Conflict and Law Enforcement*, Vol. 12, No. 1 (Spring 2004).

10. United States Central Intelligence Agency, *Long-Term Demographic: Reshaping the Geopolitical Landscape*, Washington, DC, July 2001.

11. Mats Utas, *Sweet Battlefields: Youth and the Liberian Civil War.* Dissertation for the Degree of Philosophy in Cultural Anthropolgy presented at Uppsala University, Uppsala, Sweden, 2003, p. 39.

12. Ibid., p. 138.

13. Edward Mogire, *A Preliminary Exploration of the Linkages between Refugees and Small Arms* (Bonn, Germany: Bonn International Center for Conversion, 2004).

14. Taya Weiss, *Local Catalysts, Global Reactions: Cycles of Conflict in the Mano River Basin* (Pretoria, South Africa: Institute for Security Studies, June 2005).

15. Sinclair Dinnen, *Law and Order in a Weak State: Crime and Politics in Papua New Guinea* (Honolulu: University of Hawai'i Press, 2001); Laurie Gunst, *Born Fi' Dead* (New York: Henry Holt, 1995).

16. The reference is to a swampy town in southern Sudan which, in 1898, became the center of a crisis between France and Britain as both claimed imperial sovereignty over the otherwise unimportant spot.

Chapter 2

1. The M16 is the fielded rifle of the United States military. The FAL (Fusil Automatique Legere) was the most common battle rifle of the 1950s and 1960s.

2. Small Arms Survey, *Small Arms Survey 2001* (Oxford: Oxford University Press, 2001), p. 63.

3. Some sources quote a higher figure of 28 rounds per minute. Lee Enfield Rifle Association, http://www.leeenfieldrifleassociation.org.uk.

4. Bruce Canfield, *Complete Guide to United States Military Combat Shotguns* (Woonsocket, RI: Mowbray, 2007), pp. 41–44.

5. Peter Senich, *The German Assault Rifle 1933–1945* (Boulder, CO: Paladin Press, 1987), p. 83.

6. Ibid.

7. Observations by author on visit to the weapons destruction warehouse in Maputo in 2000.

8. Interview, TAE officials, Maputo, 2000.

9. Christina Wille, *How Many Weapons Are There in Cambodia?* (Geneva: Small Arms Survey, June 2006).

10. Yem San Oeun and Rebecca F. Catella, *I Live In Fear: Consequences of Small Arms on Women and Children in Cambodia* (Phnom Penh: Working Group for Weapons Reduction, June 2001).

11. *Asia Times*, April 3, 2007.

12. The M16 has been produced under license in the Philippines, South Korea, Singapore, and Belgium.

13. For a good account of the evolution of the AR15/M16 see R. Blake Stevens and Edward Ezell, *The Black Rifle: M16 Retrospective* (Canada: Colector Grade Publications, 1994).

14. Australian Broadcasting Corporation, AM Radio Show, transcript, May 3, 2006.

15. "US Quietly Shifts Iraqis from AK-47s," *Wall Street Journal*, October 8, 2007.

Chapter 3

1. Except where noted, all factual detail and quotations on the Wazan affair are from the official report, *Commission of Inquiry into Alleged Arms Transactions between ARMSCOR and One Eli Wazan and Other Related Matters*, Johannesburg, June 15, 1995. This document became known as the Cameron Report and will hereafter be referenced as such.

2. *Rapport*, September 18, 1994, as quoted in Cameron Report, p. 2

3. Ibid., 79.

4. Ibid., Appendix 6.

5. Ibid., 30–37.

6. Ibid., 102.

7. "Anatomy of a Sting," *Time*, June 24, 2001.

8. "The Heart of the Illegal Trade," *Forbes*, May 10, 1993.

9. "Light Arms Trading in SE Asia," *Jane's Intelligence Review*, April 2001. This report indicated that Cambodia might have 900,000 small arms within its territory, with another report indicating that there were 250,000 weapons in private hands.

10. "Khmer Arms Find Market with Burmese Minorities," *Bangkok Post*, December 6, 1995.

11. "Land Where a Grenade Sells for a Few Dollars," *South China Morning Post*, March 7, 1993.

12. Pasuk Phongpaichit, Sangsit Phiryarangsan, and Nualnoi Treerat, *Guns, Girls, Gambling, Ganja: Thailand's Illegal Economy and Public Policy* (Bangkok: Silkworm Books, 1999).

13. "Dhaka Terror Attack Highlights Gun Problem," *Daily Star* (Dhaka), August 8, 2002; "Bangladesh: Breeding Ground for Terror," *Asia Times*, September 21, 2002.

14. "Arms Smuggling into Bangladesh," *Saudi Gazette*, April 22, 1996; *Dainik Janakantha*, July 16, 2000.

15. Federal Research Division, Library of Congress, *Terrorist and Organized Crime Groups in the Tri-Border Area (TBA) of South America* (Washington, DC: USGPO, July 2003).

16. Ibid.

17. "In the Party of God," *New Yorker*, October 28, 2002.

18. "Jungle Hub for Worlds Outlaws," *Los Angeles Times*, August 24, 1998.

19. "Gun Runners from Miami Give Brazilian Drug Gangs Lead in Arms Race," *New York Times*, February 23, 1992.

20. *O Globo* (Rio de Janeiro), May 10, 1998.

21. Latin American Regional Reports: Southern Cone, Latin American Newsletters, Ltd, *Brazil and US Act to Halt Arms Flow*, October 17, 1996.

22. Ken Silverstein, *Private Warriors* (New York: Verso, 2000), p. 140.

23. Cameron Report, 31, 33.

24. "The Commission heard the following allegations from Armscor and other sources: Wazan was wanted by the Lebanese government on various criminal charges; Der Hovsepian had threatened the life of Steenberg and Vermaak; and Prince Anwar had been involved in drug smuggling," Cameron Report, 85–86.

25. Cameron Report, 39.

26. Ibid., 72–73.

27. Cameron Report, 52–53; "UK Firm Linked to 65 Million Pound Bosnia Arms Shipment," *Sunday Times* (London), July 18, 1993.

28. "Croatia Built Web of Contacts to Evade Weapons Embargo," *The Independent* (London), October 10, 1992.

29. "Illicit Arms Exports Go Unchecked," *The Independent* (London), June 22, 1992.

30. "Senate Sub-Committee Report Criticises Belgian Arms Exports," *Reuters*, November 14, 1991.

31. "Bulgaria Admits Arms Sales to Iraq," *UPI*, September 8, 1992.

32. Cameron Report, 52.

33. Ibid., 49.

34. *New York Times*, November 9, 1986.

35. Cameron Report, 32.

36. Ibid., 37–46.

37. Douglas Farah, "Victor Bout: Merchant of Death," *Foreign Policy* (November/December 2006), 38–47.

38. United Nations, *Report of the Group of Experts on the Democratic Republic of Congo*, S/2005/30, New York, January 25, 2005.

39. UK House of Commons, All Parliamentary Group on the Great Lakes Region, *Arms Flow in Eastern DR Region*, APPG-03-04, London, December 2004.

40. Farah, "Victor Bout: Merchant of Death."

41. Cameron Report, 36–62.

42. Ibid.

43. Ibid., 135.

Chapter 4

1. David Keen, *The Economic Functions of Violence in Civil Wars* (London: International Institute for Strategic Studies, 1998).

2. Paul Collier, *Economic Causes of Civil Conflict and Their Implications for Policy* (Washington, DC: World Bank, 2000).

3. UK Prime Minister, Edward Heath, 1970.

4. United Nations, *Report of the Monitoring Group on Somalia*, S/2005/153, New York, February 14, 2005, p. 13.

5. Ibid. See also Sabrina Grosse-Kettler, *External Actors in Stateless Somalia* (Bonn, Germany: Bonn International Center for Conversion (BICC), 2004).

6. Ibid.

7. Ibid., pp. 19–22.

8. Hussein Abdilahi Bulhan, *Survey of Small Arms in Somaliland* (Hargeisa (Somaliland): Center for Creative Solutions, 2004).

9. Ekkehrad Forberg and Ulf Terlinden, *Small Arms in Somaliland: Their Role and Diffusion* (Berlin: Berlin Information Center for Transatlantic Security, March 1999), pp. 39–42.

10. "Philippine City's Illegal Economy Rests on Firearms' Longstanding and Lucrative Allure," *San Jose Mercury News*, March 4, 2001.

11. Philippine Center on Transnational Crime, *Illicit Trafficking and Manufacturing of Firearms: Philippine Context* (Cebu, undated).

12. "Rest, Work and Play by the Gun," *Financial Times*, April 19, 1997.

13. "Aiming for Legitimacy," *Asiaweek*, January 19, 1996; "Filipino Gunsmiths Are Making a Killing," *Taipei Times*, May 7, 2005.

14. "Clandestine Firearms Calling the Shots in Delhi," *Times of India*, May 27, 2003.

15. "Killing with Kattas," *The Week*, September 13, 1998.

16. M. Krishnan, *Gunsmiths' Cottage Industry Poses Growing Threat*, at http:www.oneworld.org/Gemini/feb98/India.html.

17. "The Kraal Shotgun: A Nifty Killer," *Africa News*, December 5, 1997.

18. United Nations Development Program, *Burundi: The Impact of Small Arms and Armed Violence on Women*, 2004.

19. Ibid.

20. Umalt Dudayev, "Chechnya's Homemade Weapons Fuel War," Institute for War and Peace Reporting, April 15, 2004.

21. In Yerevan (Armenia) the author viewed homemade weapons that the Armenian militias used during the Nagorno-Karabakh conflict. The weapons were inventive, crude, and lethal.

22. "IRA Factories Used to Develop Weapons," *The Irish Times*, August 18, 1997.

23. The Home Office gave testimony that in every case where an automatic weapon had been used in a crime in the UK between 1995 and 2000 every weapon was a legally deactivated weapon that had been illegally re-activated. UK House of Commons, Minutes of Evidence before the Select Committee on Home Affairs, London, January 12, 2000.

24. U.S. Department of Labor, Bureau of Labor Statistics, at http://www.bls.gov/oes/current.

25. United Nations, *Report of the Panel of Experts on Somalia*, S/2003/1035, New York, November 4, 2003, p. 11.

26. United Nations, *Report of the Monitoring Group on Somalia*, S/2005/625, New York, October 5, 2005, pp. 25–27.

27. Ibid.

28. Tamuna Shonia, "Abkhazia: Lucrative Farms Attract Mafia," Environment News Service/Institute for War and Peace Reporting, August 25, 2003.

29. UN Report, S/2005/625, pp. 27–28.

30. Global Witness, Same Old Story: *A Background Study on Natural Resource in the Democratic Republic of Congo* (Washington, DC: Global Witness, 2004).

31. Ibid., pp. 19–23.

32. United Nations, *Group of Experts on the Democratic Republic of Congo Report*, S/2005/30, New York, January 25, 2005; United Nations, *Group of Experts on the Democratic Republic of Congo*, S/2004/551, New York, July 15, 2004.

33. "A Dream Perverted," *The Guardian* (London), June 29, 2005.

34. United Nations Office for the Coordination of Humanitarian Affairs, IRIN, "Nigeria: Focus on the Menace of Student Cults," August 1, 2002.

35. Human Rights Watch, *Emergence of Armed Groups in Rivers State*, New York, January 2005.

36. Human Rights Watch, *The Warri Crisis; Fueling Violence*, New York, November 2003.

37. Ibid.

38. "War Talk in Nigeria Shakes Oil Markets," *Business Day Africa*, October 8, 2004.

39. "Greed and the Trail of Death," *The Independent* (London), May 25, 2006.

40. World Health Organization, *Report of WHO/FAO/OIE Joint Consultation on Emerging Zoonotic Diseases* (Geneva: WHO, May 2004).

41. "WHO Issues Alert on Ebola in Congo," CNN.com, September 11, 2007.

Chapter 5

1. David Isby, "Afghanistan: Low Intensity Conflict with Major Power Intervention," in *Low Intensity Conflict: Old Threads in a New World* (Boulder, CO: Westview, 1992), p. 206.

2. Chris Smith, "Light Weapons and Ethnic Conflict in South Asia," in Jeffrey Boutwell, Michael Klare, and Laura Reed (eds.), *Lethal Commerce: The Global Trade in Small Arms and Light Weapons* (Cambridge: American Academy of Arts and Science 1, 1995), p. 64.

3. Congressional Research Service, *Afghan Refugees: Current Status and Future Prospects* (Washington, DC: January 26, 2007).

4. BBC News, March 2, 2005.

5. Robert Wirsing, *The Baluchis and Pathans*, Minority Rights Group Report No. 48, London, 1987.

6. George Thayer, *The War Business* (New York: Simon and Schuster, 1969), p. 150.

7. "Experts Back Startling Heroin Claim," *The Guardian* (London), October 3, 2001.

8. "Woman Killed, Another Injured in Landmine Blast," *The Frontier Post* (Peshawar), December 4, 1999.

9. "Thirteen Killed in Different Incidents," *The Frontier Post* (Peshawar), December 6/7, 1999.

10. "Three Killed as Rival Afghan Groups Clash," *The Frontier Post* (Peshawar), January 24, 2000.

11. "A Menacing Edge to Pakistan's Cities," *International Herald Tribune*, March 15, 1996.

12. "The Rise and Fall of a Drug Lord," *Forbes*, October 16, 1997.

13. "Villagers Appeal to President and PM to Stop Hoodlum," *Daily Times* (Pakistan), October 22, 2004.

14. "Gunmaker Feels Pain of Law and Order," *Asia Times*, May 30, 1997; "Pakistan Ordnance Factories to Build Arms Factory at Darra," *Dawn* (Pakistan) October 28, 2000.

15. "Pakistan Plans to Take Over Arms Bazaar," *The Independent* (London), July 31, 1998.

16. Ibid.

17. Rauf Kiasara, *Deweaponisation of Afghan Refugee Camps Ordered in Pakistan*, London, International Action Network on Small Arms, November 25, 2001.

18. In a previous nationwide attempt to retrieve unlicensed Kalashnikovs in 1989 the authorities had only been able to retrieve 486 weapons. " Kalashnikov Culture," *Far Eastern Economic Review*, February 22, 1990.

19. "Call to Relax Ban on Licensed Weapons," *The Frontier Post*, March 17, 2000.

20. "Ten Million Illegal Weapons in Civilian Hands," *Daily Times* (Pakistan), June 9, 2005.

21. "Tribal Areas: Gunsmiths Leave Their Profession, Look for New Jobs," *Weekly Independent* (Lahore), July 7–13, 2005.

22. *The Frontier Post*, December 21, 1999.

23. "Mosque Blast Kills 47," *Asia Times*, July 9, 2003.

24. Arif Hasan, "Karachi and the Global Nature of Urban Violence," *The Urban Age*, I(4) (Summer 1993).

25. Ibid.

26. "Sectarian Killing Persists," *Dawn* (Pakistan), March 28, 2001.

27. O. Verkaaik, *Migrants and Militants* (Princeton, NJ: Princeton University Press, 2004), Chapter 4.

28. *Agence France Presse*, March 2, 1999.

29. "Guns for Hire Fuel Pakistan's Ethnic Battles," *Reuters*, June 2, 1990.

30. "Ethnic Tensions Grip Hyderabad," *Los Angeles Times*, October 5, 1988.

31. "Corruption in Pakistan's Schools," *Boston Globe*, May 23, 1999.

32. BBC News, July 27, 1999.

33. "A Nation Challenged," *New York Times*, October 29, 2001.

34. "Bomb Hits Karachi Mosque," *Pakistan Times*, June 1, 2004.

35. "Two Suicide Bombings," *Dawn* (Pakistan), June 9, 2004.

36. Amnesty International, *Targeted Killings of Health Professionals in Pakistan*, London, December 17, 2000; *Dawn* (Pakistan), May 23, 2002.

37. "In Skulduggery's City, Afghan Feuds Find Home," *New York Times*, November 20, 1989.

38. "Pakistan Fights to End 'Kalshnikov Culture,'" *The Washington Times*, August 20, 2002.

39. "Kalashnikov Culture Keeps Feuds Alive," *Chicago Tribune*, November 27, 2001.

Chapter 6

1. Harold Ingrams, *Uganda: A Crisis of Nationhood* (London: Her Majesty's Stationery Office, 1960), pp. 289–291.

2. Neville Dyson-Hudson, *Karimojong Politics* (Oxford: Clarendon Press, 1966), pp. 230–237.

3. Ibid., pp. 242–249.

4. "70 Killed In Raid, Women and Children," *The Monitor* (Kampala), June 2, 1997.

5. "500 Killed by Rustlers in Northeast Uganda Since March," *Agence France Presse*, September 9, 1997.

6. Charles Emunyu Ocan, *Pastoral Crisis in North-Eastern Uganda: The Changing Significance of Cattle Raids* (Kampala: Centre for Basic Research, 1992), p. 14.

7. The distinction between "redistributive" and "predatory" raiding is made in Jeremy Armon and Robin Mearns, *Conflict and Vulnerability and Famine: Livestock Raiding in Turkana, Kenya* (London: International Institute for Environment and Development, 1998), pp. 8–10.

8. Michael D. Quam, "Creating Peace in an Armed Society," *African Studies Quarterly*, Vol 1, No 1 (1997), 5.

9. Ibid.

10. Ali Mazrui, *Soldiers and Kinsmen in Uganda: The Making of a Military Ethnocracy* (Beverly Hills/London: Sage Publications), p. 61.

11. Ingrams, *Uganda*, p. 298.

12. Quam, "Creating Peace in an Armed Society," p. 5.

13. "UPDF Miss Bull's Eye in Karamoja," *The Monitor* (Kampala), September 22, 1999.

14. Benjamin White Haefele, *Islamic Fundamentalism and Pagad: An Internal Security Issue for South Africa?* (South Africa: Centre for Military Studies, University of Stellenbosch, 1997).

15. "Gangsters Declare War on Mandela," *Sunday Times* (London), May 17, 1998.

16. Ibid.

17. "Vigilante Group Sweeps the Suburbs," *Mail & Guardian* (Johannesburg), January 25, 2000, "We Must Work on Their Buttocks," May 15, 2000.

18. "Vigilante Group Faces Split," *Mail & Guardian* (Johannesburg), May 9, 2000.

19. Hendrickson, Armon, and Mearns, *Conflict and Vulnerability*, p. 11.

20. "Police Form Anti-Stock Theft Unit," *The Monitor* (Kampala), September 22, 1999.

21. Integrated Regional Information Network (IRIN), *Focus on Growing Tensions in Karamoja* (Nairobi: United Nations Office for the Coordination of Humanitarian Affairs), March 22, 2000.

22. "Cattle Rustlers Kill Five Soldiers in Uganda," BBC World Service, April 11, 1998.

23. New African, *Mob Justice in Karamoja*, May 1998.

24. "Up to 400 Dead in Ethnic Fighting," IRIN, March 22, 2000.

25. "Raid on Bokora Clan Leaves 140 Dead," IRIN, Weekly Roundup, August 7–13,1999; "Corpses of 500 Ugandans Left to Rot," *Sunday Times*, South Africa, September 19, 1999; "Police Form Anti-Stock Theft Unit," *The Monitor*, September 22, 1999.

26. "Karimojong Take Up Arms Ready for Renewed Fight," *The East African*, October 12,1999; "30 Feared Dead in Inter-Clan Clashes," *New Vision*, May 4, 2000.

27. See Michael Bollig, "Ethnic Conflicts in North-West Kenya: Pokot-Turkana Raiding 1969–84" (Zeitschrift fur Ethnologie, 1990); "Kenya-Population: Arms Race among the Nomads," *Inter Press Service*, June 7, 1995.

28. "Cattle Wars: Poverty, Ignorance Causes," *The Nation (Kenya)* April 26, 1998.

29. "Kenya-Population: Arms Race among the Nomads," *Inter Press Service*, June 7, 1995; "Cattle Rustlers Slaughter 50 in Northeast Kenya," *Agence France Presse*, December 6, 1996.

30. Hendrickson, Armon, Mearns, *Conflict and Vulnerability*, p. 9.

31. "Moi Order on Cattle Rustling," *The Nation* (Kenya), December 23, 1999.

32. "Law and Order Gives Way To Violence," *Mail & Guardian* (Johannesburg), May 10, 1996; "Violence on Rise in South Africa," *Associated Press*, March 25, 1999.

33. "Gun Trade Rampant in Kenya," *Xinhua News Agency*, October 27,1996; "Over 5,000 Unlicenced Guns in Nairobi," *Daily Nation*, July 12, 1999.

34. Hendrickson, Armon, Mearns, *Conflict and Vulnerability*, pp. 9 & 12.

35. Human Rights Watch, "Global Trade, Local Impact: Arms Transfers to All Sides in the Civil War in Sudan," *HRW*, Vol 10, No 4 (August 1998).

36. "Rising Armed Crime in Kenya Linked to SPLA Guns," *The East African* (Nairobi), September 13, 1999.

37. "Slaughter in Turkana," *News Stands Weekly Review*, September 26, 1997.

38. Kenyan Television Network, May 5, 1998.

39. "Who's Fuelling Cattle Rustling By the Pokot?" *The East African* (Nairobi), February 14, 2000.

40. "More Than 280 Assorted Firearms and 1,301 Rounds of Ammunition Have Been Recovered," *The Nation*, July 17, 1998.

Chapter 7

1. Mark Huband, *The Liberian Civil War* (London:Frank Cass, 1998), p. 61.

2. For the most comprehensive coverage of the role of traditional religion in the region's conflicts, see Stephen Ellis, *The Mask of Anarchy* (New York: New York University Press, 1999).

3. See Paul Richards, *Fighting for the Rain Forest: War, Youth and Resources in Sierra Leone* (Oxford and Bloomington: James Currey and Indiana University Press, 1996).

4. Ibid.

5. George Packer, "Gangsta War," *New Yorker*, November 3, 2003.

6. Frances Fukuyama, "The End of History?" *The National Interest*, Summer 1989.

7. Ibid.

8. Mats Udal, *Sweet Battlefields: Youth and the Liberian Civil War*, Dissertation for the degree of Doctor of Philosophy in Cultural Anthropolgy presented at Uppsala University, 2003, pp. 119–138.

9. M. Thabane, "Liphokojoe of Kao: A Study of a Diamond Digger Rebel Group in the Lesotho Highlands," Journal of Southern African Studies, Vol 26, No 1 (March 2000), 105–121.

10. For additional commentary on the social dimension of banditry in Africa, see Donald Crummey, ed., *Banditry, Rebellion and Social Protest in Africa* (London and Portsmouth, NH: James Currey and Heinemann, 1986).

11. Richards, *Fighting for the Rain Forest*, pp. 100–103.

12. United Nations, *Report of the Panel of Experts Appointed Pursuant to Security Council Resolution 1306 (2000), Paragraph 19, in Relation to Sierra Leone, S/2000/1195*, New York, December 20, 2000.

13. For a discussion on weaponry and war in West Africa see John K. Thornton, *Warfare in Atlantic Africa 1500–1800* (London: University College Press, 1999).

14. Small Arms Survey, *Small Arms Survey 2001: Profiling the Problem* (Oxford: Oxford University Press), p. 63.

15. United Nations, *Report of the Panel of Experts Appointed Pursuant to Security Council Resolution 1408(2002), Paragraph 16, Concerning Liberia, S/2002/1115*, New York, UN Security Council, October 25, 2002, pp. 18–22.

16. Ibid.

17. United Nations, *Report of the Panel of Experts pursuant to Security Council Resolution 1343(2001), Paragraph 19, Concerning Liberia, S/2001/1015*, New York, UN Security Council, October 26, 2001, pp. 46–47.

18. Human Rights Watch, *Easy Prey: Child Soldiers in Liberia* (New York: Human Rights Watch, 1994), p. 5.

19. Udal, *Sweet Battlefields*, Chapter 4.

20. See Angela Veal and Aki Stavrou, *Violence, Reconciliation and Identity: The Reintegration of Lord's Resistance Army Child Abductees in Northern Uganda* (Pretoria: Institute for Strategic Studies, 2003).

21. Global Witness, *For a Few Dollars More: How al Qaeda Moved into the Diamond Trade* (London: Global Witness, April 2003).

Chapter 8

1. Paul Dresch, *Tribes, Government, and History in Yemen* (Oxford: Clarendon Press, 1989), pp. 38–42.

2. R.B. Serjeant, "South Arabia," in van Nieuwenhuijza (ed.), *Commoners, Climbers and Notables* (Leiden: E.J. Brill, 1977), pp. 228–229.

3. Dresch, *Tribes, Government and History in Yemen*, p. 109.

4. "Random Armed Killing Is Common in Yemen," *Yemen Times*, May 10–16, 1999.

5. Dresch, *Tribe, Government and History in Yemen*, pp. 39–42.

6. "Multiple Efforts to Solve an Old Tribal Dispute," *Al-Ehya' Al-Arabi*, November 15–21, 1999.

7. "Staggering Crime Facts in Yemen," *Yemen Times*, November 22–28, 1999; *Al-Ehya' Al-Arabi*, November 15–21, 1999.

8. *Yemen Gateway*, Security Incidents in Yemen 1998/99, http://www.al-bab.com/yemen/data/incident.

9. Ibid.

10. George Thayer, *The War Business* (New York: Clarion/Simon and Schuster, 1969), pp. 147–149.

11. "Yemen's Tribes Rule with Absolute Power," *Agence France Presse*, September 28, 1999.

12. "North Yemen: Second of Three Part Series," *Christian Science Monitor*, January 13, 1983.

13. Ibid.

14. This figure has, however, been disputed by a reputable source, which estimates that there are only 6–9 million arms or 40 weapons per hundred people in private hands in Yemen; Derek Miller, "Demand, Stockpiles and Social Controls: Small Arms in Yemen" (Geneva: Small Arms Survey, May 2003).

15. Dresch, *Tribe, Government and History in Yemen*, p. 374.

16. "Taiz Deserves Much More." *Yemen Times*, August 30–September 5, 1999.

17. "A Positive Role of the Press Signalled by Yemen Times Seminar," *Yemen Times*, November 15–21, 1999; "North Yemen," *Financial Times*, November 26, 1984.

18. "Qat in Yemen," *Al-Jadeeda*, May 27, 1998.

19. "Qat Farmers Drain Most of Nation's Underground Water," *Yemen Times*, January 18–24, 1999.

20. "Chewing through a Yemeni Afternoon," *The Economist*, May 29, 1999.

21. "Yemen's Love Affair with Guns," *Yemen Observer*, November 1, 1999.

22. "Chewing through a Yemeni Afternoon," *Economist*, May 29, 1999.

23. "Yemen's Tribes Rule with Absolute Power," *Agence France Presse*, September 28, 1999.

24. "North Yemen," *Financial Times*, November 26, 1984.

25. *Yemen Times*, Interview—Sheikh of Jahm Explaining the Importance of Weapons for Tribes, July 31–August 7, 2000.

26. Dresch, *Tribes, Government and History in Yemen*, p. 374.

27. "Yemen Police Chief's Son Slain in Arms Dispute," *Agence France Presse*, September 4, 1999.

28. Ibid.; "Interview-Sheikh of Jahm," *Yemen Times*, July 31–August 7, 2000.

29. "Border Timetable Agreed," *Yemen Observer*, July 4, 2000.

30. "Tribes and State in War at Border," *Yemen Times*, August 21–27, 2000.

31. *Report, Kidnapping Statistics 1999*, Colombian Armed Forces, April 2000.

32. "Philippine Rebels Free Five Hostages," *The Guardian*, August 28, 2000.

33. "How Long Will This Continue?" *Yemen Times*, August 23–29, 1999.

34. "Jail Discovered in Sanaa University," *Yemen Times*, July 31–August 7, 2000.

35. Ibid.; http://www.al-bab.com/yemen/data

36. "Where To?" *Yemen Times*, December 13–19, 1999.

37. "German Captives Speak of Their Ordeal," *Yemen Times*, December 13–19, 1999.

38. "Military Machine Crushes Jahm," *Yemen Times*, July 3–9, 2000.

39. "Hostage to Fortune and Yemeni Guns," *The Guardian,* December 30, 1998.

40. "Military Machine Crushes Jahm," *Yemen Times*, July 3–9, 2000.

41. "Renewal of Battles in Serwah, Mareb," *Yemen Times*, July 10–16, 2000.

42. Ibid.

43. *Al-Ayyam*, June 14, 1998.

44. "Is the Government Sincere in Its Campaign?" *Yemen Times*, September 6–12, 1999.

45. *SIPRI Yearbook 1999* (London: Stockholm International Peace Research Institute, 1999), p. 321.

46. United Nations, *Statistical Yearbook 1996* (New York: United Nations, 1999), pp. 40, 83; "Military Spending Cuts," *Reuters*, July 19, 2000.

Chapter 9

1. Eric Hobsbawm, *Bandits* (London: Weidenfeld and Nicholson, 2000).

2. Philip Dinham, "Jamaica 2004 Review," *Jaimacans.Com*, January 1, 2005, www.jamaicans.com/articles/priemarticles/yearreview/2004.shtml.

3. Laurie Gunst, *Born Fi' Dead* (New York: Henry Holt, 1995), p. 84.

4. John Davison, *Gangsta* (London: Vision, 1997), p. 61.

5. Caroline Moser and Jeremy Holland, *Urban Poverty and Violence in Jamaica* (Washington, D.C.: World Bank, 1997), p. 2.

6. The Supreme Court, Ministry of Justice, Jamaica, www.moj.gov.jm/node/view/37

7. Davison, *Gangsta*, Chapter 4.

8. World Bank, *Violence and Urban Poverty in Jamaica: Breaking the Cycle*, Report 15895-JM (Washington, D.C.: World Bank, January 31, 1997), p. 15.

9. James Perl, "Guns of Jamaica," *New York Times*, August 12, 1980.

10. Moser and Holland, *Urban Poverty*, p. 17.

11. World Bank, *Violence and Urban Poverty in Jamaica*, p. 41.

12. "The State Is Collapsing," *Jamaica Gleaner*, Kingston, July 16, 2001.

13. "Illegal Guns, Ammo Fetch High Prices," *Jamaica Gleaner*, Kingston, July 1, 2001.

14. Anthony Harriott, "Mission Effectiveness, Environmental Change and the Reconfiguration of the Jamaican Security Forces," *Security and Defense Studies Review*, Vol 2 (Summer 2002), 19–45.

15. Davison, *Gangsta*, chapters 1 and 7.

16. Karyl Walker, "Guns Silent as Army/Police Move into August Town," *Jamaica Observer* (Kingston), March 20, 2005.

17. Ibid.

18. Sean Dorney, *Papua New Guinea: People, Politics and History Since 1975* (Sydney: ABC Books, 2000), pp. 26–38.

19. Sinclair Dinnen, *Law and Order in a Weak State: Crime and Politics in Papua New Guinea* (Honolulu: University of Hawai'i Press, 2001), p. 49.

20. Ibid., p. 190.

21. Sinclair Dinnen, "Law, Order and State," in Laura Zimmer-Tamakoshi (ed.), *Modern Papua New Guinea* (Kirksville: Thomas Jefferson University Press, 1998), p. 338.

22. Ibid., p. 74.

23. "Not Hard Cop, Not Soft Cop, But Still Firmly into PNG," Hugh White, *Sydney Morning Herald*, September 23, 2003.

24. Dinnen, "Law, Order and State," p. 340.

25. World Health Organization, *Papua New Guinea*, June 2005, at http//:www.who.int/3by5/support/june2005/_png.pdf

26. Dorney, *Papua New Guinea*, Chapter 5.

27. "PNGDF Mutiny," *Post Courier*, March 16, 2001.

28. James Sterba, "Rain Forests and Lots and Lots of Guns," *Wall Street Journal*, April 1, 1998.

29. Philip Alpers and Conor Twyford, *Small Arms in the Pacific* (Geneva, Switzerland: Small Arms Survey, March 2003), p. 53.

30. "Torres Strait Remains Most Vulnerable Border," *AAP Newsfeed*, February 24, 1998; Joint Standing Committee on Foreign Affairs, Defence and Trade, *Seminar on Papua New Guinea* (Canberra: Commonwealth of Australia, November 12, 1996).

31. Alpers and Twyford, *Small Arms in the Pacific*, p. 22.

32. Robert Muggah, *Diagnosing Demand: Assessing the Motivations and Means for Firearms Acquisition in the Solomon Islands and Papua New Guinea*, Discussion Paper, Research School of Pacific and Asian Studies, Australian National University, 2004, p. 9.

33. Alpers and Twyford, *Small Arms in the Pacific*, p. 20.

34. Dinnen, *Law and Order in a Weak State*, pp. 135–136.

35. Joint Agreement on Enhanced Cooperation between Australia and Papua New Guinea, Port Moresby, June 30, 2004, Department of Foreign Affairs and Trade, Canberra, Australia.

36. Julio Jacobo Waiselfisz, *Mortes Matadas Por Armas de Fogo No Brasil 1979–2003* (Brasilia: UNESCO, June 2005).

37. Ibid.

38. *Orfeu Negro*, director Marcel Camus, released 1959.

39. Carlos Marighella, *Minimanual of the Urban Guerrilla* (Boulder, CO: Paladin Press, 1980).

40. Carlos Amorim, *Comando Vermelho: Historia Secreta do Crime Organizado* (Rio de Janeiro: Distuidadora, 1993).

41. Patricia S. Rivero, *The Value of the Illegal Firearms Market in the City of Rio de Janeiro* (Rio de Janeiro: Viva Rio, 2004).

42. Luke Dowdney, *Child Combatants in Organized Armed Violence: A Study of Children and Adolescents Involved in Territorial Drug Faction Disputes in Rio de Janeiro* (Rio de Janeiro: ISER/Viva Rio, 2002), p. 72.

43. Diana Jean Schemo, "In Paraguay Border Town, Almost Anything Goes," *New York Times*, March 15, 1998.

44. Benjamin Lessing, *The Demand for Firearms in Rio de Janeiro* (Rio de Janeiro: ISER/Viva Rio, 2004).

45. Dowdney, *Child Combatants in Organized Armed Violence*, p. 34.

46. Ibid., p. 46.

47. Human Rights Watch, *Police Brutality in Urban Brazil* (Rio de Janeiro: HRW, April 1997).

48. Larry Rohter, "String of Street Shootings Kill 30, Including Youths, in Rio Suburb," *New York Times*, April 2, 2005.

Chapter 10

1. *Report of the United Nations on the Illicit Trade in Small Arms and Light Weapons in All Its Aspects*, New York, July 9–20, 2001, A/Conf. 92/15.

2. Statement by John R. Bolton, U.S. Statement at Plenary Session, Under Secretary of State for Arms Control and International Security Affairs, UN Conference on the Illicit Trade in Small Arms and Light Weapons in All Its Aspects, July 9, 2001, http://disarmament.un.org/cab/smallarms/statements/usE.html.

3. Ibid.

4. Ibid.

5. Ibid.

6. It was estimated that 550,000 weapons and more than 830 million rounds of ammunition were taken from the armories at that time. Tanani, Agim, *Albania: Cash-for-Guns Plan Misfires*, Institute for War and Peace Reporting, November 4, 2002.

7. Sami Faltas and Wolf-Christian Paes. *'You Have Removed the Devil from Our Door': An Assessment of the UNDP Small Arms and Light Weapons Control (SALWC) Project in Albania* (Bonn, Germany: Bonn International Center for Conversion (BICC), October 23, 2003), p. 30.

8. William H. Godnick, *Goods for Guns Program, MPCD of El Salvador*, Program of Arms Control, Disarmament and Conversion at the Monterey Institute of International Studies, July 1998.

9. Sami Faltas and Wolf-Christian Paes, *Exchanging Guns for Tools: The TAE Approach to Practical Disarmament—An Assessment of the TAE Project in Mozambique* (Bonn, Germany: BICC, 2004).

10. Christopher Dickey, "How Extremists Get Their Weapons," *Newsweek* (New York), August 20–27, 2007.

11. "Gun Sculpture Unveiled by Museum," BBC News, London, February 2, 2002.

12. Adedeji Ebo, *Small Arms Control in West Africa* (London: International Alert, October 2003).

13. Ibid.

14. Mariam Kandeh, "West Africa: Ecowas Urged to Ratify Convention on Small Arms," *Concord Times* (Freetown, Sierra Leone), September 6 2007.

15. Inter-Press Service, *Mozambique-South Africa: Arms Trafficking Worries Governments*, Maputo, Mozambique, October 27, 1993. Kalashnikovs were reported as available for less than $40.

16. Interview, Superintendent Stan Joubert, Illegal Firearms Investigation Unit, SAPS, 2000.

17. Martinho Chachiua, *Arms Management Programme: Operations Rachel 1996–1999*, ISS Monograph Series # 38 (Pretoria, South Africa: Institute for Security Studies, June 1999).

18. SaferAfrica, "Arms Management: Destruction—Mozambique," Pretoria, South Africa, 2006.

19. Ana Leao, *Weapons in Mozambique: Reducing Weapons Availability and Demand*, ISS Monograph # 94 (Pretoria, South Africa: Institute for Security Studies, January 2004), p. 15.

20. "Drop Your Guns," *Yemen Times*, March 21/23, 2005.

21. UN Office for the Coordination of Humanitarian Affairs, *Yemen: When Cultural Norms Underpin Gun Ownership*, New York, July 26, 2007.

22. Shaun Overton, "The Yemen Arms Trade: Still a Concern for Terrorism and Regional Security," *Terrorism Monitor*, Vol 11, No 9, Jamestown Foundation, May 6, 2005.

23. "Conflict Continues between Army and Houthis," *Yemen Times*, August 15, 2007.

24. Overton, "The Yemen Arms Trade."

25. Find UN report, 2006.

26. U.S. Department of State, *Yemen: Security Assistance*, Washington, D.C., July 12, 2007.

27. "Security Authorities Remain Silent While War Continues for Four Years between Two Tribes," *Yemen Times*, June 9–12, 2005.

28. Abdul-Aziz Oudah, "Thousands of Weapons Seized and Destroyed," *Yemen Observer*, July 14, 2007.

29. Harriet Namisi, *Peacebuilding and Conflict Resolution in the Teso/Karamoja Region* (Development Network of Indigenous Voluntary Associations, July 2006).

30. Ibid. One report estimated that there were 30,000 firearms in Karamoja, BBC News, January 19, 2007.

31. United Nations, *Report of the United Nations High Commissioner for Human Rights on the Situation of Human Rights in Uganda: Situation in Kotido, Karamoja, from 29 October to 15 November 2006*, New York, 2006.

32. Ibid.; UN High Commission for Human Rights, *Update Report on the Situation of Human Rights in Karamoja, from 16 November 2006 to 31 March 2007*, New York, 2007.

33. Ibid., p. 8.

34. *The Statute of Disarmament: Law No. 10,826/03*, Sao Paulo, Instituto Sou Da Paz, 2003.

35. The vote against the referendum was 64 percent. *Brazil Gun Referendum Defeated*, International Action Network on Small Arms (IANSA), October 24, 2005.

36. *Estado de Sao Paulo*, October 23, 2005.

37. Human Rights Watch, *Fighting Violence with Violence: Human Rights Abuse and Criminality in Rio de Janeiro* (New York: HRW, January 1996).

38. "Army to Be Deployed against Drug Gangs," *New York Times*, May 6, 2004; "19 Are Killed as Drug Gangs Conduct Attack in Brazil," *Reuters*, December 29, 2006; "Brazil Police Kill 11 in Raid on Rio Slums," *Reuters*, January 4, 2007.

39. "Brazil Pays for Inequality with Violence," *Reuters*, April 13, 2007.

40. Loretta Bondi and Elise Keppler *Casting the Net?: The Implications of the US Law on Arms Brokering* (Washington, DC: The Fund for Peace, 2001). As of mid-2007 it is unclear whether anybody has been charged under the 1996 U.S. law relating to arms brokering.

41. Douglas Farrah, "Merchant of Death," *Foreign Policy* (November/December 2006), 39–47.

42. J. Macalesher and R. Parker, *Bulgaria's Arms Transfer Control System at EU Accession* (London: Saferworld, February 2007).

43. The Nairobi Declaration, Global Policy Forum, New York, March 15, 2000.

44. Kenya was ranked jointly 142 out of 163 countries in the Transparency International corruption index for the year 2006, Transparency International Corruption Perceptions Index, Berlin, 2006.

Bibliography

Alpers, Philip and Conor Twyford. *Small Arms in the Pacific* (Geneva: Small Arms Survey, March 2003).

Amorim, Carlos. *Comando Vermelho: Historia Secreta do Crime Organizado* (Rio de Janeiro: Distuidadora, 1993).

Bollig, Michael. "Ethnic Conflicts in North-West Kenya: Pokot-Turkana Raiding 1969–84." *Zeitschrift fur Ethnologie*, 115, 73–90, 1990.

Bondi, Loretta and Elise Keppler. *Casting the Net: The Implication of the U.S. Law on Arms Brokering* (Washington, D.C.: The Fund for Peace, 2000).

British American Security Information Council (BASIC). *Deadly Rounds: Ammunition and Armed Conflict* (London: BASIC, 1998).

Buchanan-Smith, Margie and Jeremy Lind. *Armed Violence and Poverty in Northern Kenya* (Bradford: Center for International Cooperation and Security, University of Bradford, 2005).

Bulhan, Hussein Abdilahi. *Survey of Small Arms in Somaliland* (Hargeisa (Somaliland): Center for Creative Solutions, 2004).

Canfield, Bruce. *Complete Guide to United States Military Combat Shotguns* (Woonsocket, RI: Mowbray, 2007).

Central Intelligence Agency (CIA). *Long-Term Demographic: Reshaping the Geopolitical Landscape* (Washington, D.C.: CIA, July 2001).

Centre for Conflict Research (CCR) (Kenya) and International Alert (UK). *The Great Lakes Parliamentary Forum on Peace (Amani Forum: Fact Finding Mission on Urban Conflicts in Kenya—The Case of Kibera, Nairobi)* (Nairobi: CCR/International Alert, 2002).

Chabal, Patrick and Jean-Pascal Daloz. *Africa Works: Disorder as Political Instrument* (Oxford: James Currey, 1999).

Chachiua, Martinho. *Arms Management Programme: Operations Rachel 1996–1999*, ISS Monograph Series # 38 (Pretoria: Institute for Security Studies, June 1999).

Clapham, Christopher, ed. *African Guerrillas* (Oxford: James Currey Limited, 1998).

Cohen, Stephen Philip. *The Idea of Pakistan* (Washington, DC: Brookings Institution Press, 2004).

Collier, Paul. *Economic Causes of Civil Conflict and Their Implications for Policy* (Washington, DC: World Bank, 2000).

Commission of Inquiry into Alleged Arms Transactions between ARMSCOR and One Eli Wazan and Other Related Matters, Johannesburg, June 15, 1995.

Congressional Research Service. *Afghan Refugees: Current Status and Future Prospects*, Washington, DC, January 26, 2007.

Cragin, Kim and Bruce Hoffman. *Arms Trafficking and Colombia* (Santa Monica, CA: RAND, 2003).

Crummey, Donald. *Banditry, Rebellion and Social Protest in Africa* (London and Portsmouth, NH: James Currey and Heinemann, 1986).

Davison, John. *Gangsta* (London: Vision, 1997).

Dinnen, Sinclair. *Law and Order in a Weak State: Crime and Politics in Papua New Guinea* (Honolulu: University of Hawai'i Press, 2001).

Dorney, Sean. *The Sandline Affair* (Sydney: ABC Books, 1998).

———. *Papua New Guinea: People, Politics and History Since 1975* (Sydney: ABC Books, 2000).

Dowdney, Luke. *Child Combatants in Organized Armed Violence: A Study of Children and Adolescents Involved in Territorial Drug Faction Disputes in Rio de Janeiro* (Rio de Janeiro: ISER/Viva Rio, 2002).

Dresch, Paul. *Tribes, Government, and History in Yemen* (Oxford: Clarencon Press, 1989).

Dyson-Hudson, Neville. *Karimojong Politics* (Oxford: Clarendon Press, 1966).

Ebo, Adedeji. *Small Arms Control in West Africa* (London: International Alert, October 2003).

Ellis, Stephen. *The Mask of Anarchy* (New York: New York University Press, 1999).

Faltas, Sami and Wolf-Christian Paes. *"You Have Removed the Devil from Our Door": An Assessment of the UNDP Small Arms and Light Weapons Control (SALWC) Project in Albania* (Bonn, Germany: Bonn International Center for Conversion (BICC), October 23, 2003).

———. *Exchanging Guns for Tools: The TAE Approach to Practical Disarmament—An Assessment of the TAE Project in Mozambique* (Bonn, Germany: Bonn International Center for Conversion (BICC), 2004).

Farah, Douglas. "Victor Bout: Merchant of Death." *Foreign Policy*, 38–47, November/December 2006.

Federal Research Division, Library of Congress. *Terrorist and Organized Crime Groups in the Tri-Border Area (TBA) of South America* (Washington. DC: USGPO, July 2003).

Ferme, Mariane C. *The Underneath of Things: Violence, History and the Everyday in Sierra Leone* (Berkeley: University of California Press, 2001).

Fleisher, Michael L. *Kuria Cattle Raiders: Violence and Vigilantism on the Tanzania/Kenya Frontier* (Ann Arbor: University of Michigan Press, 2000).

Forberg, Ekkehard and Ulf Terlinden. *Small Arms in Somaliland: Their Role and Diffusion* (Berlin: Berlin Information Center for Transatlantic Security, March 1999).

Fowler, William. *Operation Barras: The SAS Rescue Mission Sierra Leone 2000* (London: Weidenfeld and Nicholson, 2004).

Fukuyama, Frances. "The End of History?" *The National Interest*, 3–18, Summer 1989.

Gamba, Virginia, ed. *Society Under Siege: Crime, Violence and Illegal Weapons* (Pretoria: Institute for Security Studies, 1996).

———. *Society Under Siege: Licit Responses to Illicit Arms* (Pretoria: Institute for Security Studies, 1998).

Global Witness. *Taylor-made: The Pivotal Role of Liberia's Forests and Flag of Convenience in Regional Conflict* (London: Global Witness/International Workers Federation, 2001).

———. *Branching Out: Zimbabwe's Resource Colonialism in Democratic Republic of Congo* (London: Global Witness, 2002).

———. *The Logs of War: The Timber Trade and Armed Conflict* (London: Global Witness, 2002).

———. *For a Few Dollars More: How al Qaeda Moved into the Diamond Trade* (London: Global Witness, April 2003).

Godnick, William H. *Goods for Guns Program, MPCD of El Salvador* (Monterrey: Program of Arms Control, Disarmament and Conversion at the Monterrey Institute of International Studies, July 1998).

Godnick, William and Helena Vazquez. *Small Arms Control in Latin America* (London: International Alert, 2003).

Gray, Sandra, Mary Sundal, Brandi Wiebusch, Michael A. Little, Paul Leslie, and Ivy Pike. "Cattle Raiding, Cultural Survival, and Adaptability of East African Pastoralists." *Current Anthropology*, Vol 44, 513–522, December 2003.

Greene, Owen. "Examining International Responses to Illicit Arms Trafficking." *Crime, Law and Social Change*, 33, 151–190, 2000.

Grosse-Kettler, Sabrina. *External Actors in Stateless Somalia* (Bonn, Germany: Bonn International Center for Conversion (BICC), 2004).

Gunst, Laurie. *Born Fi' Dead* (New York: Henry Holt, 1995).

Haefele, Benjamin White. *Islamic Fundamentalism and Pagad: An Internal Security Issue for South Africa?* (South Africa: Centre for Military Studies, University of Stellenbosch, 1997).

Handelman, Stephen. *Comrade Criminal* (New Haven, CT: Yale University Press, 1995).

Harriott, Anthony. "Mission Effectiveness, Environmental Change and the Reconfiguration of the Jamaican Security Forces." *Security and Defense Studies Review*, Vol 2, 19–45, Summer 2002.

Hasan, Arif. "Karachi and the Global Nature of Urban Violence." *The Urban Age*, Vol I, No 4, Summer 1993.

Hendrickson, Dylan, Jeremy Armon, and Robin Mearns. *Conflict and Vulnerability and Famine: Livestock Raiding in Turkana, Kenya* (London: International Institute for Environment and Development, 1998).

House of Commons (UK). *Report of the Sierra Leone Arms Investigation* (London: UK Stationery Office, 1998).

House of Commons (UK), All Parliamentary Group on the Great Lakes Region. *Arms Flow in Eastern DR Region*, APPG-03-04, London, December 2004.

Huband, Mark. *The Liberian Civil War* (London, Frank Cass, 1998).

Hudson, Rex. *Terrorist and Organized Crime Groups in the Tri-Border Area (TBA) of South America* (Washington, D.C.: Library of Congress, 2003).

Human Rights Watch. *Easy Prey: Child Soldiers in Liberia* (New York: HRW, 1994).

————. *Fighting Violence with Violence: Human Rights Abuse and Criminality in Rio de Janeiro* (New York: HRW, January 1996).

————. *Police Brutality in Urban Brazil* (Rio de Janeiro: HRW, April 1997).

————. "Global Trade, Local Impact: Arms Transfers to All Sides in the Civil War in Sudan." HRW, Vol 10, No 4, August 1998.

————. *Money Talks; Arms Dealing with Human Rights Abusers (Bulgaria)* (New York: HRW, 1999).

————. *Playing with Fire: Weapons Proliferation, Political Violence, and Human Rights in Kenya* (New York: HRW, 2000).

————. *Youth, Poverty and Blood: The Lethal Legacy of West Africa's Regional Warriors* (New York: HRW, 2005).

Ingrams, Harold. *Uganda: A Crisis of Nationhood* (London: Her Majesty's Stationery Office, 1960).

Institute for Security Studies (ISS). *Controlling Small Arms Proliferation and Reversing Cultures of Violence in Africa and the India Ocean* (Pretoria: ISS, 1998).

International Consortium of Investigative Journalists. *Making a Killing: The Business of War* (Washington, D.C.: Public Integrity Books, 2003).

International Crisis Group (ICG). *Afghanistan: The Problem of Pashtun Alienation* (Brussels: ICG, 2003).

————. *The State of Sectarianism in Pakistan* (Brussels: ICG, April, 2005).

Isby, David. "Afghanistan: Low Intensity Conflict with Major Power Intervention." In Edwin G. Corr Stephen Sloan (ed.), *Low Intensity Conflict: Old Threats in a New World* (Boulder, CO: Westview, 1992).

Job, Brian, ed. *The Insecurity Dilemma: National Security of Third World States* (Boulder, CO: Lynne Rienner, 1992).

Kan, Paul R. "Webs of Smoke: Drugs and Small Wars." *Small Wars and Insurgencies*, 148–162, June 2006.

Katumanga, Musambayi with Lionel Cliffe. *Nairobi—A City Besieged: The Impact of Armed Violence on Poverty and Development* (Bradford: Centre for International Cooperation and Security, University of Bradford, 2005).

Keen, David. *The Economic Functions of Violence in Civil Wars* (London: International Institute for Strategic Studies/Oxford University Press, 1998).

————. "'Since I Am a Dog, Beware My Fangs': Beyond a 'Rational Violence' Framework in the Sierra Leonean War." Crisis States Programme, London School of Economics, Working Paper No. 14, August 2002.

Kiasara, Rauf. *Deweaponisation of Afghan Refugee Camps Ordered in Pakistan* (London: International Action Network on Small Arms, November 25, 2001).

Klare, Michael and David Andersen. *A Scourge of Guns: The Diffusion of Small Arms and Light Weapons in Latin America* (Washington, DC: Federation of American Scientists, 1996).

Kratil, Saverio and Jeremy Swift. *Understanding and Managing Pastoral Conflict in Kenya—A Literature Review* (Brighton, UK: University of Sussex, 1998).

Laurance, Edward and Rachel Stohl. *Making Global Public Policy: The Case of Small Arms and Light Weapons* (Geneva: Small Arms Survey, 2002).

Lessing, Benjamin. *The Demand for Firearms in Rio de Janeiro* (Rio de Janeiro: ISER/Viva Rio, 2004).

Macalesher, J. and R. Parker. *Bulgaria's Arms Transfer Control System at EU Accession* (London: Saferworld, February 2007).

Marighella, Carlos. *Minimanual of the Urban Guerrilla* (Boulder, CO: Paladin Press, 1980).

Mazrui, Ali. *Soldiers and Kinsmen in Uganda: The Making of a Military Ethnocracy* (Beverly Hills/London: Sage Publications).

Miller, Derek B. *Demand, Stockpiles and Social Controls: Small Arms in Yemen* (Geneva: Small Arms Survey, 2003).

Mirzeler, Mustafa and Crawford Young. "Pastoral Politics in the Northeast Periphery of Uganda: AK-47 as Change Agent." *Journal of Modern African Studies*, 38(3), 407–429, 2000.

Mkutu, Kennedy. *Pastoralism and Conflict in the Horn of Africa* (London/Nairobi: Africa Peace Forum, Saferworld, University of Bradford, 2002).

———. *Pastoral Conflict and Small Arms: The Kenya–Uganda Border Region* (London: Saferworld, 2003).

Mogire, Edward. *A Preliminary Exploration of the Linkages between Refugees and Small Arms* (Bonn, Germany: Bonn International Center for Conversion (BICC), 2004).

Monaghan, Rachel. "One Merchant, One Bullet: The Rise and Fall of PAGAD." *Low Intensity Conflict and Law Enforcement*, Vol 12, No 1, 1–19, Spring 2004.

Morgensen, Michael, Sharene Mackenzie, Kenneth Wilson, and Steadman Noble. "Corner and Area Gangs of Inner City Jamaica." *Children in Organised Violence (COAV)*, undated.

Moser, Caroline and Jeremy Holland. *Urban Poverty and Violence in Jamaica* (Washington, D.C.: World Bank, 1997).

Moser, Caroline and Cathy McIlwaine. *Urban Poor Perceptions of Violence and Exclusion in Colombia* (Washington, DC: The World Bank, 2000).

Muggah, Robert. *Diagnosing Demand: Assessing the Motivations and Means for Firearms Acquisition in the Solomon Islands and Papua New Guinea*, Discussion Paper, Research School of Pacific and Asian Studies, Australian National University, Canberra, 2004.

Namisi, Harriet. *Peacebuilding and Conflict Resolution in the Teso/Karamoja Region* (Development Network of Indigenous Voluntary Associations, Uganda, July 2006).

National Security News Service (NSNS). *Central Africa: The Influx of Arms and the Continuation of Crisis* (Washington, DC: NSNS, 1998).

Niger Delta Project for Environment, Human Rights and Development (NDPEHRD). *A Harvest of Guns; Rivers State (Niger Delta, Nigeria)* (Ogale-Nchia: NDPEHRD, 2004).

Ocan, Charles Emunyu. *Pastoral Crisis in North-Eastern Uganda: The Changing Significance of Cattle Raids* (Kampala: Centre for Basic Research, 1992).

Oeun, Yem San and Rebecca F. Catella. *I Live in Fear: Consequences of Small Arms on Women and Children in Cambodia* (Phnom Penh: Working Group for Weapons Reduction, June 2001).

Organization of American States (OAS). *Report of the General Secretariat of the Organization of American States on the Diversion of Nicaraguan Arms to the United Defense Forces of Colombia* (Washington, DC: OAS, 2003).

Osamba, Joshia O. "The Sociology of Insecurity: Cattle Rustling and Banditry in North-Western Kenya." *African Journal on Conflict Resolution*, Vol 1, No 2, 11–37, 2000.

Packer, George. "Gangsta War." *New Yorker*, 68–80, November 3, 2003.

Pkalya, Ruto, Mohamud Adan, and Isabella Masinde. *Indigenous Democracy: Traditional Conflict Resolution Mechanisms—Pokot, Turkana, Samburu and Marakwet* (Eastern Africa: Intermediate Technology Development Group, 2004).

Quam, Michael D. "Creating Peace in an Armed Society." *African Studies Quarterly*, Vol 1, No 1, online, unpaginated, 1997.

Rabasa, Angel, Steven Boraz, Stephen Boraz, Peter Chalk, Kim Cragin, Theodore Karasik, Jennifer Moroney, Kevin O'Brien, and John E. Peters. *Ungoverned Territories: Understanding and Reducing Terrorism Risks*. (Santa Monica, CA: RAND, 2007).

Reno, William. *Warlord Politics and African States* (Boulder, CO: Lynne Rienner, 1998).

Richards, Paul. *Fighting for the Rain Forest: War, Youth and Resources in Sierra Leone* (Oxford and Bloomington: James Currey and Indiana University Press, 1996).

Rivero, Patricia S. *The Value of the Illegal Firearms Market in the City of Rio de Janeiro* (Rio de Janeiro: Viva Rio, 2004).

Rodgers, Dennis. *Youth Gangs and Violence in Latin America and the Caribbean: A Literature Survey* (Washington, DC: The World Bank, 1999).

Security Research and Information Centre (SRIC). *Small Arms Trafficking in the Border Regions of Sudan, Uganda and Kenya* (Nairobi: SRIC, 2001).

Senich, Peter. *The German Assault Rifle 1933–1945* (Boulder, CO: Paladin Press, 1987).

Serjeant, R.B. "South Arabia." In van Nieuwenhuijza (ed.), *Commoners, Climbers and Notables* (Leiden: E.J. Brill, 1977).

Shultz, Richard H., Douglas Farah, and Itamara V. Lochard. *Armed Groups: A Tier-One Priority* (Colorado Springs, CO: USAF Institute for National Security Studies, 2004).

Silverstein, Ken. *Private Warriors* (New York: Verso, 2000).

Singer, P.W. *Children at War* (Berkeley: University of California Press, 2006).

SIPRI Yearbook 1999 (London: Stockholm International Peace Research Institute, 1999).

Small Arms Survey. *Small Arms Survey 2001* (Oxford: Oxford University Press, 2001).

Smith, Chris. "Light Weapons and Ethnic Conflict in South Asia." In Jeffrey Boutwell, Michael Klare, and Laura Reed (eds.), *Lethal Commerce: The Global Trade in Small Arms and Light Weapons* (Cambridge, MA: American Academy of Arts and Science, 1995).

Smyth, Marie and Patricia Campbell, "Young People and Armed Violence in Northern Ireland." *Children in Organised Armed Violence* (COAV), undated, Institute for Conflict Research, Belfast, Northern Ireland, 2005.

Stevens, R. Blake and Edward Ezell. *The Black Rifle: M16 Retrospective* (Canada: Collector Grade Publications, 1994).

Thabane, M. *Liphokojoe of Kao: A Study of a Diamond Digger Rebel Group in the Lesotho Highlands." Journal of Southern African Studies*, Vol 26, No 1, 105–121, March 2000.

Thornton, John K. *Warfare in Atlantic Africa 1500–1800* (London: University College Press, 1999).

United Nations. *Statistical Yearbook 1996* (New York: United Nations, 1999).

———. *Report of the Panel of Experts Appointed Pursuant to Security Council Resolution 1306 (2000), Paragraph 19, in Relation to Sierra Leone*, S/2000/1195, New York, December 20, 2000.

———. *Report of the Panel of Experts Appointed Pursuant to Security Council Resolution 1408(2002), Paragraph 16, Concerning Liberia*, S/2002/1115, New York, 2002.

———. *Report of the United Nations on the Illicit Trade in Small Arms and Light Weapons in All Its Aspects*, New York, 2002.

———. *Report of the Panel of Experts on Somalia*, S/2003/1035, New York, November 4, 2003.

———. *Group of Experts on the Democratic Republic of Congo Report*, S/2005/30, New York, January 25, 2005.

———. *Report of the Group of Experts on the Democratic Republic of Congo*, S/2005/30, New York, January 25, 2005.

————. *Report of the Monitoring Group on Somalia*, S/2005/153, New York, February 14, 2005.

————. *Report of the United Nations High Commissioner for Human Rights on the Situation of Human Rights in Uganda: Situation in Kotido, Karamoja, from 29 October to 15 November 2006*, New York, 2006.

United Nations High Commissioner for Refugees. *Analysis of Refugee Capacity: Kenya* (New York: United Nations, 2005).

U.S. Agency for International Development (USAID). *Assessment and Programmatic Recommendations: Addressing Pastoralist Conflict in the Karamoja Cluster of Kenya, Uganda and Sudan* (Washington, DC: USAID, 2002).

Utas, Mats. *Sweet Battlefields: Youth and the Liberian Civil War*, Dissertation for the Degree of Philosophy in Cultural Anthropolgy presented at Uppsala University, Uppsala, Sweden, 2003.

Veal, Angela and Aki Stavrou. *Violence, Reconciliation and Identity: The Reintegration of Lord's Resistance Army Child Abductees in Northern Uganda* (Pretoria: Institute for Security Studies, 2003).

Verkaaik, Oskar. *Migrants and Militants: Fun and Urban Violence in Pakistan* (Princeton, NJ: Princeton University Press, 2004).

Weiss, Taya. *Local Catalysts, Global Reactions: Cycles of Conflict in the Mano River Basin* (Pretoria: Institute for Security Studies, June 2005).

Wille, Christina. *How Many Weapons Are There in Cambodia?* (Geneva: Small Arms Survey, June 2006).

Windybank, Susan and Mike Manning. "Papua New Guinea on the Brink." *Issue Analysis*, No 30, all pages, March 12, 2003.

Woodward, Susan L. "Failed States, Warlordism and 'Tribal' Warfare." *The Naval War College Review*, 55–68, Spring 1999.

World Bank. *Violence and Urban Poverty in Jamaica: Breaking the Cycle*, Report 15895-JM (Washington, DC: World Bank, January 31, 1997).

Index

About the Author

CHRISTOPHER CARR is Associate Professor of International Security at the U.S. Air War College. He has written and researched on the trade in arms and on the impact of light weapons proliferation on vulnerable societies and is the author of *Security Implications of Microdisarmament* (2000). He is a contributor to James Forest's *Countering Terrorism and Insurgency in the 21st Century*, 3 Volumes (Praeger Security International, 2007). Carr earned his Ph.D. in International Relations from the London School of Economics and Political Science.